A CAPITALIST IN
NORTH KOREA

A CAPITALIST IN NORTH KOREA

MY SEVEN YEARS IN THE HERMIT KINGDOM

FELIX ABT

TUTTLE Publishing

Tokyo | Rutland, Vermont | Singapore

Published by Tuttle Publishing, an imprint of Periplus Editions (HK) Ltd.

www.tuttlepublishing.com

Copyright © 2014 Felix Abt
All images in this book are the property of the author, unless otherwise noted.

Library of Congress Control Number: 2014938523

ISBN 978-0-8048-4439-0

Distributed by

North America, Latin America & Europe	**Japan**
Tuttle Publishing	Tuttle Publishing
364 Innovation Drive	Yaekari Building 3rd Floor
North Clarendon	5-4-12 Osaki Shinagawa-ku
VT 05759-9436, USA	Tokyo 1410032, Japan
Tel: 1 (802) 773 8930	Tel: (81) 3 5437 0171
Fax: 1 (802) 773 6993	Fax: (81) 3 5437 0755
info@tuttlepublishing.com	sales@tuttle.co.jp
www.tuttlepublishing.com	www.tuttle.co.jp

Asia Pacific
Berkeley Books Pte Ltd
61 Tai Seng Avenue #02-12
Singapore 534167
Tel: (65) 6280 1330
Fax: (65) 6280 6290
inquiries@periplus.com.sg
www.periplus.com

18 17 16 15 14   10 9 8 7 6 5 4 3 2 1   1405RP

Printed in China

Contents

Preface: On the Verge of *Glasnost*? 7

PART I

Chapter 1   Into the Heart of Darkness 17

Chapter 2   Malaise into Opportunity 37

Chapter 3   Look to the Party, Young Revolutionary, and Buy 51

Chapter 4   Healing the Great Leader's Children 77

Chapter 5   Same Bed, Different Dreams 95

Chapter 6   A Manchurian Candidate? 109

PART II

Chapter 7   Southerners, Yankees, and "Chinese Lips" 125

Chapter 8   Feeding the People 145

Chapter 9   Flowers of the Nation 167

Chapter 10   Nurturing Revolutionaries 187

Chapter 11   Coming and Going 209

Chapter 12   Partying, Pyongyang-Style 233

PART III

Chapter 13   The Price of Glory 257

Chapter 14   The Loss of Innocence 285

Epilogue: Winds of Change 299

Acknowledgments 319

On the Verge of *Glasnost*?

In December 2011, North Korea's long-time leader, Kim Jong Il, collapsed on a train and died from a heart attack. Western intelligence agencies had been speculating for about two years that the Dear Leader's health had been deteriorating. Still, by most accounts, the news came as a shock to Korea watchers. His youngest son, Kim Jong Un, immediately took the throne from his father, who was declared, in the unique North Korean tradition of necrocracy, the "eternal general secretary" of the Korean Workers' Party.

"Lil' Kim," as *Time* magazine jokingly called him on its cover, set out to reform one of the world's last five communist countries. Coming off the retrenchment of state-centric conservatism since the mid-2000s, he curbed the power of the military and surrounded himself with a top-level civilian cadre interested in a *glasnost* for the country. "Officials should work with a creative and enterprising attitude ... [and] resolutely do away with the outdated ideological viewpoint and backward method and style of work," he declared before a crowd. John Delury, a Yale-educated historian of China at South Korea's Yonsei University, compared that rhetoric to Deng Xiaoping's famous December 1978 speech that launched China's reforms, in which he called on party members to be "pathbreakers who dare to think, explore new ways, and generate new ideas."

For seven years, I worked in North Korea, hoping that injecting a business culture would help the regime nudge itself toward the world. But my romantic longing only made my life harder. People called me a "useful idiot" for one of the world's most isolated and militarized governments. They accused me of being an idealist gone blind, or a greedy capitalist trying to fill my pockets at the expense of the suffering North Korean people. Yet during my seven years living and working in the capital of Pyongyang, I was given enormous insight into a country better known for its famine and nuclear bombs than for the stories of its regular people, and all their hopes and dreams that transcend politics.

It is hard for Westerners to imagine this, but I became heavily involved as a point man for investments behind the world's last Iron Curtain. I didn't deal in arms and drugs, as many would jokingly assume. Rather, I was involved in a number of everyday projects that don't quite match the prevailing international image of North Korea. I was involved in the purchasing of domestic goods such as garments, liqueurs, metals, and minerals. I sold items ranging from machines to infrastructure items to dyestuff to foodstuff and pharmaceuticals. I was involved in setting up and running all sorts of representative offices and companies. I advised investors looking into noodle production, mineral water from the country's "holy mountain" of Paekdu, precious metal extraction, software design, and medicine production. My commercial activities promoted good business practices that included, for example, enhanced safety standards for North Korean miners. The foreign engineers who represented equipment manufacturers from other countries refused to enter unsafe mines to install and repair equipment, so we had to find a solution.

As the cofounder and director of Pyongyang's first business school, I went on an excursion into the political and business minds of senior cadres. Many of them had given up on the national myth of a pure past and a perfect socialist economy and were looking beyond North Korea's tight borders for new ideas that would spur growth and innovation. Part of the new mindset was a response to the famine and economic problems of the 1990s, when the Kim regime could no longer rely on Soviet subsidies to prop up its economy.

The institute encouraged the world's most centrally planned economy to dare to take a few steps into the world of free enterprise.

I also helped start and became the first president of the European Business Association in Pyongyang, the country's first foreign chamber of commerce. The position threw me into the role of lobbyist for investments from Europe and around the world. Part of the job required me to campaign for better investment conditions for foreign businesses, which sought ways to more easily hire employees, reduce their taxes, and gain more direct access to local suppliers and customers without the red tape. In short, we were pushing for the emergence of the rule of law, a system that would legally require the state to protect enterprises and citizens, open the markets, and create a level-playing field for Koreans and non-Koreans. It was both a challenge and an adventure, and the sort of endeavor that could create real change in the North Korean government.

Some readers will be surprised to learn that the North Korean authorities and my business partners were not brainwashed. They acted as normal and rational people would. In our meetings, they behaved fairly and with pleasant etiquette, and I will keep a good memory of them. On the other hand, perhaps I was fortunate to have dealt with people who were not out to rip me off. I have met other businesspeople who were distraught over their experiences, and I will discuss this trickier side of expatriate life later. As I don't want to hurt, anger, or offend any of my North Korean or foreign colleagues, I will sometimes redact their real names and details of our meetings. Other facts I will not disclose to protect their reputations.

Given the growing political tensions in the mid-2000s, all this business appeared to be the wrong thing in the wrong place at the wrong time. In 2002, George W. Bush placed North Korea on his infamous "axis of evil" list. In 2008, the South Korean government halted all food aid to the regime, distressing relations even more in a way that would lead to tragedy. In response, in 2006 and 2009, the Kim Jong Il regime tested two nuclear weapons. Then, in 2010, North Korea was accused of torpedoing a South Korean naval corvette, the

Cheonan, killing forty-six sailors—a claim that it continues to deny.

Both sides have hardened their stances with each confrontation, and the deaths of those sailors would certainly be unforgivable if North Korean forces were indeed behind the attacks. Unfortunately for the hawks, the evidence is still conflicting. In 2012, a prominent Korean seismologist and an Israeli geologist suggested, based on an analysis of seismic and acoustic waves, that the ship probably hit a South Korean mine.

This all plays into a bigger picture of geopolitical bullying. The government, I found in my experience meeting local people, was cornered and needed to protect itself. The regime was reacting to United Nations sanctions and to condemnations from the international press. Legitimate business in North Korea—the sort that could help the country grow out of its impoverished rut—was being harmed in an attempt to go after a tinier and perhaps more extreme contingent of hawkish military commanders.

Those political challenges were among the most difficult of my life, because there's no other place like North Korea. I say that having lived and worked in nine countries on three continents. That's in addition to the dozens of other places I've visited for business and leisure—a smattering of countries throughout Africa, Asia, and the former Soviet Union and its communist allies. My travels gave me insights into the vastness of the human experience, showing me how people are shaped by their diverse cultural practices and political systems. North Korea is one example of how seclusion has shaped the attitudes of a people, and this book will show how international politics isn't reassuring for them.

That said, Pyongyang may be isolated from the world, but it's far from being the begrimed center of poverty that the world makes it out to be. Pretty much every year the human resources consulting company ECA International releases rankings that place Pyongyang among the least hospitable cities for expatriate business people. The North Korean capital falls into a tier that includes Kabul, Afghanistan, and Karachi, Pakistan—a characterization that doesn't strike me as reasonable. While the capital can hardly match the glamour of London and New York, it's nevertheless a decent place to live if you're a foreigner. Expatriates can sit back free from worries about crime, terrorism, and the safety of their children. Pyongyang is clean and secure, even if it sometimes lacks reliable electricity and running water. To be fair, those shortages are to be expected of any metropolis in a poor country—including the rising industrial powerhouses of Beijing, Ho Chi Minh City, and Jakarta.

Given the country's troubled history and estranged political position, it would be fair to look at the isolationism and socialist red tape from the view of North Koreans. North Korea is the most heavily sanctioned nation in the world, and no other people have had to deal with the massive quarantines that Western and Asian powers have enclosed around its economy. These penalties are upsetting from a business standpoint and have only worsened the country's prospects for developing economically. One time, for instance, I lost a multi-million dollar contract for a project to rehabilitate Pyongyang's water and sewage system. Any capital in the world, regardless of its political system, should have a sewage system that protects its residents from waterborne diseases like cholera, a scourge of the developing world. The project was funded by the Kuwait Fund for Arab Economic Development, a financing body for development projects run by the Kuwaiti government. But certain types of software that were needed for the project were hit by sanctions from Washington. The American embargo was structured so that multinational companies that do business in North Korea could lose their stakes in the U.S., and could face future legal hurdles there. Because those companies were nervous, the Kuwaiti government awarded the contract to smaller Asian suppliers that didn't need to fear the ire of Uncle Sam.

On another occasion in 2008, I had to fear for the survival of my pharmaceutical factory, PyongSu, a company into which I put my heart and soul. I was its managing director around the same time the United Nations slapped even more sanctions on North Korea in the mid-2000s in protest of its nuclear tests. Because of a very poorly timed move by international groups, I was no longer allowed to import certain chemicals for laboratory tests even though they were designed to bring better health care to the countryside.

It's just one example of how sanctions, applied in a shortsighted way, can hurt regular people who need health care instead of the government they're targeting. Though in theory health care and medicine is free for all in North Korea, the practice of bribe-taking means, in practice, that people depend on an irregular supply of pharmaceuticals from foreign donors and nongovernmental organizations (NGOs).

Despite all my efforts to cope with sanctions, my biggest headaches didn't come from dealing with the nations that had blacklisted Pyongyang. Even more problems, to my surprise, came from ill-informed investors, employers, principals (a term for the business owners who appointed me as their agent), customers, suppliers, and journalists who, for the most part, didn't make much of an effort to understand North Korean society, choosing to fall back into stereotypes. The country itself was, quite often, of marginal and contemptible importance to them. They showed up eager to invest in what they thought would be another emerging market that followed the rise of China. But they didn't shake off the cookie-cutter views that all North Koreans were Stalinist ants. They sneered at my business queries and explanations as to how the country works and degraded the abilities of North Koreans to think for themselves.

Apart from the business side of things, I had a pleasant family life. My wife and my young daughter stayed for some time with me in Pyongyang, moving back and forth between there and our other home of Vietnam. We enjoyed ourselves despite the lack of running water and electricity, and managed to live with the absence of dairy products in the summertime. (The lack of refrigeration in hot summer months cut back the supply of these items.)

Still, with my long working hours, I very much regret not always spending enough time with my family. I therefore dedicate this book to my wife and daughter.

North Korea gave them great life experiences too. For some time, my Vietnamese spouse worked as a Swiss government-sponsored consultant to the Ministry of Light Industries. She led a project aimed at building up the small leather industry, using as its basis the valuable skins of the two million goats that were left unprocessed after being slaughtered. Unfortunately, the project did not materialize. Our toddler, who learned to walk in Pyongyang, spent about three hours every day at the kindergarten of the Korea International School. While there, foreign children were surprised to learn from their North Korean teachers that Kim Il Sung, the founding father of the nation, is also the symbolic father of all children in Korea.

Even with that propaganda, I realized that North Koreans are first and foremost human beings, not robots who follow the dictates of the Dear Leader. They experience the same sorrows and worries, happy and sad moments, and hopes and aspirations of humans all over the world.

In this book I will share with you my unforgettable experience. For some readers, my story will be an entertaining plunge into this strange, alien world, while for those of a scholarly bent, it could reveal much about the inner workings of this remote nation.

Regardless of what you take from this memoir, I hope you'll be inspired to put aside the perceptions you may have about North Korea. Life in the hermit state is difficult, but it is not as outlandish as they say. The nation, unknown to many, is full of opportunities for curious foreigners, like business, tourism, teaching English, and even training sports teams in Pyongyang.

In the end, this "useful idiot" earned a comfortable living and happily shared his knowledge and skills for the good of regular North Koreans. He tried to be a sort of cultural translator, clearing up misunderstandings and building bridges between the state and the outside world. He was happy bringing good-quality but inexpensive medicine to this impoverished country and teaching North Koreans to do business in an ever globalizing world. And as the young Kim ascends to power, that globalization is taking a greater toll on a nation many think is stuck in the cold war. As with Deng Xiaoping before him, business is the way forward for Kim's country; with that, we begin my story.

Felix Abt
Nha Trang, Vietnam
December 2012

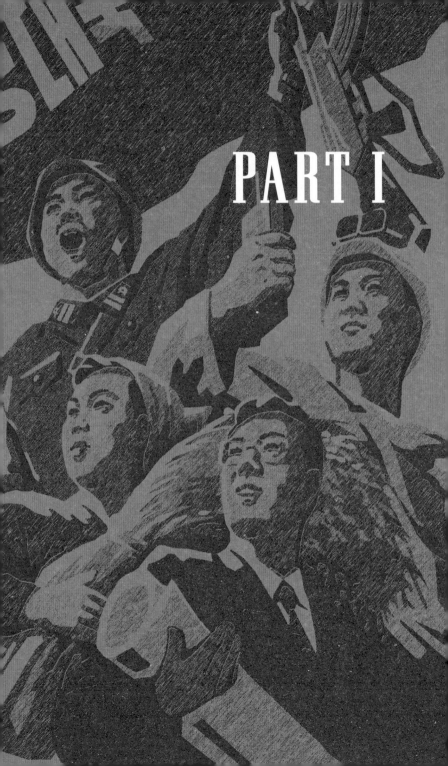

PART I

Chapter 1

Into the Heart of Darkness

After the rain, good weather.
In the wink of an eye,
the universe throws off its muddy clothes.

— Ho Chi Minh

Sitting in the Beijing airport, I felt an eager and exciting tingle while awaiting my first flight with the North Korean national carrier, Air Koryo. In an introduction to the country's superstition, I waited at terminal 2, gate 16, an area reserved specifically for North Korean airplanes. The number, 2.16, is sacred in the so-called hermit kingdom. It signifies February 16, a national holiday and the official 1942 birthday of the late supreme leader Kim Jong Il.

It was July 2002, the beginning of a seven-year journey into what the Western press has painted as Joseph Conrad's "heart of darkness." The experience would become the most fascinating period of my life. But it was a bittersweet time. I met all sorts of friendly North Koreans. They included laborers and mining engineers, the staff of food-processing factories, farmers in food cooperatives, and elites such as academics and top officials. The distance between them and me—the foreign "capitalist"—was wide. My approach of making a profit was something new to them. They had become so accustomed to meeting foreign donors from the fraternal socialist countries and Western nongovernmental organizations (NGOs), like the World Food Program and United Nations.

I sat down, and the diversity of passengers immediately struck me. About a third of the people waiting were North Koreans; half were Korean-Americans, South Koreans, Chinese, and other Asians; and the rest were Caucasians like myself. The North Koreans stood out from all the other groups. Their ethnicity was obvious based on the pins they wore on their jackets, tiny portraits of the country's founding father, Kim Il Sung. He's the eternal president who, under the Constitution, rules North Korea from his grave—making North Korea the world's only necrocracy.

I also realized the sad fact that foreign companies would treat my presence in North Korea as a crippling risk. Air Koryo was blacklisted from operating in the European Union because of its safety record, a measure partially lifted in 2010. But I didn't worry about the safety of the airplane itself. Rather, I feared my health insurance provider could have used this flight as a reason to deny me coverage in case of an accident.

My trepidation was partly realized. Years later, my life insurance company suddenly dropped my plan, arguing that my North Korean residency wasn't appropriate and couldn't be covered. Then, after I opened a profile with a North Korean address on LinkedIn, the account was cancelled. A fellow expatriate, I should add, had his credit card revoked once he disclosed his Pyongyang address.

Those companies weren't seeing the entire picture; my first impression was that the country and its people, and even its airplanes, seemed quite "normal," for lack of a better word, like when I was greeted by a warm smile.

The airplane was one of several Ilyushin Il-62s that were bought in the Soviet Union in 1982. The seats were larger than those of other Asian airlines, which greatly added to the comfort of the tall and overweight Westerner that I was. The cabin looked clean and well maintained. Though the model itself was the oldest aircraft I've ever flown, invented in 1963, it had a solid safety record compared to its later generations. Pilots today even note that it flies smoothly and is famous for steady mechanics alongside scarce electronics.

The standards were indeed what would be expected with any global airline. When I opened my laptop aboard another flight, a nervous hostess immediately rushed over and ordered me to shut it down. She apparently feared the equipment would interfere with sensitive electronics that the airplane did not even have! Precaution was the name of the game here. I was also impressed by the flight skills of the pilots, especially in spring, when they dealt with enormous high winds and dust storms from China. When the airplane was shaking in a storm that, at times, was quite a frightening experience, I always knew in the back of my mind that the pilots were highly professional in their work.

Before takeoff, revolutionary and patriotic music whistled over the loudspeakers. Instead of the *International Herald Tribune*, the *Financial Times*, or *Time* magazine, I was given a copy of the English-language government mouthpiece, the *Pyongyang Times*.

I wasn't surprised at the stories that were splashed all over the newspaper. The front page boldly carried a portrait of the then-leader Kim Jong Il, which is a daily ritual in the North Korean press. The papers themselves are pillars of national glory that foreigners were expected not to step on or throw away—or else they'd take the next flight home. Below Kim's likeness, the paper boasted, "Kim Jong Il, general secretary of the Workers' Party of Korea, chairman of the DPRK [Democratic People's Republic of Korea] National Defense Commission, and supreme commander of the Korean People's Army," was inspecting army units.

Clearly, North Korea was a place where important things happened, I thought with a chuckle. And misguided foreigners like me still hadn't learned of the worldwide significance of the Dear Leader's grand inspections. Other news items of great excitement to any rational individual ranged from "Pyongyang to host Kimjongilia [a flower species named after Kim Jong Il] festival," to "Young builders at power station construction site" and "Fodder additive developed" to "Company increases food output." Other pieces raised hackles about the dangers of a militant Japan and the ghastly human rights records of the American government.

I closed the newspaper. I had no more doubts about where I was heading.

To its credit, Air Koryo was generous, and even Western airlines came off as stingier. The stewardesses served a full free meal with a beverage. The lunch was not exactly a feast, but it was edible. The fried fish, although cold, was tasty. It came in a dark salty sauce with rice, canned fruit, kimchi, and sponge cake. Years later, in the mid-2000s, when at long last fast food became popular in North Korea, Air Koryo gave me a sandwich that resembled a hamburger and, to Korean customers, minced meat bread. The burger joints that later emerged in Pyongyang used the same expression, "minced meat bread," on their menus in lieu of our Western "hamburger."

All the flight attendants were young and attractive females. When I tried to engage in some conversation, I noticed that they got shy. Their vocabulary was limited to a few essential sentences that a North Korean flight attendant was supposed to know, and the airline probably didn't want them to converse with outsiders beyond the politically correct lexicon they were given. After all, they could never be sure about who was sitting in the airplane and what intentions they harbored.

In business class, flight attendants wore the bright red *chosŏn-ot*, the traditional Korean dress known more popularly in South Korea as a *hanbok*. Other flight attendants were dressed in bright red jackets. Red had a strong meaning for North Koreans, since it was on their national flag. Their hair was pulled tightly back and they were all wearing white gloves. Their faces were powdered to make the skin appear white, a look that is considered pristine and proper all over East Asia.

When the airplane crossed over the Yalu River—the geographic boundary that separates China from North Korea—a proud flight attendant joyously proclaimed that we were officially in the pure and revolutionary country. "Fifty-seven years ago, our president, Kim Il Sung, came across the river with great ambition for his country and to liberate his country from Japanese imperialism," she said over the loudspeaker. Over the coming years I would hear that sentence spoken in North Korean airplanes so often that I learned it by heart.

Pyongyang Sunan International Airport was moderately busy with, on average, one to two international flights per day–a number that seems small but is impressive given the political isolation of North Korea.

An hour and a half after takeoff, we arrived at the Pyongyang Sunan International Airport. The government always had the same routine. First, uniformed officers led the passengers to the bus that brought us to the airport hall. Immigration officers were sitting in three closed cabins, equipped with curtains, looking down on the person whose passport details they were checking. Years later, perhaps in a public relations move, these cabins were replaced by friendlier, transparent cabins without roofs, allowing the officers better eye contact with their "customers."

After giving up my mobile phone and slogging through customs, I was welcomed by three North Koreans with winsome smiles. Two of them were my new staff members, and the other man was the director of the foreign relations department of the then-Ministry of Machinery and Metal-Working Industries (the organization that sponsored my visa). That role carried a heavy burden because if I behaved poorly, he would be held responsible.

The weight of my actions didn't seem to bother them. The gleeful employees whisked me away in a minibus to Pyongyang. An exciting journey in this very special country was just beginning.

On the road downtown, I was greeted with a banner that read,

"Independence, Peace, Friendship." These slogans were commonplace, but they give the impression to most foreign visitors that North Koreans are brainwashed. I knew all the clichés spread by the media, and arrived with healthy skepticism toward claims that North Koreans are mindless henchmen.

WAKING UP TO KIMCHI

I will never forget my first breakfast, bright and early at 7 A.M. in Pyongyang. I munched on the staple of the Korean diet, kimchi, which is usually a pickled China cabbage mixed with chili, ginger, garlic, and sugar. It came with rice, eggs, and soup and tasted raw, sweet, and spicy. Like many Westerners, I found the kimchi unbearably hot and ordered another coffee to wash the chili down.

Nevertheless, the taste grew on me, leading me to become something of a kimchi aficionado. My Vietnamese wife, Huong, also enjoyed the dish and learned to make it in all sorts of ways, both spicy and not spicy, from our North Korean maid, Ms. O.

Ms. O was highly educated, and as a medical doctor by training she spoke English and had many talents, such as fixing toilets and calming down fussy children. Even though she was a doctor, working for a foreigner brought in a better income and working conditions. One perk was a daily warm shower in the employer's house, which wasn't available in most other workplaces. She kept our house in good order and was a lovely nanny to our child.

After Huong learned to make kimchi, my family returned the favor to Ms. O by offering her, along with my other staff, some excellent (though foreigner-made) kimchi. They were surprised and delighted, claiming the taste was as good as theirs.

THE PYONGYANG PRIVILEGED

Pyongyang is considered by its residents, known as "Pyongyangites," to be the capital of the Korean revolution against the Japanese occupiers of the first half of the twentieth century. Among North Korean cities, it's the more privileged hometown inhabited by former anti-Japanese guerilla fighters, soldiers, and other Koreans who locals will tell you performed great deeds in the struggle against the Japanese colonial rule and the revolution. The Korean Workers' Party calls this clique of former revolutionaries the "core class." This honorific distinguishes them from the so-called "hostile class," a bedeviled group that includes male ancestors who were landowners, entrepreneurs, and administrative staff working for the Japanese colonial regime (or as the party would say, "pro-Japanese collaborators").

The third social group in this class society is the "wavering class," a sort of middle ground between the first two. This one isn't quite loyal enough to the people's government, making it highly suspect. When the new class system was introduced in 1970 at the Fifth Party Congress, they were officially banned from staying in Pyongyang as well.

Living in Pyongyang, then, is a privilege for the core class of North Koreans. The city itself is a symbol of revolutionary struggle, having been flattened during a fire-bombing campaign by some 1,400 American aircraft during the Korean War. In the 1950s, the capital was rebuilt from scratch with a massive, almost inhumane effort that sacrificed countless lives. The North Korean people were lucky in one way, though, when they began receiving generous economic and technical help from Soviet Russia and other fraternal socialist states. This legacy would continue through the cold war: the DPRK was the biggest recipient of aid from socialist countries until the collapse of the Soviet Union in 1991.

Unlike most foreigners living in Pyongyang, I traveled through large parts of the country and realized that the Koreans living in the capital, who accounted for 10 percent of the country's total population, were by comparison very lucky. Food, housing, and infrastructure were substantially better than what I came across throughout the rest of the country. The gap between Pyongyang and other cities was not huge, but distant rural areas had unpaved roads, no bridges, no cars, no railways, no power pylons, and no cell phone towers. Indeed, Pyongyang gave off a triumphant and stately air. It reminded me of the metropolises in Eastern Europe's socialist nations in the 1960s. Like them, Pyongyang had wide alleyways and streets, blockish apartment buildings, and a welter of revolutionary monuments. Everywhere I looked, the stone faces of memorialized soldiers, workers, and farmers stared back at me, their faces etched with expressions that appeared self-confident about the future of their country. The atmosphere undoubtedly made people feel proud to be North Korean.

PYONGYANG'S BUILDINGS AND MONUMENTS

Pyongyang is a city of grandiosity, and the sheer ingenuity of the buildings and monuments overwhelmed me. The Grand Theater, with a surface area of 322,920 square feet (30,000 square meters)—an area larger than five American football fields—allows 700 artists to perform in front of 2,200 spectators. The Grand People's Study House, one of the world's largest libraries, extends across a space of 1,076,391 square feet (100,000 square meters) and can hold up to thirty million books.

North Korea is also known for its two circuses: one run by the military and another—and some would say even more impressive—troupe that performs on a surface area of 753,473 square feet (70,000 square meters), holding daily performances in front of up to 3,500 spectators. The Mansudae Assembly Hall, where North Korea's parliament, known as the Supreme People's Assembly, holds its sessions, has an area of 484,375 square feet (45,000 square meters). It's a stretch equivalent to eight football fields. The Tower of the Juche Idea (Juche Tower), built on Kim Il Sung's seventieth birthday, is covered with 25,550 pieces of granite, each representing a day in the life of the Great Leader.

The Mangyongdae Children's Palace is a six-story building where youngsters can dabble in extracurricular activities like martial arts, music, and foreign languages. It's at the Street of the Heroic Youth and contains hundreds of rooms that can accommodate 5,400 children. One iconic luxury building and the second-largest operating hotel in

The statues of Kim Il Sung and Kim Jong Il stand before the mosaic of Paekdu Mountain. Kim Il Sung's statue was built in 1972 in honor of his sixtieth birthday. According to Confucian tradition, the sixtieth birthday is a particularly celebrated event because it closes a cycle, at the end of which the names of the years are repeated in Chinese and Korean.

the country, the Koryo Hotel, sits in central Pyongyang with a total floor space of 904,170 square feet (84,000 square meters), comprising two 470-foot (143-meter)-high connected towers with revolving restaurants on top. Up to 1,000 guests can stay in 504 rooms on 45 floors—a height that some would consider an urban feat in Pyongyang.

In addition to the behemoth buildings, I gasped at the surfeit of monuments. The most recognizable shrine—lined across foreign newspapers and photographs of this people's republic—is the 60-foot (18-meter)-high bronze statue of the eternal president, Kim Il Sung. His figure stands triumphantly in front of a mosaic on a wall, a dense packing of stones that make up a panorama of Paekdu Mountain, known as the birthplace of the Korean people. That image also has a special meaning in North Korean culture because Kim Il Sung and his guerrillas fought the Japanese colonialists from this mountain. In April 2012, authorities revealed a second bronze figure of the late leader Kim Jong Il, positioned next to his father's statue (please see illustration on previous page).

What strikes visitors here is the embellishment of the Kims' features, making their statues look manlier and stronger—in a manner similar to how sculptors emphasized the rakish qualities of Roman emperors. North Korean publications call the Kims the "peerless leaders." They are presented as benevolent rulers who, according to Confucian belief, have earned gratitude and loyalty. Confucianism was the dominant value system of the Chosun Dynasty from 1392 to 1910, before Korea was colonized by Japan until 1945.

Although the Korean Workers' Party rejected the Confucian philosophy, which stemmed from feudal China, the authoritarian strain from Confucianism did not disappear. Rather, it was transformed by the wave of socialism and Juche, the ideology of self-reliance. In other words, the old Confucian tradition of repaying debts of gratitude with unquestioned devotion is firmly upheld today, as seen in the numerous visitors bowing in front of the statues.

Other effigies take on mythical qualities, drawing on the potency of Korean legend to uphold the glory of the state. The statue of the Chollima, the Korean equivalent of a winged horse or Pegasus and the largest of its kind in Pyongyang, is 50 feet (16 meters) high and stands on a 110-foot (34-meter)-tall granite footing in a 53,820 square foot (5,000-square meter) park. According to a Korean myth, this untamed horse could travel 245 miles (393 kilometers), about the equivalent of the north-south length of the entire Korean Peninsula, in a single day. On the back of the horse sits a worker with a message from the party Central Committee and a female farmer with rice, flying up to the skies to spread the party's glorious message all over the country.

The Chollima symbol has also been used on other occasions, such as to promote rapid economic development with the slogan "Charge forward with the speed of the Chollima!" which is meant to inspire people to work hard. The Chollima movement in the 1960s was the Korean version of the Chinese Great Leap Forward movement in the

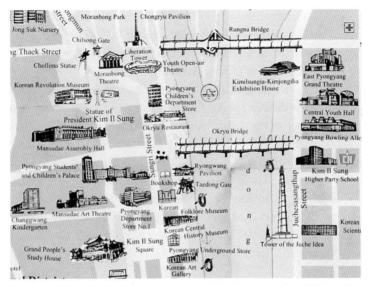

A small section of the Pyongyang city map, marking just a handful of its many grand buildings.

late 1950s. But Kim Il Sung's economic drive was more successful than the Chinese model. North Korea completed its 1957-61 five-year plan two years ahead of schedule, which it celebrated in 1961 by building the bronze Chollima statue.

Not every building in North Korea is a drab, Soviet-style block. The People's Culture Palace and the People's Grand Study House have impressive traditional Korean tiled roof designs. Parts of the city even have a slight European touch: Greek-style theaters, neoclassical congress halls, and an Arch of Triumph have been built, the final as a tribute to Korean resistance fighters against Japanese colonialism from 1925 to 1945. The arch is similar to Paris's Arc de Triomphe, a testament of national power commissioned by Napoleon in the early nineteenth century.

The only minor difference is that it is 30 feet (10 meters) higher, but overall it gives an international flair to the narrative of North Korean glory. Other examples aren't quite façades of antiquity, but give off a more contemporary chic vibe. Wavelike and cylindrical apartment blocks line the relatively affluent neighborhoods along Liberation Street (in Korean, Kwangbok Street), located about 5 miles (8 kilometers) west of the city center.

In 1991, Kim Jong Il coined the term "Juche architecture," which he defined as the expression of *"the harmony of national virtues and the modernity in the design."* It was meant to develop a distinctive national identity, separate from the rest of the world, although Soviet influence was imposed on North Korean edifices.

These projects also display a sort of North Korean craft-excellence, the ability of the efficient command government to pool together labor and resources and to impress their imagery on citizens. In most laissez-faire economies, scarce resources usually aren't allocated so quickly and efficiently.

NEIGHBORHOOD LIFE

Apartment blocks could go somewhat high to forty floors, a minor feat that places Pyongyang ahead of poor but growing cities like Phnom Penh, Cambodia, and Yangon, Burma. Still, while many around the world enjoy the view of a penthouse flat up top, North Koreans preferred, for more practical reasons, modest rooms near the bottom. Elevators frequently broke down thanks to the regular power cuts, a nightmare because they'd instead have to take a dozen flights of stairs.

When there was no electricity to operate the water pumps, residents carried empty buckets and tubs to taps on the street, or they fetched their water from rivers for cooking and washing. In the countryside, where everyday life remains starkly different from that of the capital, people get water from simple old village wells. During the wintertime, people carry water upstairs as water pipes are bound to freeze, at least in the upper floors of unheated buildings.

Regardless of power supplies, I had to get used to the fact that we didn't have running water all the time. I had to adjust to my new schedule, as a privileged foreigner, in which I could enjoy running water only three times a day in tandem with meals: between 7 and 8 A.M., at noontime for an hour, and from 6 to 8 P.M.

Having water did not necessarily mean we had *hot* water either, so I got used to cold showers. I felt more healthy and fit, particularly in winter. Cold showers not only activated my immune system, according to folklore, but led to a life free from colds, flu, and a runny nose. Average Koreans, however, were not as lucky as me. My home, unlike theirs, was almost always heated. This sad reality came back to me in a very direct way. I realized there was a reason behind the soaring winter sales of cold, flu, and respiratory tract infection medicine produced by my pharmaceutical company, PyongSu.

Neighborhood units called *inminban* dominate every apartment block, guarded by volunteers who are usually elderly women or men sitting at the entrance. Their duty is to greet and keep an eye on every visitor to "prevent undesirable elements from gaining a foothold," as described by local media. Such "undesirable elements" include people with a potential political agenda, vendors, and burglars. The citizens, called *dong mu* (a comrade at the same level or below the speaker) and *dong jie* (a comrade at a higher rank than the speaker), are from time to time reminded in newspapers and through propaganda posters to, according to one poster I saw, "heighten revolutionary vigilance."

Whenever I passed by and saw the old guards, one of the most famous claims I came across in foreign media came to my mind. Pyongyang, some newspapers alleged, had been "cleansed" of old people—along with the handicapped as well as pregnant women—who were relocated to the countryside to gentrify the city. If this were really the case, the rules must have been relaxed after I arrived in Pyongyang. The city was home to more diversity than the mass media claimed.

The residents were also responsible for keeping their neighborhoods clean. Indeed, the order and cleanliness of Pyongyang is exemplary. On my walks around the capital, I observed locals, mostly women of various ages, cutting and yanking out the grass sprawling chaotically on streets and pavement. Since the city authorities didn't have lawnmowers, the same manual procedures were applied at parks. Hedges were always neatly trimmed. Not only were streets and pavements spotless, but the pavement edges and trees were painted a very pure and clean white and surrounded by small stones. The rivers running through the city did not have rubbish floating around, and unlike other poor Asian cities such as Manila and New Delhi, I never came across garbage dumps.

Because of the difficulty of nonfunctioning elevators, the elderly lived in apartments on the first few floors of the buildings, while stronger, younger people were expected to live on higher floors. Those who were rich by North Korean standards and who owned a bicycle carried it up and down the stairs, which was no easy task for residents in buildings with twenty or thirty floors. While bicycles were safe in the apartments, thieves took them quickly on the ground floor.

This does not mean that violent crime is rampant, although petty wallet and bike thefts do happen. To give one example of the atmosphere, North Koreans never left shoes in front of their doorways. A Korean joked to me that if they did, the shoes would "walk away all

The view of Pyongyang from the top of the television tower, which is home to a bar and a restaurant. At a distance the capital looks impressive with its high-rise buildings.

In the "backyards" of the best buildings in Pyongyang, small buildings in poor shape line the streets.

by themselves." Over the years, I observed iron bars being erected outside windows and balconies of lower-story apartments, a sign that either thefts were on the rise or people were becoming less trustful of each other. Or both.

The best buildings in Pyongyang and other cities are built along main streets. In the "backyards," small buildings in poor shape line the streets. Shoddy buildings in the "backstreet areas" are surrounded by walls, and the streets in these areas are mostly unpaved (please see illustration on following page). The Pyongyang People's Committee, the official name for the city government, is trying hard to replace these, although it has few resources to do so. New four- and five-story buildings that emerge in these areas are usually constructed by hand, the impact of which is clearly visible because the quality standards aren't consistent.

Around the time I arrived, the North Korean government had set the year 2012 to be a milestone for the development of Pyongyang.

The shoddy buildings in the backstreet areas of Pyongyang are surrounded by walls.

Mr. Pak, who was vice director of the country's leading design institute and who helped construct the building for one of my cofounded companies, explained the rationale to me: "Our great founding leader and president, comrade Kim Il Sung, will then be one hundred years old," he proclaimed. "In his honor, we will make a huge effort to modernize our capital and build new buildings." The plan was a partial success, but did not reach its full potential thanks to the scarcity of resources.

He explained to me that 100,000 apartments in high-rise buildings should be built by 2012, and that each flat should be at least 1,075 square feet (100 square meters) with what sounded like Western-style kitchens and bathrooms. On the balconies, the units would even have storage areas for kimchi jars.

I thought this was an excessively bold plan, taking into account the country's dearth of resources like steel, cement, and scaffolding.

I followed the developments with interest from a distance; by the time they were to be completed, I would not be living in Pyongyang anymore, but I would surely see any results on my future visits.

Despite resource scarcities, it turned out that, in true North Korean fashion, thousands of able-bodied workers were "mass mobilized." Universities, for instance, were shut down in 2011 so students could work on construction sites until April 2012.

It was truly a remarkable spectacle of the ability of this government, and its people, to so swiftly get things done. The government called it the "New Pyongyang Speed Battle," in a reference to the massive reconstruction campaign after the Korean War. The state cleared out land with short notice and evicted residents to their relatives' and other apartments. With hundreds of laborers putting efforts into each edifice on rotating shifts, a new floor popped up every two days.

On the other hand, the facelift had an underbelly. The number of fatalities among untrained workers had probably not been small, although the exact numbers go unreported. And the quality of new buildings has sometimes visibly suffered from the hasty construction. I occasionally noticed cracks on walls and ceilings or paint dripping down onto window glass. Then there's the very visible strain on the capital's aging infrastructure, which has created regular interruptions of the supply of power, water, and heating.

But for the government, this revolutionary project gets the job done. Visitors are often taken aback at the city's modern façade, belying the common description of this capital being stuck in a terrible Stalinist age.

My walks through Pyongyang during the day and night gave me glimpses into apartments, and therefore clues about daily life. Whether affluent or poor, North Koreans seemed to live simply and with few possessions. Although the size and quality of the predominantly state-owned houses varied according to the social status of the dwellers, a typical apartment had two cozy rooms plus a small kitchen not exceeding 325 square feet (30 square meters).

In smaller cities and in the countryside, where there were more one-story houses for families, the living rooms were slightly larger. As four to five family members often lived together, the living room was also used for sleeping. In less luxurious apartment blocks, dwellers shared toilets and showers, which were usually one each per floor.

Most homes do not yet have a telephone. According to 2011 statistics, there were 1.1 million fixed-line phones installed in this country of 24 million inhabitants. They are predominantly used in government offices, state-owned enterprises, and collective farms. The country has been considered a technology backwater, and I have come across hand-cranked phones for communications in a number of facilities. However, three years after the launch in 2008 of a telecom joint venture's 3G cell phone network, it hit 1 million subscribers. According to a study of the U.S.-based Nautilus Institute for Security and Sustainability, 60 percent of Pyongyang residents aged twenty to fifty now use cell phones. By 2013 the number of subscribers doubled to 2 million.

Overall, the quality of life improved during my seven-year stay. I eventually noticed more exhaust pipes from makeshift heating devices heating what would otherwise have been bitterly cold apartments in the winter. More balconies were used by families to cultivate animals to be sold for a profit or to generate meat for the family, a sign of the privatization of the socialist economy discussed in depth later.

Items as diverse as war memorabilia and Japanese Hello Kitty bags were scattered around the rooms. To cope with frequent power cuts after nightfall, flashlights, candles, and matches were common. When I was in charge of a pharmaceutical joint venture, we took advantage of that need by giving away small pocket flashlights as promotional gifts. They were quite a hit, a small gadget that solved a regular problem for North Koreans.

Blankets were another household item, providing warmth during the harsh winters. The walls were usually covered with rough wallpaper from recycled paper, and floors used to be covered by paper. They're now more often covered with plastic-like vinyl, which is cheaper than hardwood, tiles, or carpets and more durable and easy to keep clean.

Like the country itself, apartments were kept meticulously clean. Until the 1990s a so-called sanitation month was proclaimed by the government twice a year, during which all homes had to be repaired and scrubbed down. Now campaigns are less frequently held and less followed, but homes are still amazingly tidy given the shortage of water and detergent.

Everything had a cover: a cover for the radio, the fan, the sewing machine, and the television, often beautifully embroidered, as many North Korean women learn to embroider during their childhood. A large number of dwellers used to embellish their homes not only with embroidery but also with potted houseplants and even aquariums with various kinds of fish. In a country better known for its food shortages than for its livability, there were popular specialized shops that sold aquariums and accessories. It was not the North Korea I saw on CNN. Nor was it the "heart of darkness" that I anxiously awaited ten years ago.

Chapter 2

Malaise into Opportunity

When written in Chinese, the word "crisis" is composed of two characters. One represents danger and the other represents opportunity.

— John F. Kennedy

How did North Korea get where it is today, carrying through the end of the cold war, surviving a devastating famine, and remaining a bastion of communism in a world rapidly turning to the free market?

In the 1960s, there were only two industrialized countries in Asia: Japan and the Democratic People's Republic of Korea. The latter was founded in 1948 on the ashes of Japanese occupation from 1910 to 1945, following the devastation of World War II.

But despite all the destruction and mayhem, socialist North Korea managed to prop up one of Asia's fastest-growing economies from the 1950s until the beginning of the 1970s. For a long time the country's growth and gross domestic product (GDP) per capita rivaled that of capitalist South Korea's, which for a long time was an agrarian and fractious state that depended on the American military presence for protection.

North Korea bolsters a mainly state-run economy, with all bodies reporting to one of three national pillars: the Korean Workers' Party, the Korean People's Army, and the Council of Ministers headed by the prime ministers.

But more interesting are the North Korean companies that resemble the South Korean *chaebol*, conglomerates like Samsung and

Hyundai. The government oversees some 200 businesses that, by North Korean standards, would be considered medium and large enterprises, employing at least a few hundred but in some cases more than 10,000 employees.

Some groups, such as the Korea Sonbong Export & Import Company (exporting marine products and importing foodstuffs) and the Korea SEK Company (exporting cartoon films on order and importing movies and fine-art materials), are more focused on a handful of core operations. Other conglomerates have diversified into a wide range of non-core business activities, such as the Korea Rungrado General Trading Corporation (Sindok spring water, marine products, knitwear, clothes, metallic and nonmetallic minerals, natural shell buttons) and the Korea Kwangmyong Trading Group (agricultural produce, marine products, vessel equipment, nonmetallic minerals, clothes, essential oil, processed jewels).

Although diversification tends to be wasteful, companies added business lines partly as a measure to diversify risks in economically uncertain times "due to hostile foreign forces," according to the government. The diversification also forced businesses into tougher competition with each other, a move that was seen as a countermeasure against waste, as Mr. Ham, a senior official of the State Planning Committee, explained to me. In short, the state didn't want to have all its eggs in one basket in case a crisis erupted.

With the support of the Korean residents living in Japan since the time of the Japanese colonization, Kim Il Sung founded the country's largest conglomerate, the Korea Daesong Trading Group. Today it continues to operate under party provision. Daesong was to become a model group for the rest of the North Korean companies, dabbling in a kaleidoscope of sectors like mining, light industrial factories, ginseng cultivation, shops, and even a large and well-managed ostrich farm, which I visited. Like the South Korean *chaebol*, Daesong also has its own bank that's set up as a separate business unit but that helps finance its vast operations.

During the first few decades of its existence, the DPRK boasted significant development progress with fast electrification and mechanization. By 1984 the state had six to seven tractors per 100 hectares. It also saw widespread "chemicalization"—that is, more widely used fertilizers and pesticides in agriculture and land irrigation, which increased from 227,000 hectares in 1954 to 1.2 million hectares in 1988.[1]

As there were no economic incentives to flee to South Korea, defectors rarely ran off during that period. In fact, the opposite was more common. Among the South Koreans who defected to the North, Ri Sung Gi and Choe Deok Sin were the most famous. Ri, a chemist, ran away in 1950 and was later accused of being involved in North Korea's nuclear weapons programs when he headed the North Korean Atomic Energy Research Institute. He also played a leading role in setting up the massive Vinalon Complex in Hamhung, producing a garment material that became a symbol of national pride and, as many scholars have argued, the material embodiment of Juche. The DPRK-produced Vinylon, also known as "Juche fiber," that was produced there has become the national fiber of North Korea and has been used for the majority of textiles. It has outstripped the use of cotton and nylon. Choe was a South Korean foreign minister who defected in 1986 with his wife to North Korea.

Other prominent defectors were O Kil Nam, a South Korean economist who defected with his family in 1985 to Pyongyang and asked for political asylum in Denmark one year later. The final one was Ryu Mi Yong, current chairwoman of the North Korean Chondoist Chongu Party, who defected in 1985 with her husband to Pyongyang.

PATCHING UP THE ECONOMY

Things took a dramatic turn downward in the 1980s, when North Korea's annual growth dropped substantially to a modest 3 percent per year on average. In the 1990s, the country suffered a further setback when its economy shrank by an annual average of about 4 percent. Most scholars attribute the collapse to the fall of the Soviet Union and Eastern European states, which previously offered food and fuel subsidies to the regime. Combine that with the huge natural calamities such as a drought in the 1990s and, last but not least, structural problems like its obsolete, underinvested state economy.

While global geopolitical changes in the 1980s kick-started China and Vietnam on the road to economic reform, North Korea took no such path. Three reasons explained why the DPRK was less willing to reform than China and Vietnam. First, the U.S. refused to sign a peace treaty with the DPRK, which made the country feel threatened and froze it in a militarized, defense-oriented state. Second, Vietnam was reunited under northern rule in 1975, while mainland China was also a single entity at relative peace (not counting Hong Kong, Macao, and Taiwan). Unlike North Korea, China and Vietnam did not face a significant external political threat, which allowed the two nations to open up gradually without fear of overthrow.

Chinese leaders like to remind their North Korean colleagues of this history. That's because Beijing hopes to put North Korea on a Chinese growth model. At diplomatic meetings, they explain to North Koreans that the socialist countries in Eastern Europe collapsed because of their reluctance to reform, whereas Vietnam and China undertook pragmatic even if unpopular changes. The official line is that the reforms led them on a path to development, prosperity, and strength. In the eyes of the Vietnamese and Chinese neighbors, socialist countries like North Korea and Cuba needed to make up their minds quickly.

One analysis by Bank of America-Merrill Lynch, published in early 2012, argues that serious economic reforms would most likely trigger an annual growth rate of 10 to 12 percent—a remarkably high average that exceeds the roughly annual growth of 5 to 8 percent in China and Vietnam. The firm further noted that liberalization would close the income gap between "rich" South Korea and "poor" North Korea. In forty years North Korea may be just over three times poorer than its southern neighbor, compared to forty times poorer if no changes are enacted soon. The report added that the DPRK can achieve this goal if it follows the steps of other emerging economies that decided to join the global economy. It also said that market opening does not necessarily lead to reunification, as the North may opt for a partial open market system like China.

Western advice to the North Koreans is suspected as a sugar-coated plot to overthrow the socialist system, in particular during periods when tensions with the U.S. and South Korea are high. Still, in my own private discussions with senior cadres, they admitted the need to "learn from other countries and adopt elements from them that are beneficial for our country."

Lately, reform-minded cadres have been getting a new boost from "Kim Jong Un, who has an interest in the knowledge economy and is carefully watching economic reforms in various countries, including China," said Yang Hyong Sop, vice chairman of the Supreme People's Assembly, to the Associated Press in a rare interview on January 16, 2012.

North Korea's official economy began a modest recovery in the 2000s, but annual average growth was meager at 1.5 percent per year during the 2000s. As in countless other poor countries, the informal or "shadow" economy without a doubt grew multifold during the same period. In the absence of reliable statistics, the figures I've compiled from different sources, combined with my on-the-ground observations, are merely approximations and not precise data.

But being in the field, I've captured a general idea of economic trends that the statistics don't fully reveal because the government doesn't publish them. There are emerging bicycle repair spots across the country and more people selling cigarettes, drinks, food, and other goods along streets outside the capital.

But number-crunching didn't encapsulate the breadth of what was going on. In February 2012, for instance, the South Korean Hyundai Research Institute reported that North Korea's GDP grew the previous year by a surprising 4.7 percent from a year earlier. But take the figure with a grain of salt. It was based on the think tank's calculations of grain production, which according to the U.N. Food and Agriculture Organization[2] grew by 7.2 percent from the previous year. Combine that, the organization argued, with a lower infant mortality rate—a combination of trends that, from an economist's standpoint, signify growing per capita income and prosperity. The country's heightened efforts to meet its goal of building "a strong and prosperous nation by 2012" was another cause for this growth rate, although it will be unsustainable without future economic reforms. There were other chance factors, like a good harvest that year and the efforts made in preparation for Kim Il Sung's birthday.

There appears to be no end in sight for the severe economic problems of the world's most centrally planned economy. Chronic underinvestment from both foreign investors and the government led to an industrial capital stock that was run down to a critical level. Over the past two decades, countless factories have closed; those that continue to run often do so at low-level capacities, thanks to a shortage of raw materials. (North Korea is relatively resource-rich, but the country needs heavy investment to exploit the metals and minerals, as well as foreign equipment and spare parts.) Add that to chronic electricity shortages, and economic prospects get even worse; the lack of electrical power is the largest bottleneck to any industrial development of North Korea. I have visited provincial factories far from the capital where workers slept in the factory at night so they could wait for sudden electrical bursts. When the power came back and the lights went on, the workers jumped to their feet to operate the machines for a couple of hours until the next blackout. They'd sometimes go without electricity for the remainder of the day.

Historically, North Korea had difficulties propping up its industrial economy without sufficient electricity, but the situation was always better before the cold war ended. Thanks to flooding, hydropower generation dramatically dropped until the mid-1990s. In addition, the coal supply declined and wasn't enough to feed thermal power plants, because of the end of Soviet subsidies and because many coal mines were flooded in the 1990s.

In the late 1980s, North Korea generated its peak electricity output, estimated at 30 terrawatt-hours. (1 terrawatt-hour is 1 billion kilowatt-hours, the equivalent of the amount of energy that is produced by a 1 million megawatt generator over a period of 1 hour.)

Surprisingly, the World Resources Institute estimated in 2010 that North Korea's electricity consumption per capita was 600 to 800 kilowatt-hours per year, compared to 402 in India and merely 74 in Myanmar. The estimates seemed impressive, but flawed. They may be based on nominal electricity generation and distribution capacities, versus a much lower actual electricity production and distribution. About two thirds of the power came from dams built mostly under Japanese rule, and the remainder from coal plants—two sources that add up to a decent output, but not enough for the entire country.

In the 1990s, the total power production dropped below 20 terrawatt-hours, according to most estimates. ABB, a firm I represented that worked on power technologies, suggested that the loss of power during transformation and distribution amounted to up to 25 percent. We recommended that the Ministry of Energy Production and Coal Industry allocate more resources for fixing up the country's electrical infrastructure. The approach would have been far more cost-effective than adding new power stations, and total savings would have corresponded to a substantial double-digit percentage.

Logistics (or the lack of it) has as much to do with North Korea's food shortages as it does with power shortages. North Korea is home to hundreds of thousands of what were once pristine agricultural machines and trucks. This was because mechanization of agriculture as well as modern transportation (in addition to electrification) was one of Kim Il Sung's most important goals for the socialist country. After the 1990s, they fell into disrepair. Many are still out of order, and the country can't get enough spare parts or fuel. A team of foreign experts from the Swiss Development and Cooperation Agency and NGOs estimated that up to 20 percent of the annual harvest rots in the fields and never reaches consumers in the cities. That made the food shortages of the 1990s even worse.

Throughout the 2000s, the state-led business sector has been trying to repair and set up new power stations. The situation today has improved over that of a decade ago, when I arrived in North Korea. Several power stations are being built along the Huichon River, and after 11 years of construction, the largest one, with a power capacity of 300,000 kilowatts, was completed in 2012. Pyongyang is the main beneficiary, and it will suffer from fewer blackouts as a result. The dams will help protect cultivated land and residential areas along the river that have been regularly flooded in the past, helping bring about devastating food shortages. But the total power output remains substantially below the record output at the end of the 1980s, and it's not clear when or if the nation will return to those days.

North Korea's ailments partially grow out of its "military first" policy, which gobbles up funds that could go to infrastructure and education and instead puts them in the hands of the nation's military. The U.S. government put forward figures, possibly exaggerated, suggesting that North Korea is the world's most militarized country: about a million people, or 20 percent of men aged seventeen to fifty-four, serve in the regular armed forces. That number doesn't include the substantial reserve force of seven to eight million soldiers out of a total population of twenty-four million. The number pretty much includes every person in their twenties and thirties, who are ready to fight at a moment's notice.

In addition to being a strong deterrent for potential aggressors, a nuclear arsenal is relatively cost-effective compared to legions of obsolete weaponry and a massive defense force, a senior party official explained to me.

WILL NORTH KOREA STRIKE GOLD?

For all the errors and mismanagement, there's reason to be hopeful for the future. The North Koreans are very pragmatic people, coming from a long tradition of industrialism in its economic alliance with the Soviet Union. During the cold war, the DPRK even boasted a higher percentage of industrial workers than its former socialist ally, which is an important measure of "socialist progress." That factor, combined with the population's 99 percent literacy rate, can bring about a swift reconstruction of industry once economic reforms are carried out.

All over the countryside I saw that people were in some ways not living agrarian lives. Their skills were clear, for example, when they would weld with pinpoint precision, something only well-trained and experienced craftsmen do. More extraordinary was their ability to weld in the dark, despite not having undergone professional training. Factories were better organized and cleaner than those I've seen in other socialist countries in the past, such as those in Czechoslovakia and Hungary.

I was also impressed by the electrical and mechanical engineers who explained to me how they built a hydropower station, which included turbines and generators. The construction was based on one dam in a simple 1970s Russian leaflet with a few photos, but without detailed drawings and technical specifications. A team of ABB experts whom I led on a delegation were amazed at the ingenuity and called the station an engineering masterpiece.

The good work ethic comes from the party's sophisticated governance system, which uses awards and high-level visits. One system, called the *Ch'ŏngsan-ri* management method, started in the 1960s. It was first introduced in the Chongsanri agricultural cooperation in 1960 before it was applied as an agricultural management system for collectivized farms. Essentially, the system was designed to give workers ideological and spiritual rather than material incentives. It urged officials to emulate Kim Il Sung by doing field inspections during which they addressed farmers' grievances and listened to their ideas.

For factories, the *Taean* work system was introduced and aimed at streamlining bureaucratic management. This system was first introduced in 1961 at the Taean Electric Machinery Plant, which put a party committee at the head of an enterprise. The members were to debate and decide collectively the directions and methods to be applied in the company. As in the case of Chongsanri, the party committee had not only a supervisory role but also an inspirational one to permanently motivate workers to achieve production goals. Observers in the West may see an approach like this as paternalistic and backwards, but stripping it of all moral judgments, it gave North Koreans reason to work hard when times were difficult.

These socialist management systems were, with the exception of those of Mao's China, the most radical ones. Even Stalin's Soviet Union gave material benefits to high-performing workers. In addition to these methods, mass production campaigns like the Chollima movement that started in 1958 were introduced, which exhorted the workers to achieve production targets. To this effect it included "socialist competition" among industries, companies, farms, and work units, where the winners earned praise for their outstanding socialist and patriotic deeds.

The Korean Workers' Party also has mass campaigns extolling workers to labor and to meet the planned targets. And last but not least, the top leaders regularly inspect factories, farms, shops, and military units, where they offer guidance and mix with exemplary workers, farmers, and soldiers. To memorialize such a historical visit, the local committee always erects a commemorative stone at factory entrances, schools, and other places that have what they would call the privilege of benefiting from the leader's personal guidance.

The most exemplary workers are honored with the award of a "labor hero" title, while others get other awards and medals. State-run factories, companies, and army units are also given Kim Il Sung medals and Kim Jong Il medals "in the struggle to construct the state," as the award reads. A small elite of senior party cadres, artists, sportsmen and sportswomen, and scientists who have done extraordinarily great deeds for the country are honored with golden watches carrying the leader's signature, cars with the leader's birthday number (216) on the license plate, and sometimes even houses. On a side note, material objects also, such as buildings, tractors, trucks, etc., are "rewarded" with stars and other symbols of recognition when their planned life span has been exceeded.

Everybody in the production line, from regular workers to chief engineers all the way up to senior ideological leaders, held a fervent belief in technology. They believed that it could solve pretty much every problem in their businesses. It's a myth that has been cherished by all socialist countries—that science and technology can bring about an affluent socialist society—which also has influences in Confucianism. They constantly chattered using trendy acronyms like CNC (computer numerical control, meaning computer-controlled machine tools) and IT (information technology), and terms like "biotech," implying some level of sophistication.

In 2009, I began hearing choirs sing a propaganda song praising the greatness of CNC machines. It was striking that the North Koreans, otherwise proud of conserving the purity of the Korean language, used even the English expressions CNC and CAD (computer-aided design) and not a Korean euphemism stripped of any foreign tinge. That was because everybody agreed, at least on the surface, that the DPRK did not require social and economic reforms. The fatherland was perfect, but the economy suffered because it didn't have state-of-the art technologies. They blamed that problem on Western embargoes.

North Korea has the potential to experience a windfall of wealth from natural resources—but the problem is, unfortunately, that it's not selling metals and minerals systematically. An important cause of this is the lack of electricity and materials, along with the worn-out equipment, antiquated facilities, and poor maintenance. This made even the country's most important facilities operate at about 30 percent or less of their capacity only in the mid-2000s, according to the assessment of some mining equipment companies I represented in North Korea. The country has impressive deposits of more than 200 different minerals.

North Korea's magnesite reserves are the world's second largest after China's, and magnesite is a particularly valuable mineral because of its importance for industry. It has a wide range of uses such as in insulating material in the electrical industry, as slag in steelmaking furnaces, and even in the preparation of chemicals and fertilizers.

The country's iron ore mine in Musan, near the Chinese border, is Asia's largest. Iron is the most commonly used metal, used for construction, including bridges and highways; means of transportation, such as cars, trains, ships, and aircraft; and tools such as machines and knives.

Its tungsten deposits are likely the sixth largest in the world, and North Korea is China's second-largest coal supplier. While coal is primarily used for producing steam in electric power plants or by the steel industry for coke making, tungsten is used for mining and drilling tools, cutting tools, dies, bearings, and armor-piercing projectiles. In countries like the United States and Germany, tungsten is widely used in the production of cutting tools and wear-resistant materials.

North Korea is also home to substantial deposits of rare earth minerals, which are difficult to find around the globe but are increasingly in demand from growing powers such as China and India. They are particularly valuable because of their omnipotent potential: they're present in pretty much every piece of consumer electronics, such as computer disc drives, X-ray imaging, flat-screen televisions, iPhones, wind turbines, halogen lights, and precision-guided missiles, to name but a few. The country is also home to an estimated 2,000 tons of gold, 500 billion tons of iron, and 6 billion tons of magnesite, with a total value running into the trillions of U.S. dollars. At least that's according to a 2009 report titled *Current Development Situation of Mineral Resources in North Korea* by South Korea's government-owned KORES Korea Resources Corporation.

North Korea feared losing control of its glamorously valuable natural resources, and as such was reluctant to sell raw materials to neighboring countries. As a result, only a few foreign and North Korean-invested mining joint ventures have been doing the extractions in the last ten years. When I suggested upon my arrival in North Korea to the senior officials in the then-Ministry of Metal and Machinery Industries, which owned the large Musan Iron Ore Mine at the Chinese border, to open it up to Chinese investment and exploitation, the answer was that "it is a part of the Korean heritage which we cannot give away." Over the following years I witnessed the government turn down a dozen or so foreign requests to invest in mines.

But change is in the air, and North Korea is getting serious about profiting from metals and minerals. The *China People's Daily* reported in September 2011:

> According to China's General Administration of Customs, the value of direct exports to China from the DPRK last year was $1.2 billion, a 51 percent increase year-on-year, attributed to China's robust demand for iron ore, coal, and copper. At present, the DPRK mainly imports grain and oil from China. In 2010, China's exports to its peninsula neighbor reached $2.3 billion, an increase of 21 percent from a year earlier.

The prospect was unthinkable just a couple of years earlier, but North Koreans are now rolling out the red carpet for Chinese investors. They're also building manufacturing outposts along the border where China can hire cheap North Korean labor, where dealings are more relaxed than in Kaesong. (More on Kaesong later.)

China is making an effort, too, to develop its desolate northern provinces by taking advantage of cross-border exchanges. These provinces are now booming with factories along with a construction frenzy to build roads and railways that move outside of North Korea, but China supports the construction and maintenance of some roads into North Korea as well.

Some unlikely spots are being developed for joint manufacturing projects. Hwanggumpyong, a farming and military-focused island south of the Chinese border city of Dandong, and Wihwa, a smaller island in the middle of the Yalu River, are due to be turned into hubs for manufacturing, tourism, and logistics. So far, disagreements between the North Koreans and the Chinese have led to delays.

Russia, too, has moved in with construction projects that will give it access to the ice-free North Korean port of Rajin. Moscow's hope is to export Siberian coal and import Asian goods that it will eventually transport to Western Europe. (Russian Railways operates the world's second-largest network after that of the U.S., reaching from North Korea's border well into Western Europe.) Of course, North Korea stands to get significant cuts from the project.

Many South Koreans fear that China is encroaching on North Korea with money, hoping to swallow it up and turn it into a de facto Chinese province. The accusations are unfounded; I just don't see convincing evidence that the investments—made by individual companies and not the government itself—are part of a political conspiracy driven by common defense interests or a grand geopolitical strategy on the Korean Peninsula.

Trade and investment are bigger priorities for China. That will improve the standard of living of its northeastern provinces, as well as promote stability in its immediate neighborhood. Too much pessimism can block out this sort of objective view, and there's much to look forward to in China-North Korea relations.

NOTES

1. Data from http://www.country-studies.com/north-korea/agriculture.html.
2. Data from U.N. agencies and *The World Factbook* 2013-14. Washington, DC: Central Intelligence Agency, 2013.

Chapter 3

Look to the Party, Young Revolutionary, and Buy

*Only the mob and the elite can be attracted by
the momentum of totalitarianism itself. The
masses have to be won by propaganda.*

— Hannah Arendt

"He looks like a monkey," Mr. Kim, a customer, said while giggling during our lunchtime one day, as he watched a Western aid worker at another table. I laughed as I found both the foreigner funny as well as the reactions of the two Koreans.

The foreign aid worker had piercings all over his face, on his eyebrows, nose, lips, and even cheeks. His untidy long hair was patched with dyed colors. He wore a ridiculous-looking cap that was too small and had a zany insignia, and tattered clothes, including the typical torn jeans in vogue for Westerners.

He wasn't the only unkempt Westerner I knew in the expatriate community, and people like him reinforced the stereotype. They seemed to forget that they were, in fact, guests in a foreign country, and not there to take advantage of some tributary vassal state in the Far East.

Mr. Kim's superior, Mr. Son, looked at him sternly, disapproving of his remarks. Mr. Son probably thought exactly the same thing. But Mr. Kim was not supposed to express his thoughts about a foreigner in front of another foreigner. Reading between the lines, I understood what both of them were really thinking. What Korean would ever want to become like him?

Meanwhile, patriotic songs were constantly blaring on public loudspeakers, on television, and at military parades. But one piece in particular got stuck in my head, played over and over as the country's most popular melody. At a gymnastics performance, the tune buzzed on once again, prompting me to turn to a friend for an explanation.

Mr. Pang, a chief beer brewer working at a beer factory, responded that he was shocked that this Swiss expatriate wasn't familiar with it.

"You don't know this tune?" he answered with genuine surprise. "It's called 'No Motherland without You.'"

"What is it about then?" I inquired.

He went into an impassioned but short speech, showing off his patriotism for the fatherland. "It's about our General Kim Jong Il. It says without him we cannot exist, as he has extraordinary talents and virtues, and that's why we Koreans love him. It was him who further developed the Juche idea created by our Great Leader president Kim Il Sung, and it was him who introduced the Songun (military first) politics to protect our motherland and the Korean people."

Mr. Pang then translated the core sentence that is repeated in the song: "We cannot exist without you, Comrade Kim Jong Il! The motherland cannot exist without you!"

For all his faults, Kim Il Sung did everything in his power to preserve Korean arts and culture. His ideas were even supported by ardent overseas Koreans who opposed the regime.

North Koreans consider themselves to this day as ethnically pure and intrinsically superior, far more than do the people of other nationalistic regimes in Japan and China. They believe that they are the world's most upright people living in the world's most exceptional nation.

The mindset is a natural extension of their history. A national experience of foreign dominance by China, Japan, and the U.S. has, in the eyes of the North Koreans, wrecked the purity of their southern neighbors; today, North Koreans have taken sole guardianship of what they see as true "Koreanness."

The attitude is reflected in North Korean propaganda, and taking a look at the myriad of posters and leaflets reveals much about the mindset. Pyongyang is home to the Korean Workers' Party's Propaganda and Agitation Department, which controls far-reaching ideological campaigns. The state sees propaganda as particularly valuable, giving it the needed resources that take up a good chunk of the gross national product—although the precise data haven't been published.

To be fair, all over the world businesses engage in another form of propaganda: advertising. The only difference is that it advances a cause of consumerism rather than politics. North Korea had banned the unsocialist practice until 2002, when advertisements were allowed. The opening suggests at least a partial embrace of market ideas.

Still, it's only a little creek compared to the vast sea of state-sponsored information: PyongSu, my pharmaceutical company, launched its first radio commercial for its painkiller PyongSu Spirin in 2005. For a short while in 2009, television stations surprised their viewers by broadcasting commercials for beer, ginseng, hairclips, and a Korean restaurant.

The government has, unfortunately, not resumed TV commercials since then, part of a ploy by the same hard-liners who pushed for a disastrous currency devaluation in 2009. Yet it wasn't a complete reversal of the new policy: the state didn't clamp down on printed advertising, allowing PyongSu and other North Korean companies to continue distributing flyers and catalogues and advertising their products and services on the country's intranet. TV advertising was perhaps perceived as too politically sensitive by the conservative old guard since foreign visitors as well as South Koreans could watch and observe it.

However, propaganda continues to be an everyday message blurted in front of the North Korean people. And it plays a significant role in their lives.

After Kim Jong Il died in December 2011, party mouthpieces shot off a new emergent ode called "Footsteps"—and it wasn't the jazz standard performed by John Coltrane. The piece was written for Kim Jong Un, and its title signified that he was marching in the heroic footsteps of his deceased father. North Koreans attribute the song with son Kim's emergent legacy. Of course, pretty much no beautiful melody on TV, radio, or in karaoke rooms is free from ideology and propaganda. Most of them appeal to patriots, the party, and the army. They often wax philosophical on the sufferings under the yoke of the Japanese colonialists or praise the leaders.

A PROPAGANDA STATE?

It is true that Bible-like allegories have a profound impact on how North Koreans see themselves and the world, as told to me by countless locals. Posters are also a potent venue: they are the regime's most visible form of propaganda, painted with bright colors, meaningful symbols and images, and large fonts. Simple but commanding language is used.

Barbara Demick, the author of the widely acclaimed 2010 book *Nothing to Envy: Ordinary Lives in North Korea*, mentioned that in his book *1984*, "George Orwell wrote of a world where the only color to be found was in the propaganda posters. Such is the case in North Korea."[1] But her statement isn't entirely true. Half a decade before she wrote this, we had already plastered our pharmaceutical factory with a green color, because it was a well-known pharmaceutical symbol in continental Europe.

Around the same time, other buildings were being repainted in Pyongyang in a wider variety of colors. People could be seen over the years with more colorful clothes, not only during holidays, as is tradition. More young students carried colorful Hello Kitty and other fancy school bags.

In her book, Demick also claims that "*Gone with the Wind* is a dangerous, banned book."[2] But I saw people reading the novel at the Grand People's Study House in Pyongyang and in public libraries in provincial capitals. The gap between Barbara Demick's Orwellian stereotypes and the reality on the ground is widening a little every year.

Still, the signs are hung up everywhere you go: in school buildings, hospitals, factories, and farms; in magazines, paintings, films, theaters, operas; on TV and radio and on public loudspeakers. It's difficult to escape the gaze of a nationalistic worker or national leader peering down at you from his poster, urging absolute loyalty to the pure Korean race.

Posters are addressed to different groups of people. For farmers, they offer a resounding call to the fields, to boost food production amid chronic shortages. For industrial laborers, the placards urge no able body to sit idle in the withering factories, but rather encourage them to double their efforts for a strong and prosperous nation. Students are pushed to become skillful scientists who can develop sophisticated technologies and to propel the country into "a brilliant new era," to quote a common catchphrase on the posters. Nobody is left out: other targets include grandchildren being urged to care for their grandparents and rascals being cautioned against doing something dangerous.

That's not to say the propaganda is trite and childlike. Sometimes the party is clever in how it plays with imported foreign ideas. In response to George Bush's declaration of the "axis of evil" in 2002, one North Korean poster launched subtle counterpropaganda: "The world turns with Korea as its axis." Of course, not all North Koreans believed the world actually revolved around their country.

Even the newspapers play a prominent role in spreading state ideas. In North Korea, state-run publications do not compete to break the fastest and hardest-hitting news. The mass media's purpose is spelled out in the Constitution: it defines the press as "strengthening the dictatorship of the proletariat, bolstering the political unity and ideological conformity of the people, and rallying them behind the party and the Great Leader in the cause of revolution." North Korea's media correspondingly carries strict proofreading procedures. Any journalist committing an ideological "error" is quite certain to be sent to a harsh wasteland to be thoroughly "revolutionized."

Every administrative district in North Korea is home to a so-called immortality column, a reference to the immortal heroes of the revolution. Statues of Kim Il Sung adorn the special zones, usually found in provincial capitals and places of national significance. All of the effigies display the same tagline: "The Great Leader Comrade Kim Il Sung will be with us forever."

SOME PROPAGANDA SLOGANS

Instilling a sense of loyalty in the Korean Workers' Party (created in the 1980s, still fully valid):
"What the party decides, we do."

Worshipping the best:
"Worship the Great Leader, General Kim Il Sung, like the eternal sun."
"Let's thoroughly arm more and more through the revolutionary ideas of the Great Leader Kim Il Sung."
"The Great Leader Kim Il Sung will be with us forever."
"Hurray for General Kim Jong Il, the sun of the twenty-first century."
"Thank you to General Kim Jong Il, our loving father."
"Let us become human bullets and bombs guarding the Great Leader General Kim Jong Il with our lives!"
"Let us defend the party Central Committee headed by the respected comrade Kim Jong Un, at the cost of our lives."
"Let us become revolutionary soldiers boundlessly loyal to the party and Great Leader!"
"Let's accept our party's Songun (army first) revolution loyally."
"Our [Leader/ideology/military/system] is the best."

Calling to uphold Juche and Songun (army first) politics:
"Let's stick to self-sufficiency and nationalism in revolutions and construction!"
"Our country's socialism is the best!"
"Ideology, technology, and culture according to the demands of Juche!"
"Spread the ideological, fight, speed, and skill battles. [This is a literal translation from Korean, but it roughly means the battles fought everywhere such as against imperialist enemies and to build up the country.] Let's use Juche Korea's wisdom and bravery."
"Let us complete the Juche revolutionary cause under the leadership of the respected comrade Kim Jung Un!"

"Living methods, fighting spirit, new ideas, all according to the needs of Songun."

"Songun politics. The DPR Korea moves the world."

Promoting Korean culture devoid of any impure foreign content:

"Let's make the beautiful Korean clothes a way of life."

"Let's establish a social spirit for enjoying our people's clothes."

"Let's actively promote our people's traditional folk games."

Parents and teachers being asked to make Korean children more intelligent and able than they already are:

"Let's actively develop children's intelligence."

"Let's learn how to swim starting young."

"Let's all become expert swimmers."

> The book is a silent teacher and
> a companion in life.
>
> KIM IL SUNG

This quote adorns every book shop and library.

A propaganda poster at the school of the Chongsanri farm, a model farm shown to foreign tourists, praising a North Korean kids' game:

"It is exciting to play soldiers beating and seizing the Americans!"

Messages directed at farmers: the first one, issued years ago, expressing a wish that has yet to be fulfilled:

"Let's send more tractors, cars, and modern farming machines to the farm villages for the working class."

"Let's raise a great number of goats in every family."

"Let's raise a lot of livestock through multiple methods."

"Let's expand goat rearing and create more grassland in accordance with the party."

"Let us turn grass into meat!"

"Let's grow more sunflowers."

"Prevention and more prevention. Let's fully establish a veterinary system for the prevention of epidemics!"

Messages on posters, in newspapers, and on loudspeakers urging voters to take part in elections held every five years. Elections are mostly a formality, though: citizens elect the candidate for their district chosen by the Democratic Front for the Reunification of the Fatherland, which is dominated by the Korean Workers' Party.

"July 24 is day of elections for deputies to provincial (municipal), city (district), and county people's assemblies."

"Let's demonstrate the power of single-hearted unity."

"Let's all vote yes."

The first message below urged people to work at the speed of the mythical Korean Pegasus, a campaign to make Pyongyang look modern by 2012 (when the hundredth birthday of founder president Kim Il Sung was celebrated):

"Let's develop Pyongyang, the capital city of the revolution, into a world-class city."

"Electric power, coal, the metal industry, and the railroad are important to the revitalization of the people's economy."

"Let's construct small and medium power plants everywhere in our country and get energy everywhere."

"Work and live with the mind and spirit of Pegasus!"

"The twenty-first century is the age of information (communications) industry."

"Radical turn in people's livelihood improvement!" (The slogan, several years old and regularly repeated, will hopefully be realized someday in the not too distant future.)

Calling upon families to avoid wasting resources:

"In your family, let's conserve every drop of water." (The poster shows a mother closing a dripping water tap.)

These messages should make clear that North Korea is invincible thanks to its military might:

"Just as it began, the revolution advances and is victorious, through the barrel of a gun."

"The reunified fatherland is at the tip of our bayonets."

"Nobody in the world can defeat us."

"Let's be invincible in every fight."

"Let's achieve even more supremacy."

"Our missile program is a guarantee for world peace and security."

Calling for reunification of North and South:

"Kimjongilia, the flower of reunification." (The poster depicts united Korea in the shape of a sea of Kimjongilia flowers.)

"Let's quickly end the agony of division." (The poster shows a grandmother still waiting for reunification.)

"Between our people, let's rush towards a majestic and prosperous strong unified country."

Messages to keep people alert about the threats posed by the DPRK's worst enemies from day one of its existence:

"When provoking a war of aggression, we will hit back, beginning with the U.S."

"Let's take revenge a thousand times on the U.S. imperialist wolves."

"If the American imperialists attack us, let us wipe them off the map forever!"

"Death to U.S. imperialists, our sworn enemy!"

"Let's prepare thoroughly in order to defeat the invaders. The Japanese invaders slaughtered innocent, law-abiding citizens. 1,000,000 slaughtered; 6,000,000 forced arrests; 2,000,000 sex slaves."

LIFE IN COLOR

Seeing propaganda spread across every nook and cranny of North Korean society, it's easy to pass off North Koreans as mindless drones. But would such logic make sense if it were reversed? Do Americans get brainwashed by cravings for McDonald's and Starbucks, seeing their logos smothered all over the country? Do they salute every American flag?

Actually, North Koreans simply walk by propaganda posters—including new ones—without so much as a glance. Like their American counterparts who constantly drive by advertising billboards and are inundated with flashy Internet marketing, North Koreans are accustomed to the messages at political training courses, mass rallies, and in the mass media and blurted out on loudspeakers. The propaganda is reiterated—again and again—until the slogans are known by heart (just like how most young Americans bandy about the old McDonald's tagline, "I'm lovin' it").

A recent U.S. government-funded study titled *A Quiet Opening: North Koreans in a Changing Media Environment* reads: "While it remains the most closed media environment in the world, North Korea has, to a significant extent, opened unofficially since the late 1990s. North Koreans today have significantly greater access to outside information than they did 20 years ago." Young North Koreans in particular are better informed overall and take official propaganda with a grain of salt. They're less respectful of the state and less fearful of repression.

North Korea historian Andrei Lankov even argues that state subjugation overall has significantly diminished over the last two decades and that propaganda has lost some of its power of persuasion. He also stressed that "contrary to media portrayals in recent years, North Korea has actually become a less repressive place to live."[3] Keep in mind, though, that North Koreans rarely gossip about politics and that the country is still a very authoritarian state despite the loosening.

Propaganda posters twenty or thirty years earlier portrayed North Korea as an industrial powerhouse, with steel mills and factories running at full capacity. South Korea was depicted as a poor agrarian country with grim and oppressive American soldiers. Taking account of the latest developments on the Korean Peninsula that are largely known to North Koreans, newer propaganda posters are portraying the South in a reverse mode as a place where people are being suffocated by air, poisoned by its numerous factories and vehicles, and deafened by infernal noise. North Korea, meanwhile, is shown as a pristine, quiet natural paradise.

Compare the everyday experiences and struggles of North Koreans with the stereotypes coming out of the West. In 2012, Stanford professor and Pulitzer Prize-winner Adam Johnson wrote a novel set in North Korea, but included just about every negative generalization he could find on the country. He and his publishers promoted the book as "insight" into North Korea.

So much for insight: he claimed that in North Korea "no one has read a book that's not propaganda for 60 years," a patronizing falsehood. My staff, along with all sorts of other North Koreans I've met, have read foreign books such as Alexandre Dumas's thriller *The Count of Monte Cristo* and Ernest Hemingway's short stories *Men without Women*, and some of them could even recite lengthy passages. At home and sometimes at their universities, they watched foreign movies like *Gone with the Wind* and *Titanic*.

Over the years, more kids carried around backpacks and bags adorned with Mickey and Minnie Mouse and Daisy Duck. Nobody complained that the harmless characters were *miguk nom*, the Korean phrase used in official propaganda that means "American bastards." The kids also enjoyed watching *Jungle Book, The Lion King*, and *Spiderman*. I have listened to North Korean orchestras play all sorts of Western classics; the most memorable for me was "Gwine to Run All Night," more widely known as "Camptown Races." It was not composed by some communist sympathizer, but by Stephen Collins Foster, the most famous songwriter of the United States in the nineteenth century, often called the "father of American music."

A former U.S. State Department official summed up the situation: "We know less about North Korea than they know about us."

Journalist Melanie Kirkpatrick, a longtime member of the editorial board of *The Wall Street Journal*, published another North Korea book in September 2012. She portrayed North Korea as a "hellhole" that was "rife with suffering and starvation." The country, she added, "keeps its citizens in the dark ages." "Foreigners and foreign goods are kept out" is another tall claim of hers. Had that been true, I would, of course, not have been able to sell foreign goods in North Korea.

Yet looking more carefully under the veil, it becomes clear that these stories represent a single slice of North Korean society. A professor from the Australian Defence Force Academy who spent six months from 2010 to 2012 teaching English to North Korea's future leaders opposes Johnson's and Kirkpatrick's views. In *North Korea from inside the Classroom*, Professor Stewart Lone, wrote: "Having spent a good deal of time in the company of more than 400 North Korean teenagers, I dismiss the idea that everyone lives in fear and privation." He later told news.com.au: "I saw young people who were secure, contented, and proud of their society." "The stereotype of North Korea … is the contemporary version of 'the yellow peril' and follows many of its key features (irrationality, brutality, docility)," he added in his book, referring to the hysteria in Western countries over the rise of Japan in the early twentieth century.

Another American literature professor who teaches in South Korea, Bryan R. Myers, summarized North Korean propaganda in a more thoughtful—even if flawed—way in his 2010 book, *The Cleanest Race: How North Koreans See Themselves and Why It Matters*. His problem was that he took the propaganda more seriously than North Koreans do themselves. His claims were shaky: he argued that the basis of North Korean ideology is race, not the more commonly cited mix of socialism, Juche, and Songun. He even called Juche "window-dressing" for foreigners, a rather absurd claim given the reality that the state carried out huge efforts to teach Juche to its people.

During exhibitions students from different universities approached me at my exhibition booth to practice English. I often asked them what trade they wanted to take up when they finished university, and why. The answer was often quite patriotic: "I want to be an electrical engineer to help electrify my country to stand on its own feet in accordance with the Juche idea." Another said, "I want to be a medical doctor to help my countrymen to be healthier. I agree with our Juche idea, which aims at strengthening our health system and at making it independent from foreign countries." These were their actual beliefs, and didn't fit into any narrative of "window-dressing."

A few other claims are questionable. Myers claims that the North Korean personality cult is an idea imposed by Japanese colonialists. I think the concept arose out of Stalin's personality cult, or even more from a historical undercurrent stretching back to thousands of years of Chinese overlord emperors. Myers doesn't fully address how three decades of a Japanese administration could upend these more entrenched forces at work.

Myers further claims that the party, in its propaganda, portrays North Korea's leadership as motherly figures, not fathers. But he doesn't explain, then, why the Korean War is called the "Fatherland Liberation War" instead of the "Motherland Liberation War." The North Koreans who talked to me about the "father of the nation" or the "father of all Koreans," referring to their leader, never mentioned any mothers of the nation.

My company's staff members reminded me that company bosses in North Korea were expected to behave like good "fathers" with the staff. I used to reply half-jokingly that I, as their father, would expect the respect and obedience from my large family—as is typical in a traditional Confucian Korean family. Had my staff called me "mother," Myers would have been believable. The expression "father" was used not only for the English translation but also in Korean.

Other North Korea experts such as Professor Leonid Petrov and Professor Victor Cha have continued to ponder the country's isolation, especially whether collapse would come about from information entering the country.[4] It completely escaped their attention that years before, in the mid-2000s, a quiet but radical "information revolution" had already taken place in North Korea. Memory sticks and USBs became popular when they were more affordable. Foreign music, movies, and even e-books were stored or exchanged on these easily concealed sticks. More people started talking about famous movies; I was surprised that they knew films like *Kill Bill* and *The Pianist*.

At the beginning of my stay in North Korea, I offered nice gifts to prospective partners, such as a pair of fine leather shoes, a bottle of Scotch whisky, or a large box of Dunhill cigarette packs for the men.

For the ladies, I handed over a beautiful silk scarf, a brand-name perfume, or a piece of jewelry. But when people became so keen on getting a USB to watch foreign movies, I stopped offering expensive presents and gave them those tiny electronics. One male recipient laughingly told me that USBs had become so popular that women would carry them under the bra to have them well-cushioned. He didn't tell the full truth. They were being kept away from preying authorities who would have loved to know what was stored on these accessories.

A MONOLITHIC COUNTRY?

When I first arrived, I had a singular, bland image of North Korea, envisioning it as a place where everyday life is choreographed and controlled. I had learned from media and book authors that North Korea is a country where everybody marches single-mindedly to the tune of the leadership, physically as much as mentally in goose step. It was a country, I assumed, where orders would come from the top and everybody would mindlessly execute them or else risk being thrown into a gulag.

That was hardly the truth. I was in Pyongyang when there was a soccer game in 2005 between the allied countries Iran and DPRK. To my total surprise, a full stadium of North Korean fans got so excited that they started shouting abuse and throwing objects against the Iranians, a absolutely politically incorrect and outrageous act by their standards. The security forces struggled to maintain order. The Iranians even complained that they feared for their lives, a worry that they did not overstate. The world soccer governing body FIFA soon punished North Korea for crowd unrest. I knew North Koreans who were at the game and behaved like hooligans. But they did not disappear, thrown in a prison camp for potentially damaging the nation's relationship with Iran, as the Western media would have you believe.

I have also seen drivers getting out of their cars, shouting and yelling at the traffic police for perceived missives, men defiantly smoking under the watchful eye of guards of public buildings or the

Pyongyang Metro in nonsmoking areas, and farmers pushing their carts in the prohibited opposite directions of a one-way street despite the presence of police. I also knew people who traveled across the countryside even though they did not have the permits that the government still requires for moving around in the country. Some workers did not attend the compulsory weekly ideological training sessions, playing hooky so they could set up their own little capitalist businesses. In what was once the world's most radically demonetized country, American dollars, euros, and Chinese yuan were used regularly to bend laws, overcome old habits, and grease the emergence of small businesses.

So, not everyone ends up in a gulag for infractions of socialist laws. I have been told the opposite by people who believe they know North Korea better than me, and who criticize me for not sharply condemning human rights abuses in this country. While I clearly disavow any human rights abuse in North Korea and anywhere else in the world, I'm a businessman who has never visited any gulag or prison. I am not a human rights expert.

Human rights activists claim that 150,000 to 200,000 people are inmates of such camps, while the United Nations estimated in February 2014 that the number now stands at 80,000 to 120,000 prisoners. That is certainly bad, but it represents less than 1 percent of the total population. While a significant portion of the 99 percent of the population still live a life in hardship, many of them live normal lives and don't end up in horrible places.

To talk about North Korea being a single concentration camp, like Auschwitz, with a systematic extermination program through gas chambers is demagogic and is not a fair characterization of the system. I personally knew a government minister and a mechanical engineer who committed what the state called "serious crimes." They were sentenced to time in labor camps, but were released after a few years and then fully reintegrated into society. They would hardly have survived a "crime" of that nature in Stalin's Soviet Union or in Hitler's Germany.

It seems that when it comes to human rights issues in the DPRK, stories are highly dramatized for political reasons. What about all the poor souls rotting in post-genocide Rwandan prisons or Equatorial Guinea? And how about the U.S., which is home to the highest documented percentage of prison inmates in the world?

GLORY OF THE NATION

The Arirang Mass Games, as the popular event is called, takes place in the May Day stadium in Pyongyang, which is spacious enough for an audience of 150,000 people. Every year more than 100,000 participants attend—double the number of spectators. The *Guinness Book of World Records* ranked the spectacle in 2007 as the world's largest performance.

Thousands of gymnasts perform acrobatics, synchronizing their maneuvers to create wonderful kaleidoscopes on the field. Students form giant changing mosaics by turning the 150 pages of large books in their hands, to name another example. For Koreans, such glamour brings razzle-dazzle to an otherwise colorless life; the games also give tasks to the unemployed or underemployed, of whom North Korea harbors a great number. People around me seemed happier around the time of Arirang each year.

According to *Rodong Sinmun*, the party mouthpiece, millions of North Koreans and foreigners have witnessed the games, although the numbers don't quite add up and are probably part of a propaganda push. Still, it's safe to say that hundreds of thousands of people, if not more, have performed and watched the games. I visited for the first time in 2002, when the tradition started, and a few more times in the years after that.

The exhibition was bedazzling and probably quite effective propaganda that raised the profile of the DPRK. More importantly, though, it presented one interpretation of Korean history as seen by the party and its leaders; the games reflected on how they felt their nation should be regarded by the masses: the dancing and gymnastics, all in unison, gave off an image that North Korea was a happy, socialist country and a paradise. The appearance of solidarity further reflects on a notion that North Korea could mercilessly crush and destroy any foreign invader, with the entire nation standing behind a single cause.

During my first visit, I was still unfamiliar with North Korea and didn't fully understand what was going on. There were so many symbols displayed and as a foreigner I couldn't quite follow them. As time went by, I learned to better understand the Korean symbolism that played an important role in these mass games but also in many other circumstances. The sea of red flowers, for example, represents the working class, and the purple color stands for Kim Il Sung, as a purple orchid had been named after him as Kimilsungia. And the rising sun is a symbol for Kim Il Sung, venerated as the sun of humanity.

I paid around 150 euros for the second-best possible ticket, one step below the best seating. Twice I was driving my car with staff to the stadium when I was stopped every thirty meters or so by officials asking for ID. Before walking into the stadium, they ordered me to leave my mobile phone, camera, wallet, and keys in the car; it was obvious that Arirang had attracted a high-ranking guest. Indeed, I was sitting about twenty rows behind the Dear Leader himself, Kim Jong Il. He was sitting in the front row with a foreign guest and a lineup of Korean dignitaries, surrounded by plain-clothed secret service officers.

THE FLOWERS OF PYONGYANG

Flower exhibitions, sometimes consisting of thousands of blossoms, carried heavy symbolism during the two most revered public holidays: the birthday of Kim Jong Il on February 16 and the birthday of Kim Il Sung on April 15. Government agencies, organizations, and individuals exhibited flowers outside their buildings.

Two species of flower were exhibited in the Kimilsungia-Kimjongilia Exhibition Hall, a building made of bricks and mortar but that had some characteristics of a greenhouse. The center was appropriately named after the Kimilsungia and the Kimjongilia species. Kimilsungia was bred by an Indonesian botanist in 1965 and Kimjongilia by a Japanese one in 1985, and both offered them as gifts to North Korea.

I observed a flower exhibition of Kim Il Sung's birthday on April 15, 2008. In addition to the two dynastic flowers, the government put on display 7,000 various trees, plants, and flowers representing several hundred species. Everywhere the eye could see, ministry buildings, hospitals, and People's Army offices showed off their flowers on two floors of exhibition space. The booths also carried national symbols such as country and party flags, and reproduction models of important national monuments. In the center of the exhibition a plaque read: "The great leader Comrade Kim Il Sung will always be with us," "Juche," and Kim Il Sung's quote "The people are my God."

I understood how pivotal this day was to the North Korean people, so I decided to chip in on behalf of PyongSu. At the two main exhibitions every year, I brought along flowerpots of the best quality and presented them with a placard displaying my name and the PyongSu logo. The Ministry of Public Health placed my donation at its booth, and the flowerpots became famous around the country because they were the only ones offered by a foreign boss of a domestic enterprise. When journalists interviewed me, I offered praise for the showcase and added my own advertising angle: that our quality- and service-minded pharmaceutical company could never be absent from such a prestigious exhibition.

Of course, the press spun my commentary into an entertaining propaganda twist, but I didn't mind. Later on television, a euphoric reporter described me planting and growing the flowers myself—and, to add, with the loving care that is usual for patriotic Kimilsungia and Kimjongilia flower growers. I did not mind the propaganda. On the contrary, it helped boost our sales more than any advertising campaign could ever have achieved.

Western journalists have continued to write to this day that there are no advertisements to be seen in North Korea. The exceptions,

Kimjongilia flowers donated by this tributary foreigner.
The relatively small gesture was paid back multiple times.

they often write, are displayed on billboards promoting domestically assembled cars and the Koryo Link, a mobile phone telecom joint venture between the North Korean telecom and the Egyptian Orascom company.

In 2006, the government-run Korea Central News Agency (KCNA) published a fascinating news item about the newly founded Korea Advertising Company. The group reported that the company, "which is doing commodity and trade advertising activities in a uniform way, makes and sets up advertising mediums of various forms and contents in streets, stadiums, and international exhibitions and extensively advertising them through newspapers, TV, and Internet at the request of local and foreign industrial establishments and companies."

Today, the advertising firm belongs to the Foreign Trade Ministry and is run by a former student of my project, the Pyongyang Business School. No matter how harsh the socialist regime, those journalists should remember that where there are markets, there are advertisements. And by looking at opportunities in the advertising industry, North Korea made quite a leap that signifies deeper market changes.

SUBVERSION AND PROPAGANDA?

Whenever I ordered foreign literature, consisting mostly of commercial and technical books, my staff had to submit them to the authorities for a review. The censors made sure my potentially dangerous material contained no hostile propaganda.

ABB, which had a strong presence in South Korea, made a faux pas when they began sending us their Korean-language literature from Seoul. They thought it would make more sense, since those books were written in Korean and were cheaper to send. But the authorities found glamorous photographs of their southern neighbor, which looked like counterrevolutionary propaganda—the high standard of living down there, they thought, was too good to be true. To get by them, we had to remove ABB's South Korean address and replace it with ABB's Pyongyang address using stickers. The authorities noticed the tactic but didn't seem to care.

We had other awkward encounters with the ideology police, of course. I sometimes bumped into inspectors who arrived at our office after 7:30 P.M., when I was not expected to be there. They weren't naïve, but understood I was expecting them in the one-party state. Nevertheless, they came off as embarrassed and said that they preferred to review all of the foreign material in my absence. I let my Korean staff handle the matter with them behind closed doors in the meeting room. The inspectors were always upright with us, not veering zealously from their set procedure. I respected them: they had a tough and rather invasive job and just wanted to do it right.

On the other hand, DHL Pyongyang always handed me private courier deliveries on the same day they arrived. In Vietnam, however, when I received a book, like one on wildlife in East Africa sent by my mother for my birthday, DHL called me the day of the arrival and informed me that delivery would take another five days. The reason was that customs and "cultural control" procedures needed to be implemented. It's one of the many examples in which the North Korean authorities surprised me with their much less bureaucratic and more pragmatic approach.

Outside the DPRK, the government is embarking on thrusts of propaganda directed at overseas Koreans. Uriminzokkiri, which roughly means "on our own as a nation," is the official website of the Committee for the Peaceful Reunification of Korea in Pyongyang. It spreads the message that the North Korean leadership is, according to its website, "guardian of the homeland and creator of happiness" for all Koreans. But under South Korea's National Security Law, Uriminzokkiri was banned in an attempt to block communications in support of the North.

Another party-sponsored overseas group is the Committee for Cultural Relations with Foreign Countries, which is charged with disseminating North Korea's views around the globe. Unlike Uriminzokkiri, it's aimed at non-Koreans. Through its Korea Friendship Association (KFA)—a body designed to give the committee's views to foreigners—it is trying to foster constituencies abroad that are sympathetic to the plight of North Korea. The group does some business operations: it's involved in attracting funding and foreign investment for North Korea, running a body in Pyongyang called the IKBC (International Korean Business Centre). KFA's website calls itself "the Official Website of the Democratic People's Republic of Korea," which a senior cadre from a competing state organization told me is "somewhat pretentious."

A video by another organization featuring Pak Jin Jun, a beautiful student at Pyongyang Teacher's University, went viral on the Internet. Her message was clear: whereas poverty and chaos reign in the capitalist West, where people even kill themselves and die of hunger, the Korean socialist system guaranteed a life of happiness and serenity. The video showed her family, cheerfully clapping their hands and happily singing together at home. It is a masterpiece of North Korean propaganda worth watching.

THE FACE OF JUCHE

Over seven years I hosted all sorts of visitors who were hoping for insight into the so-called hermit state. The Juche Tower was almost always on their wish list. After all, it was the world's second-tallest monumental column behind the San Jacinto Monument, built in memory of the decisive battle of another revolution in the Western Hemisphere, namely the Texas Revolution in 1836. Its towering height is, of course, symbolic of its influence over the lives of North Koreans.

Over the years, I've always been impressed by the wit and fluency of the English-speaking tour guides at the tower. One pretty and affable young guide struck my attention: she graduated first at the Foreign Studies University, where she learned perfect English and sophisticated etiquette for dealing with foreigners. She must have been talented, or else she would not have received this job, which is respected in North Korea.

I met her for the first time at the Juche Tower when she was a twenty-something university graduate. During another visit a few years later, she told me that she had happily been married. A couple of years later I visited yet again, and she was gleeful that she recently gave birth to her first child. She was very effective at her work, communicating the ideas of Juche; never overzealous, she maintained a relaxed demeanor and was fully convinced of what she was representing. Her self-confidence gave her an authoritative aura on all things Juche. Tourists asked her plenty of silly, embarrassing, and sometimes even provocative questions, but nobody could ever disturb her; she had the situation under control.

This woman and her colleagues taught me the remarkable history of the monument: The 555 foot (170-meter)-high tower, designed by Kim Jong Il himself, was built in 1982 on the occasion of the seventieth birthday of his father, Kim Il Sung, the founder of the Juche idea. The government erected it on the eastern riverbank of the Taedong River, opposite the Kim Il Sung Square in central Pyongyang. The structure contains a stunning 25,550 blocks, each representing a day of Kim Il Sung's life. The slabs are dressed in white stone with 70 dividers, or lines, on all four sides of the tower. The entire edifice is capped off with a 20-meter-high, 45-ton torch that shines every night.

Visitors take an elevator to the top, where a balcony offers a 360-degree view of Pyongyang. It's one of few places where they're allowed to film and take pictures. North Koreans brag that the entire structure was erected at "Chollima speed" in only thirty-five days, and that it was dressed up in seventy-six days. In front of the tower sits more propaganda: a single, 100 foot (30-meter)-high statue comprising three figures. One man grasps a hammer, another holds a sickle, and the final one carries a writing brush. They represent the classes of workers, peasants, and intellectuals.

The word Juche or Chuch'e literally means "main subject." It often has been translated and interpreted as "independent stand" or "spirit of self-reliance" or "always putting Korean things first." To my mind, the last one is the most accurate one. Kim Il Sung explained that the Juche idea is based on the belief that, in his words, "man is the mas-

At the Juche Tower, a stone was left on behalf of my predecessor, resident ABB country director André Reussner, who passed away in 2002 in a Bangkok hospital. The North Koreans removed the plaque when the ABB group downgraded its engagement with North Korea, a sort of pragmatic move for them.

ter of everything and decides everything." And of course, in Korea, man should always be Korean and never a foreigner.

In a nutshell, Juche is, according to Kim Il Sung, the "independence in politics, self-reliance in the economy, self-defense in the military." Although Juche is the national ideology of North Korea, Kim Il Sung also recommended it as a solution to developing countries. North Korea has been organizing international seminars on Juche since 1977.

After the death of Kim Jong Il in December 2011, the North Korean media swiftly heralded Kim Jong Un as the "great successor," according to several news reports. Most importantly, the propaganda apparatus stated, the young Kim would uphold the Juche philosophy and the army first policies, creating an uninterrupted line from his father's rule.

The press went along with the story that like both his grandfather and father, Jong Un descended indirectly from Paekdu Mountain because his father was supposedly born there. That made him "the spiritual pillar and the lighthouse of hope" for all Koreans, according to all the state newspapers. The personality cult, it seemed, did not end with single personalities, but stretched across family lines.

A few days after the news broke, the managing director of a North Korean company operating in a Southeast Asian country sent me a letter that affirmed what I suspected. "I am now in great sadness to hear that our Great Leader has passed away," he wrote, "but we will push ahead our work to build up a great powerful nation by upholding the wise leadership of our new Leader General Kim Jong Un according to the lofty will of our Great Leader General Kim Jong Il."

The letter made it clear that he, like all North Koreans, understood that Kim Jong Un would be the undisputed successor. The fervor hasn't wavered.

NOTES

1. Barbara Demick. North Korea: secrets and lies. *The Telegraph*. February 16, 2010. http://www.telegraph.co.uk/news/worldnews/asia/north-korea/7249849/North-Korea-secrets-and-lies.html.

2. Barbara Demick. *Nothing to Envy: Ordinary Lives in North Korea*. London: Granta Books, 2010.

3. Luc Forsyth. Understanding North Korea—part 2. Luc Forsyth, Photojournalist. May 16, 2012. http://lucforsyth.com/tag/policy/.

4. Victor Cha. *The Impossible State: North Korea, Past and Future*. New York: Ecco, 2012.

Chapter 4

Healing the Great Leader's Children

Poverty is not socialism. To be rich is glorious.

— Deng Xiaoping

Working in Pyongyang's pharmaceutical industry was full of daunting obstacles and headaches. By the second half of 2007, when the sales of our first few pharmaceuticals began rising, I noticed a sinister oddity in our success. One of our products skyrocketed to a level of popularity far beyond that of all other pharmaceuticals.

The drug? Diazepam, a sedative used to treat anxiety and insomnia.

More familiarly, the tablet was known as Valium, launched by my former employer, Roche.

It is one of the most common drugs in the world and was put on the World Health Organization's (WHO) "Essential Drugs List," meaning it was a core pharmaceutical needed for basic health care. But it is also believed to be one the world's most abused pharmaceuticals.

Valium today is notorious for its addictive properties, and is also frequently ingested, together with alcohol or other substances, by people trying to commit suicide through an overdose. There's no proof, though, that North Koreans in particular were abusing this drug because they were more depressed than other people around the world. Rather, their usage followed a worldwide trend.

I told the sales team that only patients with a prescription from a doctor could buy the product and that we should regularly check that the pharmacies were following our directives. If they did not, we would not sell the product to them anymore. As a precaution, I later restricted the sales to our own pharmacies, where we could directly oversee how the drug was handled.

But even that move wasn't enough to smother a potentially explosive situation. One day a Belgian pharmacist and I visited the gift shop of the Pothonggang Hotel, where I was shocked and embarrassed when I saw that our diazepam was on sale. The visitor must have known that diazepam was, according to the International Narcotics Control Board, a Schedule IV controlled drug that required vigilance when sold even with a prescription. But the tablets were sold here just like the snacks and the souvenirs!

I vividly imagined waking up to foreign newspapers with the headline: "In North Korea, Valium is sold over the counter like chewing gum!" The risk that a foreign journalist would have seen this blunder in a hotel shop was high, because a large delegation of foreign reporters was in town around the same time. What a fantastic opportunity for a Western journalist to do some North Korea bashing, I thought.

How would the government react? Would PyongSu be shut down, and would I be kicked out of the country? Anything was possible. Every day I Googled the keywords "North Korea" and "diazepam" to check up on whether somebody had written about it. Luckily, this never happened.

That was my first run-in with a potential disaster, and others haven't been so lucky dealing with the North Korean market. Over several years a lineup of businesspeople tried and failed to set up a small medicinal tablet factory in Pyongyang, and even we had trouble keeping foreign talent in the country. A Filipino pharmacist gave up on this task, simply because he felt lonely in his hotel room. Then a German production pharmacist stayed a few years but left. Both were experienced at setting up and running large production sites, but PyongSu's situation turned desperate when our German pharmacist left for personal reasons.

The situation got even worse when a WHO-sponsored international inspection team visited the site and compiled a list of seventy-eight objections. They rejected the factory from getting Good Manufacturing Practices (GMP) acknowledgement, the industry's worldwide production quality standard defined by the WHO. The problem, then, was that foreign buyers (such as aid organizations) would not purchase pharmaceuticals from the factory without it meeting the baseline standard. The company was making no sales and only carried expenses.

Adding to that conundrum, PyongSu had to deal with the fallout of its low rating. PyongSu's product portfolio consisted only of large quantities of aspirin and paracetamol manufactured during the first trial production run. But they were nearing their expiration dates and were stockpiled at the warehouse unused. Investors didn't want to give the company any more support, and staff had little confidence left in the company's future. But this was only one considerable hurdle we had to overcome; we ran into all sorts of follies in setting up a business in North Korea.

TAKING THE LEAD

In October 2005, I stepped up to lead PyongSu, but others probably thought that I had taken on a suicidal mission. Indeed, they saw a bad omen: after a few months of working, the recently appointed American CEO of a large family-owned business based in Hong Kong, which was then the main foreign investor in PyongSu, "lost" the employment agreement twice over several months and could not sign it. He was supposed to agree to the terms with me—he as the employer, me as the employee—since his group was the majority investor. This was an utter nuisance to him; he was against the group's engagement in North Korea. By "losing" the contract, he was expecting the headache to be finished quickly if PyongSu collapsed. I later learned that the board of directors had not been informed by his predecessor, a family member, of the group's North Korea investment. When they did learn of it, they wanted it shut down.

Although PyongSu had decent hardware with few shortcomings, the company immediately faced a shortage of skilled staff. Few qualified doctors wanted to work for us, because we had fostered a reputation for being an unstable company with an uncertain future. And when I did hire capable, English-speaking physicians and pharmacists, or a young and organized secretary, they usually resigned after a few weeks. I saw them later working at the WHO and U.N. agencies, where the jobs were safer, better-paid, and less stressful.

It would have been difficult to get out of this hole, and if I revealed the extent of PyongSu's needs to the investors, they would have certainly axed the entire operation. And yet the correction of the seventy-eight major and minor shortcomings alone would require substantial additional financing and more than a year's worth of time until they were fixed. The two main shortcomings, namely a large water purification system as well as a microbiological test laboratory, would not only be expensive but also difficult and at worst impossible to install given the many parts from Western suppliers that most likely would refuse to sell them to a North Korean factory.

Additionally, we had, with the exception of the two painkillers previously mentioned, no products to sell, neither self-made ones nor products made by other producers, although we now urgently needed to generate income and cash. Also, we had no marketing and sales unit, which in a way made sense as we had little or nothing to sell.

Moreover, we lacked a strategy as it was not clear what the company stood for, what were its medium- to long-term goals, and how it should reach them. I knew that the last thing I should do then was to send the investors a report on the state of the business and on what needed to be done—including footing the bill—as that could have meant the immediate death knell for the joint venture.

The most difficult question, given this overwhelming fiasco, was where I should begin. In a heavily regulated industry, even the production of older, well-known generic drugs takes many months before the drugs hit the market. I started tapping into my industry network, looking for somebody willing to give me some formulations, or drug "recipes," free of charge. That would allow us to start preparing production right away, saving on enormous costs.

I wasn't sure how long, though, it would take for these medicines to reach store shelves, so I diversified by contacting traders in Asia and Europe. I received pharmaceuticals from them on a consignment basis, meaning we paid them after they were sold. At the same time, we did a terse market study and put together a strategy and a marketing plan. One of its core elements was what we called the "quality pharmacy" concept. This idea included not only quality pharmaceuticals for the treatment of more than 90 percent of all diseases, but also the provision of quality customer service and health care advice based on professionalism, expertise, and ethical integrity. It sounds simple, but reaching this pinnacle was easier said than done.

PyongSu could not compete with the lower prices set by other North Korean companies. Our competitors had the market stacked in their favor because they were politically connected and state-owned. They paid lower salaries, lower electricity and water bills, and had zero land fees. They were also privileged enough to receive raw materials that were, at times, free of charge from both the North Korean government and international donors.

As a result, our aspirin was dozens of times more expensive than that of our local competitors. For example, 20 tablets of our version of aspirin, or 250 mg in international standard packaging, were about $0.40, compared to $0.015 for the equivalent local product wrapped in a simple manner.

We had to find a way to distinguish our image as a company that churned out the highest quality of the bunch, and that meant we had to rely on "brand marketing" as much as the quality itself. Before I became managing director, I suggested as a member of the board of directors that we develop a line of branded generic pharmaceuticals. The aspirin was to become PyongSu Spirin and the paracetamol to become PyongSu Cetamol. That plan, it seemed, would give us a distinctive buzz among customers looking for an alternative to the state-produced drugs.

Dr. T.M., a Seoul-based British economic historian who was a member of the board of directors, tried to mob me out. I was a threat to his consulting firm, which he used to try to bring foreign companies to North Korea, some of which were instead contacting me. He sent alarming mails to the investors telling them, to name one instance, that "problems with Felix Abt seem to increase. The North Koreans tell me that Felix is 'poking his nose into everything' and has delayed packaging and signage."

Dr. T.M. soon resigned as a director and shareholder, which allowed me to step into the leadership role. My first task was to replace our logo with a newer one, a medicine capsule that became part of a new corporate identity. Later we regularly won contracts from the International Federation of Red Cross and Red Crescent Societies (IFRC), but they demanded that we change the logo from a red to green color. The motif was reserved for them under the 1949 Geneva Conventions and could not be used for commercial purposes. We did so with pleasure, honored to work with such a prestigious body.

We couldn't rely too much on our brand image, though. This pharmaceutical business had to be run in a polished, modern way unfamiliar to the North Korean board members. The Chinese industry became our benchmark, because it has been transforming from an outdated socialist public health system to a more market-oriented one. I took my Korean colleagues on study trips to Shijiazhuang, Shenyang, and Shanghai.

In a visit we hoped would foreshadow our future success, we visited the pharmaceutical joint venture formed between foreign and Chinese investors. To my surprise, the foreign majority shareholder of that company today remains Bristol-Myers Squibb, an American multinational. I also convinced its Chinese octogenarian architect, Henry Jin, to join our company's board of directors, because he could bring his relevant background to the table.

In the past in China, multiple government agencies used to give orders and instructions to the management of enterprises for running their daily business. While China had radically streamlined bureaucratic control and delegated power to managers, North Korean enterprises were still micromanaged by the government.

Smiling and not surprised at the query, the CEO of a large, state-owned pharmaceutical company in Shanghai responded to a question about "government management" from the North Korean members of our board: "The state owns this enterprise. The government does not give us instructions on how to run it. It expects that we are doing it in a competent and profitable way. And if we don't, they'll replace us." The lesson was that this Chinese enterprise was flourishing despite the freedom its management enjoyed. It was a challenge to the hermit state's management practices.

Even though the board of directors agreed that branding was a huge part of our plan, it was hard to get the process going in this socialist country. When I wanted to set up the marketing and sales function, the Ministry of Public Health told me that companies in the DPRK usually don't have a sales department. They looked at my request with suspicion, and then asked me to send a letter to the cabinet, which reported to the prime minister, to explain my reasoning so I could get a special permit.

MAKING HEADWAY

It took the government a few months to authorize my marketing plan, after which we started receiving products from suppliers. To sell products quickly, my first mission was to set up our first pharmacy at the entrance of a large and heavily frequented shopping mall. I first targeted the Rakwon Mall, in the city center, because it sported a clientele that could afford our higher-priced and better-quality pharmaceuticals in hard currency rather than in the local weak currency.

We also took notice of the sizable Kwangbok Department Store along eponymous Kwangbok Street. This spot was situated on the capital's periphery, which was a relatively well-off suburb full of distinguished individuals.

Since we were cash-strapped and not able to pay a fixed lease in the fall of 2006, I had to think of a plan quickly to get those pharmaceuticals on the market. I first suggested to these shopping malls that we would pay a rent taken from a 5 percent cut from the monthly sales.

My second proposal was to pay no rent at all, but rather to hand the pharmacy over to the shopping mall after one or two years. That deal came with the condition that the new owners would supply their booth exclusively with products from PyongSu, including products we manufactured as well as those we imported and distributed.

This was a kind of slimmed-down franchising. Franchisers have a detailed concept that their franchisees must apply, such as which products to sell and which advertisements to display. Our main condition was the exclusivity of using us as suppliers. We would have supported the mall's "quality pharmacy" with training and advertising, though, and it was something completely new to this country. If the first franchised pharmacy worked, we could spread our model and set up more shops elsewhere.

They liked the concept, but didn't believe us when we said we'd have the funds to make sure the supply chain would work. The group was probably "once bitten, twice shy," because Chinese and Koreans had previously brought forward business proposals that never materialized. They needed more time to think about it and to observe our practices, but they agreed to sell our products in their pharmacies in the meantime.

Other suppliers and traders were ready to give us credit, so we carefully selected pharmacies and shops throughout Pyongyang, hoping they'd become fast-turning sales points. We also hired our own sales staff, who we thought could get us cash quickly to build up our business. Our opening stages involved a great publicity effort, too. We reached out aggressively to the industry, trying to familiarize them with our pharmaceuticals.

We took advantage of the state system of "household doctors."

These physicians had a mandate to care for a cohort of some 130 families. In fact, the country has no shortage of doctors and nurses—which is somewhat surprising, given that medical professionals in places like China and India often migrate to other countries for better wages and create "brain drain." Part of the reason is coercive: North Korean doctors and nurses, like other citizens, are not allowed to migrate, lest they be labeled "defectors" by the foreign press. Still, regardless of how authoritarian the antimigration legislation is, this reluctance to leave the country made the visiting Director-General of the WHO, Dr. Margaret Chan, say in 2010 that the country's health care system was "something which most other developing countries would envy."

Though correct when comparing the numbers between North Korea and other poor countries, the statement was politically incorrect: it triggered outrage by all those citizens who expected that all news coming out of North Korea would be bad news. Adding to their rage, Amnesty International carried a damning report on the state of North Korea's health care system later that year, "based entirely on the accounts of defectors. Some of them, unfortunately, had left almost a decade before the report was compiled," the *Foreigners' Correspondence Publishing* reported.

The pharmaceutical multinational Solvay gave us samples of products that we passed on to influential doctors. They designed their own trials and published their findings in North Korean medical publications. But our own factory could not produce many products in low quantities, which would have earned us no profit. We needed to focus on fewer products that could be produced in large quantities.

This wasn't too difficult; with about three or four different antibiotics, for example, one could cover most infectious diseases. Most products we imported from producers at highly competitive prices, while others, such as traditional Korean medicines, were bought locally. In short, we needed to supply wholesalers and pharmacies with a complete range of quality medicine produced not only by ourselves but by the few quality suppliers abroad who were not afraid of working with a North Korean company.

Additionally, our sales team started visiting doctors and pharmacists to promote our products. Reaching out to this clique led to a steady increase in sales, meaning they were taking well to our products. And, of course, there was the market research side: our staff hung out at pharmacies, observing and interviewing the people there. I myself once observed a doctor and his patient crossing the street from Kim Man Yu Hospital to the opposite flower shop, which had a pharmacy that was also selling our pharmaceuticals. Inside the shop the patient opened her wallet to show the doctor how much money she had to pay for medicine. The doctor compared pharmaceuticals on sale and their prices and then advised her to buy a treatment in line with her purchasing power. The pharmaceuticals that hospital pharmacies gave free of charge to patients were mostly donated by foreign groups. When the hospitals lacked medicine, patients or their families bought it in shops and markets, where pharmaceuticals were cheaper but not as safe. PyongSu's strategy was to fill in those gaps.

Given the realities of the closed socialist system, most foreign managers were kept in a bubble, making it difficult to meet directly with North Korean customers, suppliers, and authorities. I got lucky, because the state allowed me regular access to local businesspeople and customers. For example, I met with the directors of all the most prominent hospitals in Pyongyang, as well as the main wholesalers— the best of whom I negotiated a distribution joint venture with. I also dealt with scores of pharmacy managers.

I even invited the boss of our fiercest rival, which belonged to a powerful military organization, to the founding of the European Business Association. That group trusted me because I had been doing business in the country for some years, giving them the opportunity to observe me. Her deputy became a student at the Pyongyang Business School, and I tried to help her find a foreign investor who could jointly set up an herbal medicine venture. As their company was losing customers to PyongSu, my gestures eased their potentially dangerous frustrations.

Part of my success owed to my willingness to work with local people rather than pass judgment and get involved in politics. I built up a large network of contacts that helped shape our business for the socialist economy. Compare this approach to that of my predecessor, a close friend of the British ambassador, who was a staunch advocate of regime change. He didn't get access, of course. While I could name offhand the family backgrounds of my staff, he did not even know who the party secretary at PyongSu was—and a good relationship with that gate-keeping official is key to success.

THE CHALLENGE OF KEEPING UP

We did encounter an obstacle in our production. Some groups were either not willing to enter a franchising agreement with us, as we have seen in the case of the Rakwon shopping mall, or would not allocate enough resources to set up and maintain the quality pharmacy concept. They lacked selling space, sufficient refrigeration, and the cash to buy the pharmaceuticals. We were not able to offer them products on credit terms, meaning payments after they sold the products supplied by us.

I realized that if we could not rely on franchises, we would need to run our own pharmacies to make sure the quality pharmacy concept would be implemented. Our factory was only a small tableting unit, not benefiting from economies of scale and therefore lacking the potential of making a reasonable profit. Our domestic competitors not only had larger tableting units but produced a complete range of galenical forms of drugs from injectables, syrups, and powders to creams and ointments. Even if we were to become the first company to reach the highest GMP standards, it was only a matter of time until other factories caught up and took away our competitive advantage.

We focused on service, rather, as our strength, because the state-owned factories had neither the necessary attitude nor the skills to offer good service. Wholesaling and retailing of pharmaceuticals, then, fit nicely into our business model. The wholesale margin—that is, the margin when we sold imported pharmaceuticals and those made by us to pharmacies—was 15 percent. The retail margin of the pharmacies, however, was a very handsome 43 percent. If we'd run our own pharmacies, we would have earned not only the 15 percent but also the 43 percent. In addition, if we bought pharmacy buildings at attractive locations, we could eventually sell them and make a profit multiple times the purchase price a decade later or so. Our direction was now clear: developing profitable pharmacies at good locations throughout the country.

Although PyongSu's future was to be its pharmacy business, the factory still had a role to play for the foreseeable future. In my view, the company should have had not only wholesale and retail profit centers but also a factory profit center. Still, I was aware of the fact that margins had to be small if we were to compete with foreign generic manufacturers that benefited from larger economies of scale. I aimed at substituting a portion of the imported pharmaceuticals with enough of our manufactured products to employ the factory for at least one or two shifts.

Large donor organizations such as the IFRC issued public tenders for pharmaceuticals they could use in the field, and the lowest bid from a pharmaceutical manufacturer obtained the supply contract. However, for us to participate in such tender competitions, we had to solve two crucial problems. First, we had to obtain GMP status, and second, we had to find tender specifications that were adapted to our more restricted manufacturing abilities. The tenders usually sought a large range of pharmaceuticals with a variety of packages, which given our small factory we could not produce. I urged the IFRC and other groups to break down a large tender into smaller subtenders, which would have opened the competition to us.

As a former resident regional director of Roche in West Africa, I was familiar with the product Bactrim, a Roche invention, also known by its generic name cotrimoxazole. It is a combination of two antibiotics that faces little resistance and is tolerable for children. It is used mainly against urinary tract infections and respiratory tract infections, especially during the harsh winters.

At the time it was widely used by pediatricians in the form of syrup in western Africa. IFRC agreed to create one kit with the antibiotic cotrimoxazole and the well-tolerated painkiller paracetamol for adults, and one for children, and issue separate subtenders from then on.

If those ailments were left untreated, I imagined that more people in North Korea would die from these infections than from lack of food. For this reason I became a strong advocate for cotrimoxazole and wanted to produce it. When IFRC agreed and we won tenders, it became the factory's largest product.

In 2007, we won the first IFRC contract for cotrimoxazole and paracetamol, a painkiller and antipyretic. IFRC had samples of our products tested in an independent laboratory in France. The factory order profits were not substantial, but alongside our other sales, they eventually led to our first corporate profit in my third and last year at PyongSu. For the first time, we then happily paid corporate profit taxes to the government.

The challenges weren't over, though. Before international organizations started placing orders with us, we had to make sure we could produce according to the WHO's international GMP standards. Our staff worked tirelessly to remove the objections put up by the GMP inspectors. Given the closed-off circumstances in North Korea, this wasn't an easy task. We had a major headache just trying to order a new water purification system and the microbiological test laboratory. It was pretty much impossible to buy a complete system in North Korea and China. Rather, we had to buy each component from a large number of producers around the world, including in the United States and other Western countries. I started contacting their subsidiaries and Chinese sales agents in China, but most of them refused to sell their products to a North Korean company thanks to the embargoes.

Then we went through a sudden change of foreign shareholders, who substantially cut my salary and lagged in giving us the funds to implement the GMP measures. I swallowed the bitter pill of my income reduction because I didn't want to let down my North Korean staff at this critical juncture. I haggled with investors for ten months for that money, which was a waste of time. Indeed, more than half of my contractual time at PyongSu had already elapsed, much of it spent on what would have otherwise been a minor bureaucratic hassle.

Thankfully, Henry Jin and I found a smaller Chinese pharmaceutical company that was willing to help. We solved the thorny problem by purchasing a water system and microbiological test laboratory from them; they luckily had a system similar to what we needed. In our deal, we set up a project team that consisted of representatives from both companies, and they helped install the system after taking a modest commission. It was in their interests to help us: they produced an excellent cough syrup based on herbs, which they were interested in selling during those North Korean winters.

As the company grew with the GMP label, my staff and I went more often to China to meet with suppliers. The country was a foreign environment that some would have considered politically hazardous, but as I would find out, the solid worldview of my staff wouldn't be shaken by the new environment.

In Shenyang, a provincial capital in northeastern China, we sang both North Korean and Chinese songs. But the local Karaoke machines included images and sounds from South Korea. When images of Seoul popped up on the television screen, they immediately switched to other tunes with northern themes.

In other spots, the censorship got heavier. In Shenyang, we stayed at the Chilbosan Hotel, which was owned partially by a North Korean state insurance company and, understandably, hadn't installed foreign TV channels. We strolled in during the days leading up to the U.S. presidential election in 2008, but even the main Chinese channel that was broadcasting the event was switched off. When the election results came out, the TV screen remained dark; the guests, it seemed, must have been the only people in this industrial entrepôt of eight million residents who missed the announcement that America had elected its first black president.

On the glorious day we got our certification, we were ready to produce on a regular scale, and we set up our launch plan for all sorts of pharmaceuticals: antibiotics, anti-inflammatories, antihypertensives, and painkillers, to name a few staples.

Still, competing on this global scale was new to much of the staff, and I had to be vigilant over what we Westerners would consider elementary gaffes. Shortly before shipment, I scrounged around the storeroom and opened a number of the products for a last check. I got furious when I noticed that the package insert, which was supposed to list precautions for use of the drug, side effects, and contraindications, was missing.

I immediately halted our scheduled operation. The employee charged with printing the package inserts furtively explained to me, "Korean companies don't add package inserts to pharmaceuticals, and we thought we should save the cost for the package insert." At less than half a cent, a single package insert costs peanuts.

But what irked me was that since our strategy focused on quality and service, we could never compromise on an important matter like package inserts, no matter how irrelevant it seemed to the North Korean staff.

We faced yet another hiccup when, in 2006, the U.N. passed sanctions at the behest of Washington. We were suddenly prohibited from importing certain reagents that we needed, even in small and harmless quantities. But we needed them to analyze our product samples, ingredients, and the like, ensuring they were free of contamination.

One time in the Air Koryo storage room in Beijing, Chinese authorities confiscated a parcel of reagents that we had ordered before the international community slapped its sanctions on Pyongyang. I called the Chinese embassy in Pyongyang and said that they, or government contractors acting on their behalf, would inspect the use of imported chemicals at our factory. The proposal was embarrassing to the Chinese, who didn't want to get involved in any brewing disputes with Western countries. Nor did they want to be accused of taking a lax stance on North Korea. Luckily, we found suppliers within

North Korea, so we could avoid the headache and legal risks of importing the supposedly "illegal" products ourselves.

In the end, the rise of PyongSu was a rigorous project that, of course, was not free of the disputes that affect most businesses. I quarreled most often with its foreign investors, who had misconceptions about doing business in North Korea. One of the disputes was over how I treated my staff.

PyongSu had, like most if not all Korean companies, a canteen where the staff could eat. Some staff brought food to the workplace that they had prepared at home. It was usual for workplaces to feed the staff and their families, provided they were able to generate the necessary revenues. This was an important part of the remuneration. We regularly bought rice for our staff and the raw materials to make kimchi, sometimes in China at a lower price. Another important food item was edible oil. But the quantity of the oil we had was higher than the presumed consumption. This was because unused portions were often traded as barter.

Apart from giving away food items, we also paid salaries. As a foreign-invested joint venture company, we were obliged by law to pay 35 euros per month for ordinary workers, but higher salaries for specialists and managers, in a convertible foreign currency. I kept the salaries, fixed in euros, as low as possible. As we had to pay them out in the domestic currency at the official exchange rate, which was many times below the black market rate, the salaries of our staff became almost worthless.

To compensate for that, we were allowed to add incentives that could be paid in hard currency to our staff—provided they were not paid by the joint venture company but by the foreign investors alone. Incentives had to be declared a "gift" in acknowledgement of extraordinary performances. The incentives were indeed linked to performance targets defined by me for all staff, from the cleaning women and machine operators up to my deputy. The incentives ensured a nice income for our staff and gave them an incentive to do a good job.

The government did not agree in principle with "replacing" the (worthless) salaries with performance-related incentives, a full-blown capitalist concept. It allowed this only if the incentives were paid and declared as gifts by the foreign investors and not by PyongSu, a company under DPRK law. Call it a face-saving way out of a political dilemma. The foreign investors did not understand this background and insisted on having the company pay the incentives. As a result of this standoff, for several months I did not pay any incentives. Only when the morale of the staff dropped to its lowest, and well-trained staff started looking for other jobs, did the investors agree to pay.

Another dispute was about the necessity of having our own microbiological laboratory, as is usual in pharmaceutical factories. The investors thought it wasn't necessary for North Korea, as the standard offered by PyongSu would be higher than anything else in that country. We had to outsource bacteriological testing to university laboratories, a bureaucratic hassle. Only when the WHO inspection concluded that this was a major shortcoming on the way to becoming GMP-compliant did the group change its mind and agreed to forward the necessary funds.

What was amazing, though, was when the North Korean board members embraced, in a written letter to the owners of the company, the business strategies that I had pushed for, like my emphasis on service and quality. I sincerely enjoyed working with the Korean directors, managers, and staff of PyongSu, and it seemed they felt the same way. I will always have fond memories of these people, who were skillful and diligent, worked very hard—much harder than me in any case—and remained loyal even in difficult periods.

Chapter 5
Same Bed, Different Dreams

*Shallow understanding from people of good
will is more frustrating than absolute misun-
derstanding from people of ill will.*

— Martin Luther King Jr.

"Mr. Abt, hire saleswomen with miniskirts!" the scion of a family of multibillionaires, who had invested in PyongSu, told me in his office in Europe. He thought this tactic would boost sales, an ill-given word of advice.

The dilemma, though, was that miniskirts at the time were completely banned in North Korea. Either the law was strictly enforced or women took it upon themselves to follow it even when it wasn't enforced. I have never come across any North Korean woman wearing a miniskirt, unlike their more revealing cousins in Seoul. Still, as a caveat, North Korean girls sometimes donned short skirts during government-authorized parades, like the Arirang Mass Games.

I didn't challenge his words on the spot. As a third-generation entrepreneur, he did not build up his fortune but rather inherited it. Unlike me, he could afford to run a business as a hobby for which he could hire anybody who wore miniskirts. People close to him told me that he considered North Korea to not be a real profit-making opportunity but a so-called intellectual challenge.

Like any sensible businessman, I ignored his misinformed advice, and it turned out that he also ignored my advice on doing business in North Korea. But I wanted to give this investment a try, even if he didn't know what was best for his family's money. I would defend his

95

family fortune to the best of my abilities, because that's what I was being paid to do.

There's a Chinese saying, "Sleeping in the same bed and dreaming different dreams." It's a meditation on the tendency of people to see things in a radically different light. This was the beginning of a rather long sleep in the same bed with someone who dreamed strongly differing dreams.

The business was unprofitable, with a monthly sales income of $10. In the back of my mind I feared that, in a grisly attempt to self-medicate, I would become the only consumer of our own painkillers. I knew things could not continue along this path, as our investors were running out of patience. They were ready to let the company go bankrupt if no quick turnaround was achieved.

I responded to a question from my staff. "Yes, we are a Korean pharmaceutical company," I answered. "But nobody is going to donate raw and packaging materials, and nobody is going to pay salaries and electricity bills if we cannot do it ourselves. The foreign shareholders have fulfilled their obligations as they have made their investment according to the joint venture contract. The new company is operational. It's up to us now to make this company stand on its own feet and succeed."

I could see the huge disappointment on the faces of our staff. I had the impression they did not believe what I said. I repeated myself. "We must sell our pharmaceuticals, and from the sales revenues we will purchase the materials and pay salaries and electricity and other bills." I stressed: "Yes, we have to find customers able and ready to purchase and pay for our pharmaceuticals. And we must produce, import, and sell those pharmaceuticals they want." It was a bitter pill for them to swallow.

Gradually, after many sleepless nights, we arrived at the same dream of producing the highest-quality pharmaceuticals and services. It looked like a goal that would never come true. But it did, and after my work was done, I departed.

A clean-cut Belgian, thirty-one years old, arrived on April 14, the day before the birthday of Kim Il Sung. During that holiday North Koreans took a few days off work. The young man, my successor as the PyongSu director, inquired about the holiday and made a quick assessment. "They have so many holidays. They hardly work at all," he said.

When I picked him up at the airport, I wanted to learn more about his knowledge of North Korea. Was he up to the task of managing a company in this isolated nation? I asked him if he was familiar with the Chollima mythical horse and the meaning of the Arch of Triumph, both key landmarks of the capital. It was something anyone who read the entry on North Korea in Wikipedia would know (at least, as of August 2012).

These were questions I also asked to size up the various engineers visiting from Europe and Asia whom I had to work with. I was, to my surprise, often impressed by how much these people knew. They knew much more than the young Belgian who had graduated from London's prestigious School of Oriental and African Studies and spoke Korean.

He was offended at not knowing the answers, and during his first company meeting he got subtle revenge on me by speaking only Korean. It was a childish way of keeping me out of everyday proceedings. But his Korean language skills didn't help him. Because he was confrontational and lacked respect for the older and wiser staff, he clashed with the North Koreans during his first few days in Pyongyang.

From my office I overheard them shouting and yelling at times, and of course, he tried to challenge me over the most ridiculous and trivial issues, such as whether or not to introduce work incentives that already existed. Worse of all, he already talked about changing things in a big way before he knew how things operated, a sign of his misguided youth in a country he only understood from a language course.

The North Koreans, offended and angry, approached me before I packed my bags in May 2009. "We have never experienced such an ignorant and arrogant foreigner. We want to get rid of him!" announced one assistant manager at PyongSu. The group of managers surrounding him concurred.

"I think the foreign investors who have chosen him will not agree and may not send anybody else," I answered. "Think what that means for the company. So try to get along with him as much as you can. I am sure you can handle this."

A couple of days later they got back to me, saying: "Yes, we think we can handle him." Of course, I was sure they could. North Koreans are pragmatists when it comes to "managing" all kinds of people, including foreigners who travel in and out for a few years at a time.

The North Korean managers didn't see their own competence as an issue: they were not only fully able to produce pharmaceuticals according to international GMP standards but had built up experience professionally marketing them as well. The Belgian didn't see this. After I left and he had settled in Pyongyang, he wrote on his Facebook page, "I am surrounded by retards."

The advantage of having a foreign manager like this youthful Belgian, though, had less to do with his professional competence. His task was to keep communication lines open with foreign suppliers and customers, who needed a Western link to this "hermit state." He was a foreign messenger, no matter what he called himself on his business card, and a figure like that was absolutely necessary to keeping the outsiders in the loop.

He must have been perceived as a gift sent by the foreign investors, clearly preferred to somebody like me who was strongly—perhaps too strongly—involved in the corporate strategy and operational matters. With the foreign boss around, the company gets privileges that regular North Korean groups don't: it has its own international phone line and an e-mail system. For the foreign majority shareholders, there were even more cost-cutting benefits in hiring an inexperienced worker in his early thirties.

It allowed the North Koreans to switch to a principle dear to them: "You invest, we manage!" Thus, the pragmatic Koreans accepted the trouble of having a foreigner who spoke Korean, even though this is not welcome in North Korea because he could spread subversive ideas in the native language. But they were angrily willing to go along with the fact that he hated the North Korean system and was behaving rudely throughout his stay.

CULTURE AND ETIQUETTE

North Koreans are staunch in their abeyance to right speech and right action, Eastern norms that are dying in industrializing countries such as China and Vietnam. South Koreans, to them, appear more "decadent" and outgoing, in an inappropriate way that seems improper to most Pyongyangites.

For instance, foreigners visiting the embalmed corpse of Kim Il Sung must bow in reverence to him, although this does not necessarily mean that they are in agreement with his views. The sophisticated North Koreans are, in fact, aware that the political beliefs of foreigners may differ strongly from theirs; expecting this show of respect is merely an emic difference in values similar to taking off shoes before entering temples and mosques.

North Korean hosts appreciate genuine interest from foreigners. Outsiders can discuss controversial topics as long as they do not "teach" or try to "save" their hosts. One foreign businessman suggested to North Koreans that they "at last normalize relations with Japan and become friends." That's an outrageous idea to North Koreans because Japan has not apologized to and compensated Pyongyang for crimes committed during its colonization.

Nevertheless, the word "yes" does not mean a North Korean agrees: she or he may be confirming what was heard or showing respect even if he or she did not understand the English.

Straight talk is generally valued by Westerners but not by North Koreans and other Asians. It may threaten another person's face or the group's harmony. And furthermore, displays of anger are considered offensive by North Koreans (and most East Asians). Such a debacle would cause a loss of face, which is a serious matter in this region that values the self-worth of every human being. Patience, calm, and humor can help overcome the most challenging and unnerving situations, as I found at PyongSu.

In the Confucian tradition, respect for people who are older or are higher-ranking than you in terms of scholarship, wealth, or knowledge is an important part of the culture. North Koreans appeared to me to be self-controlled and disciplined. They lined up in front of counters and at bus stops, showing more deference to hierarchically higher persons and even bowing in front of them. They were also thorough in their fulfillment of social obligations, such as keeping the environment clean.

In this hierarchy, therefore, you would not pour your own drink first but rather pour for others at the table—starting with the oldest or most senior ones. Ladies do not go first, as in the Western tradition. Exchanging business cards or gifts is done with both hands, and business cards received should be read with attention before putting them away. And in a similar sign of respect, people should be waved over not with fingers crooked upwards but with the palm down.

THE BANKER AND THE ECONOMIST

Foreigners often remarked to me in exasperation that they couldn't figure out what North Koreans expected from them. The country, and its practices, was a break from anything they were familiar with back home. Business dealings were generally nontransparent, and this tendency caused outsiders to make wild assumptions about their partners. The results were foolish speculation and faulty assessments—two hindrances to getting any work done.

To North Koreans, though, the intentions of the foreigners were also unclear—although they were, by and large, better informed about outsiders from their own work experience and perhaps thanks to their quasi-intelligence gathering.

There was a typical story that unfolded: business partners were in high spirits after dining together at their welcoming dinners. They shared the confidence that their projects would be successful. But frequently misunderstandings, suspicions, and frustrations emerged. Even seasoned executives representing multinational corporations, who took intercultural training courses and had experience working in remote cultures, lost their temper.

Take a few examples. One psychiatrist in Pyongyang was a quirky fellow, a Hong Kong-born Chinese man who moved to Great Britain as an adolescent, from a wealthy family, and had studied to be a psychiatrist. In his twenties, he set up a business with the promising name Global Group, which supposedly achieved a good deal of success.

In 2004, the twenty-something, perhaps getting too confident, told the media that he would take over the country's only foreign joint venture bank, Daedong Credit Bank. His proclamation came as a surprise even to the bank managers themselves. The group didn't issue a public statement denying it, but its general manager and co-owner told me that he was taken aback by learning from the press about the supposed buyout.

In another twist, shortly after he publicized the future opening of his own bank, the Koryo Global Credit Bank, he told the media that a supposed 2,000 businesspeople in Pyongyang would constitute a potential customer base. Taking into account the dozens of Chinese businesspeople, most of whom would not need banking services in Pyongyang, the figure would have been more accurate at a hardly sustainable 200 customers.

This man was a donor to the British Labour party, had photographs splashed all over his website of himself with former prime ministers Tony Blair and Margaret Thatcher and a line-up of royalty and dignitaries from the U.K. and China. In fact, he always seemed to make sure a photographer just happened to be standing nearby to take a picture of the global elites shaking his hand.

On his conglomerate's website, he even claimed that world leaders asked him for advice—although he remained vague as to whether they approached him for his business "acumen" or whether they needed psychiatric help. One hint, though, is that he holds the post of Honorary Consul General representing Grenada in Hong Kong. Maybe a few Grenadian leaders desperately need his input on the island's pressing national security matters? Nobody was fooled by the titular tendency.

This was because he had trouble backing up his VIP image with business acumen. Then came the day when the young lad launched the bank's opening ceremony at the Yangak Hotel. None of the foreign businesspeople in Pyongyang, or at least the ones I knew, got an invitation, but I knew that the British ambassador got one and arrived after a delay. He must have had something urgent that day—certainly more important than a minor bank's grand opening.

Most North Korean media outlets, along with a few foreign newspapers, published stories on this event. But their pieces read more like celebrity hype heavily doctored by the company itself. My peers and I had never been contacted by the psychiatrist-cum-banker, and we also didn't know anyone who was dealing with the bank. The next developments came as no surprise. Just over a year later the bank's name board was quietly removed from its offices. At the hotel where it was based, the receptionist flatly exclaimed to me, "The bank is closed!"

After his banking business flopped, the psychiatrist moved from business into, dare I say it, North Korean politics when he became chairman of the International Kim Il Sung Foundation. In an interview with KCNA in October 2007, he was quoted as saying: "No prize in the world is as prestigious as the 'International Kim Il Sung Prize.' As chairman of the International Kim Il Sung Foundation, I will make every possible effort to carry out the noble cause started by the President, deeply aware of the mission I have assumed before the times and humankind." He was, in essence, taking on the world-riveting task of promoting "Kimilsungism" and Juche.

The dream of this psychiatrist-turned-tycoon—that is, striking business gold in North Korea—has not yet come true.

Another colleague I worked with was Dr. T.M., who strangely was a Juche sympathizer despite working as an economic historian, lecturer, and business consultant based in Seoul since the late 1970s. Earlier, he was a British parliament candidate for the now-defunct Liberal Party, a prominent group that espoused laissez-faire economics until it ended its run in the 1980s. He's also an expert on the *chaebol*, or South Korean conglomerates.

Nobody would believe this Cambridge-educated economist found a belief in socialism and Juche. But his "sympathies" were merely a form of opportunism to get him better business deals. During a ribbon-cutting ceremony in Pyongyang with the Minister of Foreign Trade, the North Korean dignitaries and foreign guests all wore Western suits. Dr. T.M., however, was the only exception, wearing a dark North Korean "Mao-style" cadre suit with a Kim Il Sung pin, a show of solidarity with the Great Leader's ideology.

North Koreans have various names for this outfit, such as "people's dress" or "combat uniform." Occasionally foreign businessmen don these outfits like Dr. T.M., although I never wore one. On the other hand, maybe he did not sympathize with Juche but was simply trying to gain the trust of his North Korean colleagues to find better business opportunities. Only he knows the answer as to why he dressed like this, but it only raises more questions.

Once I asked a senior security official what he thought when he saw foreigners strutting around in these outfits. "We appreciate it if they mean it sincerely," he answered. "But nobody can fool us, and we know when somebody puts up a masquerade." Obviously, Dr. T.M.'s opportunistic dream was far from the hopes of North Koreans, who wanted only true believers to wear these uniforms. These "fashionable" foreigners weren't terribly hurt by that prospect, though, because North Koreans don't even entertain a foreigner's antics unless they are useful. The locals just gaze at them with a giggle.

THE VIRTUE OF ENGAGEMENT

In North Korea you will always be confronted with the subject of human rights. While it is a serious issue, North Korea's foes are equally guilty of using rights rhetoric as a political tool to further isolate and corner the regime. Such a draconian stance, strongly advocated by the U.S., usually backfires.

Isolation shuts out information and ideas and makes people unable to ultimately choose the way they want to live. The countless definitions and interpretations of human rights and their abuses lead any approach to this matter to a reductio *ad absurdum*. Consequently, stricter definitions and interpretations would imply the prohibition of engagement with most if not all nations on earth, including the U.S.—the world's loudest champion of human rights. In short, it is engagement, and not isolation, that can lead to the improvement of the human rights situation.

In recent years big business has started to make human rights an issue of good corporate citizenship. *CR*, a corporate responsibility magazine, even publishes its yearly ranking called "The 100 Best Corporate Citizens." In 2012, the magazine put IBM and the pharmaceutical giant Bristol-Myers Squibb at the top of the list.[1] My former employer, ABB, was one of the initiators of the Global Business Initiative on Human Rights and motivated other multinational groups, General Electric, Unilever, and Coca Cola, to join it. In a brave move for a multinational corporation, ABB also became a member of Amnesty International. And it announced on its website: "Based partly or wholly on human rights considerations, ABB has not taken any business with North Korea and Myanmar for several years."

Is it a serious violation of an ABB employee's human rights when he is taken hostage by a country and put into prison by a government for no valid reason? For the president of Switzerland, who called it a "serious crime," the answer was yes. For the ABB Group's American chief executive, however, it was a no. I find it outrageous that a multinational company does not agree with all those who believe that innocent people should not be jailed. In legal-rational democracies this is a universally accepted rule.

Two Swiss ABB employees were indeed taken hostage in Libya, one of whom, the ABB country director, was put into jail without trial.[2] The imbroglio began when Libya's now-deceased premier, Muammar Gaddafi, was angered by the arrest of his son Hannibal in Switzerland on charges of bodily harm, threatening behavior, and coercion of his staff. Hannibal had a history of violence in the U.K. and Denmark, and Gaddafi's Libya had, according to Amnesty International, a long history of "human rights violations committed in the 1970s, 1980s, and 1990s." But the dictator wanted revenge.

Obviously, the ABB Group CEO considered all this benign and unimportant, announcing in a Swiss newspaper that ABB would continue to do business with Gaddafi's Libya after the release of the hostages. Human rights were no issue here when he explained his decision to the Swiss newspaper *Der Sonntag*, saying that there is "no need to change the business policy towards Libya as this was a dispute between Switzerland and Libya in which ABB was all of a sudden caught by chance."[3] There is a lot of hypocrisy involved in the behavior of "good corporate citizens," as they claim they want to be.

The dreams of being at the same time good corporate citizens and high-performing companies, including in oil-rich Libya, have evidently collided here. They have highlighted the dilemma businesses are faced with when Western politicians stigmatize, at will, countries they consider their enemies. That includes North Korea, despite their freely courting Gaddafi's Libya at that time.

Another mining company slammed the door on a delegation of North Korean mining customers who visited Sweden in November 2009. That was surprising because Sandvik, as it was called, was nevertheless eager to sell mining equipment to the country. I had been representing the business in North Korea beforehand. But the company demanded, like others, to be removed from the sponsoring list of the Pyongyang Business School.

These companies have switched from their commercial core business to protecting human rights in North Korea. But they aren't giving much thought to human rights in the rest of the world—such as Saudi Arabia and Zimbabwe, where many of them operate.

And, to add one problem that every executive sighs over, corruption is an issue that businesspeople must deal with both in emerging markets and in developed countries. In a perfect world, it wouldn't be a problem. The Korea Friendship Association (KFA), placed under North Korea's Committee for Cultural Relations with Foreign Countries, claimed on its website that North Korea is home to no corruption, whereas Transparency International (TI) believes, according to its 2011 Corruption Perceptions Index, that Somalia and North Korea are the world's most corrupt nations when measured by their citizens' perceptions.

While KFA's dream is, without a doubt, too good to be true, TI was excessively harsh. I have done business in Africa, the Middle East, and Asia, and have never found North Korea to be the worst in this regard.

The main lesson my experience taught me is that, all over Africa and Asia, civil servants were underpaid and needed to find side sources of income. North Korea is very much the same: its people remain economically isolated and sanctioned to the bone by foreign powers, and as long as the country does not carry out meaningful economic reforms, its ability to pay its civil servants will be hampered.

New Zealand ranked number one on TI's index, a potentially false victory that raises questions about the credibility of North Korea's placement on these corruption lists. Is it really possible that New Zealand is the world's cleanest country when, on the same day TI published its findings in 2011, the country's *Dominion Post* ran a front-page story titled "Economy's NZ$7 billion black hole"? The piece reported on missing cash that was equivalent to one quarter of North Korea's GNP. It alleged that "Cash trade jobs, crimes, wages under the table, and online trading are costing the Government more than $7 billion a year in lost tax." Revenue Minister Peter Dunne even told the reporter, "There is a vast underground economy in New Zealand, always has been: mate's rates, cash jobs, jobs in kind, all of those sorts of things which are very hard to track down."

In the PwC global economic crime survey for 2011, almost half of the New Zealand companies said they were victims of fraud in the previous year. New Zealand has more fraud than Australia and the U.S. The country has climbed in the global rankings for fraud from eighth place in 2009, out of fifty-four countries, to fourth place in 2011, out of an even greater pool of seventy-eight countries.

Moreover, a Justice Ministry paper revealed in December 2011 that more than 1,000 New Zealand companies or limited partnership arrangements have been "implicated in serious offending overseas over the past five years" including "trafficking of illegal drugs, people, and arms, money laundering and large-scale frauds." The logic doesn't add up. New Zealand has more than 1,000 companies involved in illegal overseas business, whereas there are only a few dozen North Korean companies that are engaged with the rest of the world. Even in a worst-case scenario, criminal New Zealand companies would vastly outnumber criminal North Korean enterprises. Can Pyongyang really be that evil compared to others on the list?

In an article entitled "The Black Hole of North Korea," published in *The New York Times* in August 2011, Isaac Stone Fish cheerfully admitted that a story he had written about a drug "epidemic" in North Korea was based on talking to just one North Korean defector without much corroboration. He confessed, apparently without any sense of guilt, "I painted a picture of the drug's abuse for my article: part escape from the desolation of North Korean life, part medicine in a country with practically no healthcare infrastructure. Yet after months of research I have to admit that I have no idea what is actually happening inside North Korea."

At least this journalist was brave enough to admit his ignorance. But others continue to make reckless assessments in their reports and books. Since many of these reporters have never visited, and the journalists who have gained access don't see much, they wouldn't really know for certain. Or, to quote *The Guardian*, "The lack of western sources in North Korea has allowed the media to conjure up fantastic stories that enthrall readers but aren't grounded in hard fact."[4]

NOTES

1. Jacquelyn Smith. The 100 Best Corporate Citizens. *Forbes*. April 18, 2012. http://www.forbes.com/sites/jacquelynsmith/2012/04/18/the-100-best-corporate-citizens/.

2. *The Local.* Swiss take Libya to court over hostages. June 6, 2011. http://www.thelocal.ch/page/view/267.
3. *Az Aargauer Zeitung.* ABB bleibt Libyen treu - Reiseverbot für Schweizer Mitarbeiter. September 21, 2010. http://www.aargauerzeitung.ch/wirtschaft/abb-bleibt-libyen-treu-reiseverbot-fuer-schweizer-mitarbeiter-11928016.
4. Paul Watson. South Korea good, North Korea bad? Not a very useful outlook. *The Guardian.* July 19, 2012. http://www.guardian.co.uk/commentisfree/2012/jul/19/korean-conflict-time-nuanced-view.

Chapter 6

A Manchurian Candidate?

*Supreme excellence consists in breaking
the enemy's resistance without fighting.*

— Sun Tzu, *The Art of War*

B ack home, curious outsiders often asked me questions like, "Are
you doing *more* than just business in North Korea? Why would
any foreigner move to North Korea unless they were in espionage? Are you a spy?" It's true that working in North Korea has the
flair of a James Bond movie, with all its intrigue, women, and cars.
In the 2002 flick *Die Another Day*, Bond even starts out captive in
North Korea and escapes across the Demilitarized Zone (DMZ) in
a prisoner exchange. It was a fate that I, thankfully, didn't meet.

To my surprise, no foreign intelligence agency asked me to snoop
on the North Korean government. I didn't understand why not. When
I arrived in the early 2000s, the U.S. had announced its firm intention to defeat the DPRK, a part of George Bush's "axis of evil." It
seemed like Washington would use all available military, economic,
and psychological weapons to accomplish its goal—which included,
according to the Bush administration, the exclusive right to pre-
emptive strikes against what the U.S. called "rogue states."

In that volatile environment, foreign intelligence agencies watching the DPRK should have been eyeing people like me who had access
to high-level officials. I wondered what my "market value" would
have been to these agencies, or to put it more bluntly, what rewards
they would have offered in exchange for information. Of course, I
never intended to sell my soul to any of them, which would have

meant betraying close friends in North Korea.

It was the moral fiber that I built up from doing business in hostile environments in Africa, the Middle East, and Asia. That was my way of staying sane when so much of the world was suffering under the weight of poverty, with millions of people waiving any commitment to ethics just to make a meager income.

Perhaps it's an example of "survival of the fittest" in the rawest sense, a fierce competition in which the toughest and most conniving political players rise to the top while their honest counterparts are purged. For a foreign businessman, being honest and gaining the trust of locals who deal in a cutthroat business environment is the only way to make a living. That's why working as a spy was out of the question.

Perhaps the intelligence agencies considered me unreliable, a loud figure among the business community in Pyongyang who could easily embarrass them publicly or blow their cover. Or did they simply realize that I was not interested in being recruited? Maybe they had other intelligence sources, like North Korean defectors and missionaries working along the border. Those people, of course, don't have quite the same access that businesspeople inside Pyongyang have. The Wikileaks did reveal that every U.S. diplomat was, to some extent, underhandedly gathering information when they met with expatriates in Seoul and Beijing.

The DPRK has been successful in shutting out foreign spies, suggesting that many of them simply don't have access to the inner workings of the country. Rather, the intelligence picture is usually pieced together through interviews and defectors' stories. The Central Intelligence Agency, for one, is known to gather as much as 90 percent of its intelligence from media reports.

Of course, it would be impossible for a CIA officer to actually gather information from inside Pyongyang. When the apartment of a senior official of a U.N. organization was renovated, she bluntly asked the Korean workers where the bugs would be planted. They equally matter-of-factly pointed to various spots in the flat, she later told me. When I made phone calls, I sometimes jokingly said, "Hello to you and to everybody else who is going to enjoy our conversation." In at least one instance I heard somebody giggling in the background in response. I was gleeful at this rather friendly human reaction. Among the Western powers, on the other hand, eavesdropping satellites and sophisticated e-mail interceptors always remain silent, a scary reality made bare when former NSA contractor Edward Snowden leaked the details of NSA spying operations in the summer of 2013. All North Koreans, moreover, have been systematically sensitized to the so-called threat of having contact with foreigners, and they were made keenly aware to avoid even harmless gatherings of them.

INTELLIGENCE IN THE DARK

CIA directors and military commanders have predicted the imminent collapse of the DPRK, despite the regime's surviving a famine, two transfers of power, the pursuit of nuclear weapons, and a near war with South Korea. In 1996, the director of the CIA predicted North Korea's collapse within 3 years[1]; earlier that year, the U.S. Commander of the Seventh Army in South Korea forecast collapse within "a very short period."[2] Was this a matter of having access to shoddy information?

One of the most vociferous persons in announcing the imminent implosion was a senior U.S. military commander and self-proclaimed North Korea "expert." He retired in the early nineties and fell into obscurity, while the DPRK continues to exist today. More recently, though, the regime added weapons of mass destruction to its arsenal, a deterrent that would ensure that its enemies' predictions would carry a devastating cost.

A European consultant who visited the DPRK several times, working with the Swiss Development and Cooperation Agency in Pyongyang, told me that he firmly believed every other expatriate was a spy. He did not give me his definition of the "expatriate" population. But if we lump all foreigners together into this label, while leaving out the Chinese, there would be approximately 500 residents (most of whom were diplomats). The Russian embassy, which was the country's largest, counted about 100 people in 2005—a sharp decline as it was one tenth of the number in 1990. Diplomats were not busily engaged in the promotion of bilateral economic development plans, and rarely did they spearhead cultural exchanges. Some diplomats told me they were bored because they had nothing to do.

Without much real work on the table, they instead observed and analyzed what they saw and reported it to their respective governments. If this was considered espionage—and I would not challenge this notion—then the consultant was right in his judgment. On the other hand, it's expected of diplomats to gather information about their host country in a way that wouldn't necessarily be considered spying. Journalists and businesspeople have been known to dive in and feed intelligence to their embassy; take, for instance, the famed reporter Pham Xuan An, who in the Vietnam War was a *Time* magazine correspondent and a double agent who played both the CIA and North Vietnam's intelligence bureau.

Outside of diplomatic circles, the expatriate community consisted of international donor organizations such as the World Food Programme (WFP), the U.N. Children's Fund (UNICEF), the IFRC, and the WHO. Fewer than a dozen NGOs hired foreigners in North Korea, and a third of the groups came with religious backing. The North Koreans were wary of them, because spies could be among them.

A Frenchman who was fluent in Korean, after working for an NGO in North Korea, never revealed his language skills until the day a U.N. organization offered a better paid job to another expatriate. A few weeks later, when his visa expired, the government did not extend it—without giving a reason. Foolishly hiding his Korean language skills, and potentially using them to listen to North Koreans unaware of this, was obviously considered an act of espionage.

Some ABB executives privately told me that they believed that the American woman who took care of a problem with my laptop at the group's compliance department was a CIA agent. Given how the CIA works overseas, such an allegation wouldn't be surprising if true. Historically, the agency's case officers have been notorious for convincing "agents," or freelancers working for governments and companies, to feed them information. Henry Luce, the founder of *Time* magazine, was one example of a pro-Washington conservative who allowed spies to take covers as journalists throughout the cold war.

In August 2005, state officials made a turnaround that backed their anti-spy paranoia: they announced that most expatriates not attached to diplomatic missions should pack up and leave North Korea by the end of the year. The DPRK, they explained, had received humanitarian aid that helped the country pull through the famine, but the aid had stretched on much longer than the usual two to three years typical for similar natural calamities. The result, officials rightly feared, was that do-gooders were creating a "culture of dependence," as one official said in the announcement. Using that phrase, they meant that the government needed to enact more of its own development cooperation from now on.

Still, the Koreans, in their usual pragmatic way, left open a caveat: foreign organizations could maintain their offices in Pyongyang if they were managed by Koreans. The arrangement came with all sorts of benefits, most importantly that the risk of espionage would be minimized to almost zero.

Unlike in Cambodia and Africa, there is no risk of being overrun by foreign NGOs in North Korea, as the government does its best to keep them in check. After months of negotiations with nervous foreign groups, the regime came to a compromise: U.N. organizations were allowed to stay as long as they reduced the number of foreign staff, while European NGOs were allowed to operate "undercover" with fewer staff using an EU banner.

Suddenly they had to give up their fake EU status because, as one European diplomat told me, it was a "face-saving deal" for all parties involved. Most NGOs agreed, but a minority among them decided to leave the country. This was because they did not want to lose their identity as NGOs. In their eyes, this may also have diminished their chances of being funded by private sponsors.

The benefits of continued aid and of future development projects disguised as humanitarian aid—since EU countries rejected any development cooperation as a result of North Korea's development of nuclear weapons—outweighed the risk of visitors' contaminating pure Korean minds and of spying and plotting against the Korean fatherland.

THE CIA "BRANCH OFFICE"

Over a period of seven years, the only Americans living in Pyongyang were the two successive heads of the country's WFP offices, and they were not spies. But expatriates joked about the impressive WFP compound, calling it the de facto "American embassy" or the "CIA branch office." At the time, the U.S. was the largest food donor to the country, contributing three quarters of the donated food, and all of it was funneled through the WFP. But many foreigners living in Pyongyang, including myself, would never have believed that the U.S. offered the goods out of a purely humanitarian motivation.

The reasons for the so-called humanitarianism included, of course, gathering information. All donated food was distributed throughout large parts of the country in the presence of the WFP staff to alleviate the possibility it would be diverted. Those staff had remarkable access to a large part of the country except areas considered sensitive by the North Koreans, mostly for military use, making them privy to valuable information that probably exceeded the diplomatic importance of the food aid. But the approach had its drawbacks for information gathering: in times of heightened political tensions, such as when missiles were tested, the foreign donors didn't allow food to arrive and be distributed.

This made the needy particularly vulnerable to any vacillations in global political moods. The satellites and the flights of unmanned espionage planes the U.S. sends over DPRK territory on a daily basis were of limited value; they could not make up for direct contacts with as many North Koreans as possible on the ground. The legendary U-2 "Dragon Lady," an icon of the cold war, was the airplane used by the CIA to spy on North Korea for more than thirty-five years.[3]

Were some of these American aid workers actually with the CIA? I can't say for certain, but the circumstances were sometimes suspicious. For a few years the second-in-command at the WFP in Pyongyang, a fluent Swiss-German speaker, claimed he was a Swiss national. From his suspicious remarks, he seemed convinced that the few foreign businesspeople in Pyongyang, including me, were regime-supporting opportunists involved in fishy business.

It was only later that a secret he tried to keep strictly confidential came out: he was also an American citizen. Quite a few foreigners, myself included, believed he projected his "Swiss-ness" on purpose to get more information out of people. In this sense, he could have been some sort of informant for the U.S. government, even if he was not an official employee.

A French NGO staffer was similarly put off by the humanitarian field. He told me he was surprised that his French bosses asked him so many questions that had nothing to do with the organization's work in the DPRK. After discussions with the Korean staff and officials at the time, the reason for this clicked. North Korea was watching the invasion of Iraq, preparing to fend off a potential threat to its sovereignty. They believed that charity groups in Iraq fed information to NGOs, which was then used by the U.S. and Britain to prepare for the Iraq War.

SNOOPING FOR INFORMATION

I was surprised to learn from the head of a humanitarian organization in Pyongyang, a serious man who did not tend to sensationalize stories like other expats, that American government officials had contacted some foreigners arriving in Beijing to interview them. Since it happened in broad daylight, the Chinese authorities must have known but stayed quiet.

That wasn't the first chatter I heard. A Belgian businessman who a decade earlier ran a Pyongyang-based diamond cutting business told me that he was contacted in Beijing by the former South Korean spy agency, the Korean Central Intelligence Agency (KCIA). When he told them he did not want to get involved, they tried to blackmail him by denouncing him as a "collaborator" with a North Korean security agency.

South Korea has a history of this. The now-defunct KCIA, once at the forefront of the cold war, has been forced to add nuance to its tactics after being renamed the NIS. This was especially true after South Korean president Kim Dae-jung launched his "Sunshine Policy" toward North Korea. The purpose was to focus on a more constructive engagement after the cold war ended, bringing the two rivals together via diplomacy rather than separating them through aggression.

Ironically, the spy agency was later accused of having facilitated the first historical meeting between the northern and the southern presidents by secretly delivering a payment to the northern side. Covert operations have taken on a different form, it seems!

With the post-cold war transformation, the incident that rankled the Belgian businessman would have been unthinkable when I lived in Pyongyang. The new world reality gives credibility to my estimate that virtually none of the businesspeople in North Korea are spies.

That they themselves are spied upon, however, is completely certain, and most likely by more than one country. For example, the son of the secretary to the German ambassador, a quick-witted IT student, spent his holidays in Pyongyang. I asked him to revise all the programs installed on my computer, and he removed more than a dozen Trojan and other spyware programs. According to him, the programs were of both Western and Eastern origin and could have been installed to gather political information.

E-mails, though, are like postcards that many can see, and the North Korean government is not unique in spying on its citizens. Special government services all over the world—especially the U.S.'s communications and cryptography service, the National Security Agency—have the ability to read any e-mail they choose with enough effort. The only way to fool them, for those who fancy doing so, is to include disinformation in the messages and to avoid writing and storing sensitive tidbits.

I sometimes would do that to protect my e-mail account and to attempt to annoy all those who were snooping. But with my lack of technological prowess, I didn't follow any systematic approach to misleading them. My counterparts in those agencies were certainly not amateurs like me.

DEFECTORS' TALES

Rather than targeting businessmen like me, South Korean and American spy agencies rely on the 20,000 or more North Korean defectors living in South Korea. And although they recount harrowing stories of suffering, some of the refugees are indeed feeding information to intelligence agencies and journalists. As 70 percent of them remain jobless in South Korea, they can make a living by selling dubious information.

The bias is understandable. Indeed, North Hamgyong province at the Chinese border is one of North Korea's poorest provinces, with a low level of food security. It suffered the most during the horrible famine in the nineties. Although this province has only 10 percent of the country's total population, the overwhelming majority of defectors stem from this province. Their tales have disproportionately shaped North Korea's international image. People in this province also have a grudge against Pyongyang and provinces near Pyongyang, which are much better off than North Hamgyong. The intelligence services, academics, book authors, journalists, and human rights and political activists who interview these defectors almost ceaselessly after their arrival in South Korea have an impact on their narrative, too. Those who know the North Korean refugee resettlement process in South Korea are aware of how easily individual accounts evolve over time from mild accounts of hunger or seeking economic opportunities to romantic tales of escape against all odds.

When I first heard that North Korean defectors claimed that the

DPRK was counterfeiting sophisticated U.S. superdollar bank notes, I was skeptical. This would have been the most high-tech product made in North Korea. All the machines came from Switzerland, which could not even sell them to North Korea and, for those that had already been sold, kept track of their whereabouts. The special high-tech paper and ink required to fabricate such bank notes come only from the U.S., according to the renowned bank note expert Frank Bender (see chapter 13).

Raising further questions, the U.S. also limits its bank note sales to an exclusive club of supposedly "serious" bank note printers that basically consists of people on good terms with the government. I also wondered if these defectors had forgotten that North Korea would first and foremost replace its torn and tattered bank notes adorned with the portrait of godlike Kim Il Sung. That's at least before undertaking the costly effort of printing notes that would earn the country, according to its accusers, a measly $20 million. So how could North Korea have possibly been counterfeiting dollars?

Not all defectors are making up their stories, and many of their terrible experiences are true. But some academics and authors seem to blindly accept all stories at face value, especially when they stem from North Korean defectors, even though there's no way to verify them.

This is true with the biography of one defector, Shin Dong Hyuk, a man born and raised in a labor camp from which he later escaped. *Washington Post* journalist Blaine Harden wrote his story in the book *Escape from Camp 14*, published in 2012. The problem was that he initially presented his story differently from how he told it later. The "insight," of course, isn't entirely true.

In 2007, I saw how the American government can quickly turn against its friends out of spite. The English-language media ran a big news story about Steve Park, a Korean-American man who imported the North Korean version of the liquor soju into the United States. The importer, of course, was later arrested as a spy—but, strangely, not one hired by North Korea but rather from South Korea! To my surprise, spying inside the U.S. against an enemy country is allowed and, in certain politically convenient episodes, encouraged—as long as the sleuth is registered with a U.S. government agency. The man neglected to do so and was jailed.

At first glance, it appeared that the U.S. burned a snitch who sided with the country thanks to its burdensome and unwavering bureaucracies. But it's also possible that it embarked on a cover-up to attain a hidden goal: to make the North Koreans, already paranoid enough, even more wary of spies camouflaged as investors. The idea was to make business with foreigners more difficult and to isolate the country further.

From a North Korean standpoint, then, it's understandable why the paranoia grew during the Bush administration. "Had we not built a strong deterrent, we would have been invaded like Iraq and Afghanistan, and did we not strongly control the influx of people and anything else, we would be infiltrated and sabotaged like Iran," Dong Jie Han, a top party cadre, explained to me over coffee.

He made a fair point, even if outsiders never fully grasped why the regime would pursue its massive army and weaponry. It was relatively easy to invade Saddam Hussein's Iraq, which, unlike North Korea, lacked the nuclear arsenal to deter its enemies. Iran's enemies, such as Israel, also had an easier time launching cyberwarfare, assassinations, and systematic acts of sabotage in Iran. Compared to North Korea, Tehran maintains a degree of openness.

The retrenchment against outside influences bodes ill for a future opening-up and for economic reforms. At least that's what Stephan Haggard and Marcus Noland argue in their study of North Korean refugees, *Witness to Transformation.*

The West, meanwhile, is clinging tightly to false hopes that North Korea will give up its nukes—its best deterrent, and likely to remain that way.

Yet U.S. Secretary of State Madeleine Albright, who met North Korea's former leader Kim Jong Il, wrote that she was "prepared to trade military concessions for a combination of economic help and security guarantees." A glimmer of hope remains that somebody with a good pragmatic sense will start engaging seriously with North Korea, like U.S. President Nixon did with Chairman Mao Zedong's China in the early 1970s.

An American détente would allow North Korea to relax its securitization, freeing up its behemoth resources that are currently tied to the military. That money could then be invested in the buildup of a modern infrastructure and the rehabilitation of the economy. It would also attract large foreign investments that would contribute to make North Korea a new "tiger economy," as happened in the 1960s and 1970s with South Korea, Taiwan, Japan, the Philippines, and Malaysia. (The latter two were only partially successful in their transformations, having reached a middle-income level and then stopping, but that was nevertheless an improvement compared to the gut-wrenching poverty they experienced beforehand.)

There shouldn't be any doubt that the North Korean people see patriotic national development as a priority, especially when you consider that some are known to jump into torrential floods at the risk of their lives to save portraits of Kim Il Sung. I saw their nationalistic fervor up front, but never betrayed them or spilled their secrets. Only after moving from North Korea to another country was I approached by some organizations and dubious individuals. I did not betray my principles and will take those secrets to my grave.

NOTES

1. Seung-Ho Joo. Korean foreign relations toward the twenty-first century: reunification and beyond. *American Asian Review*, Vol. XVI, No. 3, Fall 1998, p. 104.

2. Norman D. Levin. What if North Korea survives? *Survival: The IISS Quarterly*, Vol. 39, No. 4, Winter 1997-98, p. 158.

3. *Huffington Post*. U-2 spy planes keep watch on North Korea. February 29, 2012. http://www.huffingtonpost.com/2012/02/29/spy-planes-north-korea_n_1309877.html.

PART II

Chapter 7

Southerners, Yankees, and "Chinese Lips"

We oppose the reactionary policies of the U.S. government, but we do not oppose the American people. We want to have many good friends in the United States.

— Kim Jong Il

For a moment, the room came to a standstill. At a dinner in Pyongyang, Dr. Tejbir S. Walia, the Indian-Canadian head of the local WHO office, mentioned that he went on a work trip to meet with the South Korean Ministry of Unification, which was donating medical equipment to the North. While in Seoul, he bumped into a group of South Korean youngsters and asked them what they thought about the prospects for unification.

The answer wasn't optimistic. The scenario would cost too much for the South, and the southerners said they'd rather keep comfortable lifestyles. Indeed, the drastically high cost of unification was estimated by the state-run South Korean Institute for National Unification at $47 billion to $216 billion in the first year of unification alone.[1]

The North Koreans didn't respond. But their icy silence spoke a thousand words. When Dr. Walia changed the subject to tuberculosis, a great sigh of relief went through the room.

The uneasiness owes to the fact that North Koreans firmly believe in reunification—that people all over the peninsula, north and south, yearn for a single glorious state, one that has not yet been realized thanks to the U.S. imperialists, a small group of fascist South Korean collaborators, and Japan (which has, in the eyes of the North Koreans, not properly compensated the nation for its colonial-era crimes).

For the North Koreans at the table, though, Dr. Walia was a reputable source, a medical doctor by training and a public health expert who did not invent stories to support any political goal. That's why they were shocked to hear this story from him.

This scenario is probably much more costly than the reunification of Germany, which itself was nonetheless incredibly expensive at more than $1 trillion, for West Germany, as of 2009. Many East Germans were, moreover, afraid they wouldn't be able to find jobs and affordable homes. With a sudden large pool of semiskilled workers from the North, salaries would plummet and unemployment would sharply rise. South Korea would also lack sufficient funds to be allocated to infrastructure and would need to increase taxes to fund unification. Living standards in the South would be lower for many years.

If anything, the North Koreans in the room probably felt a sense of betrayal over Dr. Walia's claim. Once more, it seemed, their South Korean brethren had turned on them: South Korea was, as the government has said, long the source of their grievances, stretching back further than the Korean War. Dr. Lee, a tenured history professor at Kim Il Sung University, put it into perspective for me over lunch at his university. "For centuries the Goguryo kingdom was a powerful and flourishing state and more advanced than other kingdoms inside and outside Korea," he told me. "Geographically, it comprised what is today North Korea and most of Manchuria, which was lost to China in the seventh century when a South Korean kingdom called Silla committed a huge betrayal by making an alliance with the Tang Dynasty of China to attack and conquer it. Thereafter, Silla set up a brutal rule that oppressed the Korean people of the remainders of the former Goguryo Empire for more than two centuries. The Koryo dynasty, which followed the Silla rule in the tenth century and lasted until the fourteenth century, was largely dominated by southern clans enriching themselves at the expense of northerners."

He said that the Choson Dynasty, which was the regime that followed, lasted from 1392 to 1910. It too was dominated by southerners. The ruling house established a relationship that was, to the protest of Koreans, subservient to China. Northerners were discriminated against in an apartheid-like fashion: they could not become state officials, and they had to pay heavy taxes without receiving much food and educational benefits in return.

Much of the imbalance can be blamed on the topographic differences between the north and south, stretching back a thousand years before the post-World War II separation. South Korea was home to flatter landscapes, a milder climate, and more watered rice fields, making it a natural producer of food and thus more prosperous than the harsh north. Southerners, who dominated the political system, conscripted northerners as soldiers to fight various invaders, like the Manchurians. These mountain-dwellers were hardened by the environment and were better built to fight off the frequent raids from Manchuria to the north.

The royal court, moreover, forced northerners into slavery and prostitution. Girls from Pyongyang and elsewhere, who were poor, defenseless, and looked down upon, were routinely abducted and brought to the South. Some women were obliged to work as entertainers for public officers during the Choson Dynasty. During some period of the Choson Dynasty these women were called *ginyeo, gisaeng,* or *haeohwa* ("flowers understanding words") who had to "serve" noble bureaucrats, troops, and foreign envoys. Though officially considered musician-dancers, they became men's play toys rather than artists. This was a sort of prequel to the Korean "comfort women" abused by the Japanese colonists in the twentieth century.

The Choson Dynasty opened up to the outside world in the late nineteenth century, after French, English, Russian, and American troops started traveling up Korean rivers in their canon boats. The most successful foreign business quickly became a gold mine north of Pyongyang. Northern laborers toiled away under life-threatening conditions and earned almost nothing. Fat profits went to elites in Seoul and abroad.

To make a long story short, it's understandable why North Koreans would see things this way, even if they are telling me a single side of the story. The north's vast natural resources were plundered by foreigners with the assistance of southerners looking to make a quick profit. Corrupt officials further sold off Korea's sovereignty to Japan, which brutally colonized the country from 1910 to 1945 and left thousands of people dead. Finally, Mr. Lee noted, the anti-Japan struggle was fought mainly by northerners under the leadership of "our Great Leader, Kim Il Sung, who was born in Pyongyang."

"Only during the Korean War, which lasted from 1950 to 1953, did we accept foreign fighters on our soil," Dr. Lee added. "The Chinese helped us resist the U.S.-led aggression, as Koreans under the leadership of Kim Il Sung helped the Chinese fight the Japanese occupation forces on their soil before." He went on with the proclamation that sounded like a speech. Corrupt South Korean officials, he argued, brought in the American occupiers, who remain today. They also helped sabotage the reunification efforts by North and South Koreans.

The armistice agreement of 1953, after the end of the Korean War, stipulated that Washington was not allowed to station nuclear bombs on Korean soil. The 1968 nuclear nonproliferation treaty, signed by the U.S., similarly prohibits nuclear powers from threatening nonnuclear countries, and it is thus understandable that North Korea withdrew in 2003 to pursue its experimental nuclear weapons program.

The southern "traitors," he lamented, allowed the U.S. to stockpile nuclear bombs in the South for decades after the Korean War; they even organized joint military exercises that included nuclear attack scenarios against the North. The Kim regime perceived the displays to be bold threats rather than true "exercises." Dr. Lee came to a bitter conclusion: "Unfortunately, the history of Korea is also a history of treason and betrayal of southerners against northerners!"

Dr. Lee's speech sounded like an expression of factionalism in a country where not only ethnic homogeneity but also the rallying behind a single cause, namely the achievement of unification, is considered paramount. Yet he certainly wasn't a traitor by North Korean standards since he considered his party and leaders to be the vanguard to correct historic errors and to unite the Korean fatherland under its leadership.

Listening to Professor Lee and other North Koreans, I learned that the strained relationship went back centuries. A rapprochement suddenly looked much more difficult than what had transpired in Germany. The split between East and West Germany after World War II was far easier to overcome: from the seventeenth to the late nineteenth century the Germanic region was not a nation but a loose collection of smaller states without any clear "east-west" rivalry. Looking at the Koreas in this historical context, what the West often perceives as a hard-line standoff between the two modern countries makes more sense.

For Americans, the incredibly brutal Korean War—sometimes called the Forgotten War—has been buried underneath memories of the traumatic Vietnam War and World War II. But the Korean War was just as destructive: between two and three million civilians were killed in the fighting, out of a population of thirty-nine million people on the peninsula. In 1953, the U.N. brought an armistice to the table, but South Korea's leader, Syngman Rhee, refused to sign it. He claimed the job was not finished and that his country would rather fight until it had completely overthrown the Soviet-connected DPRK.

It is true, according to Russian archives and the National Security Archive at George Washington University, that Kim Il Sung had repeatedly talked with Stalin about igniting a war to rid the Korean Peninsula of American influence. His hope was to reunite both sides into one socialist nation before U.N. forces arrived under General MacArthur. But this history has a lesser-known side: that hostilities between the South and North exploded years before the official commencement of the Korean War on June 25, 1950, the day North Korean forces crossed the thirty-eighth parallel in the South. Because of the decision, Kim Il Sung is commonly blamed in official histories as the instigator of the conflict, but the quandary goes back further.

Since both sides agreed to a cease-fire and not a legal end to the war, they continued to fight a merciless but low-intensity conflict that continued throughout the cold war. In the late 1960s in particular, both sides launched sporadic border intrusions and fought gun battles, causing about 750 deaths among North and South Korean, as well as American, forces. North Korea also abducted Japanese civilians from 1977 to 1983, with the intention of using them to train North Korean agents to blend into Japanese society and then planting the agents in Japan with fake identities. North Korea recognized thirteen abductees, apologized, and returned five abductees still alive in October 2002. Japan claimed there were at least seventeen abductees, but North Korea insisted that its figure was correct. Japan, on the other hand, has still not recognized, apologized for, and compensated Pyongyang for the hundreds of thousands of North Koreans it abducted, some of whom became sex slaves.

During most of the cold war, South Korea was more autocratic than democratic and military rulers governed it with an iron fist. The country wasn't as democratic as Westerners generally assume, and it wasn't North Korea that had a monopoly on evil. In 1973 Kim Dae-jung, who later became the liberal South Korean president and launched an engagement with the North called "Sunshine," was to be thrown into the ocean by South Korean KCIA agents. General Park Chung-hee and allies of the U.S. wanted to have this opposition politician disappear forever. But the opposition learned about this plot in time and was able to mobilize world opinion to have it prevented. Even the U.S. saw itself obliged to intervene in favor of Kim Dae-jung by sending helicopters to the ship from which he was going to be thrown into the ocean and meet his doom.

One of the famous personalities who helped to alert the world about Kim Dae-jung's situation and to change its opinion in order to keep him alive was the South Korean composer Yun I-sang. He had studied music in Europe and was living and working in Germany. Yun became a target of the South Korean military dictatorship, too, and was abducted in 1967 in Berlin by the KCIA. He was brought to

Seoul, where he was, under the pretext of being a spy, tortured and imprisoned.

His actual "crime," of course, was that he was critical of Park's dictatorship. Yun was a friend of the heads of government in Germany and Portugal, Willy Brandt and Mario Suarez. The German government put a great deal of pressure on the South Korean government to release Yun I-sang from prison. After being set free in 1969, Yun was prohibited from returning to South Korea and lived in Germany until his death in 1995.

In exile, Yun had composed an orchestra piece called "Exemplum in Memoriam Kwangju," with which Yun protested against the Kwangju massacre, a 1980 military crackdown against protestors that left some 200 demonstrators dead. This statement drew the attention of the North Korean leadership, which from then on took an interest in Yun's music style. Yun was indeed world famous for creating a unique blend of traditional Korean music and Western classical music. The North Korean president Kim Il Sung invited him to teach classical music as well as his own compositions in North Korea. The social democrat accepted the offer, hoping to promote reunification through his music. This caused his popularity in the South to drop for a number of years.

In 2005, on the tenth anniversary of Yun I-sang's death, his daughter, Yun Chong, founded the Yun I-sang Peace Foundation. She felt sorry that she could not help her father during his lifetime, but she would be all the more active from then on to take care of his legacy and to make his music known all over Korea and beyond. She believed that many Koreans, from North and South, considered him a peace icon even if they did not sympathize with the northern regime. I attended the opening of Yun Chong's shop in Pyongyang. She used the profits generated there to support the orchestra performers and their family members in Pyongyang. I sometimes saw her arrive at the airport in Pyongyang with huge cases that contained elegant and fashionable clothes, bags, and shoes as well as fashionable and valuable jewelry bought in neighboring countries. She developed a good

Ethnic Koreans stroll about in a market in this Chinese town in the Korean Autonomous Prefecture in Jilin province, known for its large Korean population. The sympathies of these Korean residents are sharply divided between North and South Korea. Nevertheless, Chinese-Koreans oversee most business transacted between Beijing and Pyongyang. As early as 1954, China allowed the Yanbian Korean Autonomous Prefecture to conduct border trade with the DPRK, helping its battered ally to get on its feet faster after the Korean War.

business sense. We once discussed the joint opening of a pharmacy, as her clients, who could afford to buy these high-priced items, were in the same bracket.

THE CHINESE KOREANS

Most of the 2.5 million Chinese citizens of Korean descent live in northeast China, near the North Korean border. They mostly speak Mandarin, a Chinese dialect, but many of them also speak Korean among one another. Almost 1 million of these ethnic Koreans live in the Yanbian Korean Autonomous Prefecture, a special economic zone created by the Chinese government in 1952. Today's ethnic Koreans in China stem mostly from migrants who fled a famine around 1860 and continued their movement until 1945.

From my own experience in doing business, ethnic Koreans in China had a huge advantage over everyone else. They spoke both Korean and Chinese, and they had contacts and understood the customs of both countries. Of the 138 Chinese companies officially registered in 2010 as doing business in North Korea, the majority took advantage of this group to enter the challenging and closed-off North Korean market.

Foolish Western companies trying to exploit opportunities in those same areas could have taken a cue from their Beijing-based counterparts. They often arrived with the help of Western and, occasionally, Asian consultants who had only superficial knowledge of North Korea and usually only one contact in the country, namely that of their sponsoring organization. The Western European companies accepted their unverifiable claims on the assumption that they were receiving top services for their money. But these so-called consultants introduced their clients to suboptimal local business partners who were scratching the backs of their acquaintances. It was a common mismatch, and I witnessed the collapse of countless businesses within a few years thanks to poor arrangements. The Chinese executives I met failed less frequently through Chinese-Korean fixers.

A garment company from Liaoning province set up a successful operation with hundreds of North Korean workers with the help of Chinese-Korean fixers, while another Chinese company from Jilin province started a profitable fish-breeding farm with the help of ethnic Korean Chinese. Unlike other countries in Asia, where it's easier to cross-check the advice of consultants, North Korea remains opaque, and information is often unverifiable.

Here's one story that illustrates the point. A famous European textile company wanted to profit from the low production cost in North Korea and export its products from North Korea to Europe and China, among other markets. It hired a European consultant who claimed to have extensive North Korea experience and a wide network of contacts in Pyongyang. His local contact and facilitator was an employee of a ministry, who introduced the foreign company to a garment factory.

What unraveled was basically a Ponzi scheme. He told the foreign investors that it was the best garment factory in the country. Neither the investors nor the consultant was aware of the fact that there were other, better garment factories in the country, because the information was hard to find. The recommended factory belonged to the same ministry, and the boss of the factory was his relative.

Unlike other factories, it was in a desperate state and urgently needed to be upgraded. The foreign investors prematurely agreed to set up a joint venture and started pouring money into it. A chronic shortage of power, plenty of misunderstandings and diverging interests between the foreign and domestic partners, and, on top of this, a venture that became a bottomless well made the foreign investor abandon the project. Had they had the same intermediaries as the Chinese textile company, things most likely would not have unraveled.

THE PERILS OF SOUTH KOREAN OWNERSHIP

Some businesses tried to run their North Korean operations out of Seoul, an arrangement that was usually a disaster given the perilous relationship and economic blockages between the two countries. I saw the uneasy diplomacy unfold when I attended the only international trade fair at which the ABB group had a booth in 2002. Mr. Sohn, a senior South Korean engineer and the head of an ABB factory in South Korea, was dispatched to show ABB products made there. In particular, he wanted to display a new type of oil-free and therefore eco-friendly power transformer made in his factory. Other multinationals also sent staff from their subsidiaries in South Korea to this exhibition in Pyongyang.

Of course, the situation didn't go as planned. At our booth, about five or six eerily vague North Koreans showed up, whom I had never seen before and never saw again after this exhibition and whose legitimate interest in trade was questionable. The government probably saw muddy waters in the prospect of South Koreans having direct contact with North Koreans and thought the situation required a record number of minders. I noticed that some prospective customers, seeing the swarm of security types, avoided the booth—making the setup terribly bad for business.

The political views of South Koreans like Mr. Sohn didn't really matter to the government. They saw a challenge in the way they dressed, their looks, and their relaxed behavior. The South Korean attitude, embodied in Mr. Sohn, wouldn't fit into the official North Korean storyline that Seoul was repressed by the Yankee and Japanese invaders.

About a year later, when the company promoted Mr. Sohn to manage the business across several Asian countries, the North Korean government denied him a visa to visit Pyongyang alongside a business delegation. As the chief representative from his group, I was informed that all group members who were not Koreans were given a visa except him, leaving him heartbroken. I never found out the precise reason authorities barred him entry; he did a superb job and even North Korean colleagues liked him.

He was also a diplomatic fellow, understanding how to behave in the country of his supposed "enemies" so he didn't stir up trouble. Some of my most ardent North Korean friends loved him. After work one day, I was touched when my staff and Mr. Sohn went out to karaoke together. The North and South Korean guests sang together, and they even held hands and hugged. From the heartfelt display, I knew his visa refusal wasn't directed against him personally. He was probably just a victim of the sporadic spats between the two countries; around the same time, the U.S. accused North Korea of secretly pursuing a uranium enrichment program.

The official rhetoric on China is far different. According to the party line, Pyongyang and Beijing share an unbreakable friendship—lauded with the official slogan that the two countries are "as close as lips and teeth." The bond arises out of a sort of communist brotherhood that goes back to when three divisions of Korean communists, from all over the peninsula, joined Mao Zedong's forces to defeat the nationalist Guomin Dang army in China in 1949.

In October 1950, Beijing repaid the favor. About a month after the official start of the Korean War in June 1950, North Korean soldiers overran nearly all of South Korea down to Pusan, but were pushed back when General MacArthur's American forces landed at the port city of Incheon in September. The U.N. troops, comprising mostly an American contingent, swiftly fought back the beleagured northern army; it even appeared that the complete end of the DPRK was near under a unified Korean Peninsula. Yet even to the surprise of President Truman, Mao Zedong ordered a million Chinese troops into North Korea to protect its strategic northwestern flank.

In a speech to the Central Committee of the Chinese Communist Party, Mao justified China's intervention: "If the lips are destroyed," he proclaimed, "the teeth get cold!" His government named the campaign the "war to resist U.S. aggression and to aid Korea," but the country paid a high price for its brethren's independence: 183,000 Chinese soldiers died out of an army of 1 million, a significant toll that included Mao's own son Anying. Eight years after the fighting was halted, China and the DPRK signed the 1961 Mutual Aid and Cooperation Friendship Treaty, the time frame of which has been extended until 2021. Its contents are significant for their implications for any American or Japanese maneuver around the peninsula: China pledged immediate military assistance to Pyongyang against any action deemed an attack.

Yet despite the official propaganda portraying their relationship as close as teeth and lips, it was a far cry from being anything close to a "love affair." Chinese businesspeople and diplomats whom I met strongly resented that the enormous support China offered during the Korean War was barely acknowledged, and was driven by self-interest.

It was in 2009 that an editorial published by the party-run and conservative Chinese newspaper *Global Times* used the term "ungrateful" for the first time, in a reference to North Korea. It wrote, obviously in an outburst of anger after North Korea conducted two nuclear tests against China's advice, that, "If the hundreds of thousands in the Chinese People's Volunteer Army hadn't gone over and helped the Korean People's Army fight their bloody war shoulder to shoulder, there wouldn't be a North Korea today."[2]

North Korea wanted to correct its image of a "naughty, ungrateful child" in the eyes of the Chinese, and suddenly car license plates beginning with 727 started emerging in the streets. The change coincided with a sharp rise of badly needed fresh Chinese investment in North Korea. The number 727 stands for July 27 (called Victory Day in North Korea), which was the day the armistice agreement was signed. It's a belated, highly visible token of recognition for the Chinese.

But in a strategy that went less noticed by foreigners, a China chapter was added to the Arirang Mass Games in 2008 and repeated during the performances over the next four years. They expressed a kind of gratitude to China and the recognition of China's successful reform path. One of the sharpest North Korea observers, Andray Abrahamian, explained that it "explicitly encourages the audience to see China as both friendly and as a successful model that could be an option for Korea." "One party 'socialism,'" he continued, "is paying dividends in the People's Republic of China, and the people of the DPRK might reasonably expect something similar in their country."

Not only do the Chinese have a grudge against their northern neighbor, but anti-Chinese sentiment has run high in North Korea for reasons dating back much earlier than the Korean War, due to a thousand-year-old relationship that included wars and occupation. Some staff made me understand that, saying, "The Chinese cannot be trusted." Mr. Pang, a senior diplomat, told me at a cocktail party, "We Koreans have a long history of ups and downs with China, and we know how much we can trust them."

Because we were chatting informally, I asked him a pointed and very undiplomatic question: "Which of the two countries is the lips and which is the teeth?" The official, who always wore a stern face, burst into laughter and almost spilled his wine. "I'm sorry, Mr. Abt," he said. "I cannot answer this intrusive question, but ask yourself: who would like to be the lips and who would not prefer to be the teeth?" His answer was, of course, as diplomatic as it could be and very clear despite its subtlety.

I could feel the strong urge by North Koreans, like the diplomat, to outline a sharp national identity that unmistakably distinguished Korea from China. This was despite, or perhaps because of, China's strong footprints on Korea's culture. Mr. Kim, the chief mining engineer, mentioned that he had recently visited China. He spoke Chinese. I tried to engage him and the other Koreans in a discussion on China and the Chinese language. I said that with 70 percent of all Korean dictionary entries being of Chinese origin, the Chinese language shouldn't be too difficult for Koreans to learn.

That was too much of a provocation and they could not hide their irritation. One of them answered, "Kim Il Sung's father left for China to organize the anti-Japanese resistance. Kim Il Sung accompanied him. There the latter went to school and learned Chinese. But our Great Leader Kim Il Sung, then a boy of eleven years, was told by his father Kim Hyong Jik, himself a great revolutionary and patriot, that he wanted him to continue his studies in Korea as he wanted his son to know his homeland, its culture, and master its language and be aware of the suffering of the Korean people under Japanese rule."

He went on. "When he was back in Pyongyang and joined a school there, his schoolmates knew that he had been living for several years in China and that he was fluent in Chinese. They often asked him therefore to speak Chinese to them, but he refused and answered, 'Why use Chinese when we have our own language?'"

For the first time since the peninsula was divided in 1945, the first hundred South Koreans visited Pyongyang in September 2003. An unlikely business empire had organized the tour: Moon Sunmyung's Unification Church, which ran the pioneering travel company Pyeongwha, along with the Pothongang Hotel in Pyongyang. Just opposite the hotel, Moon's conglomerate ran a large building for meetings and events called the Pyongyang Peace Embassy. The five-day tour cost $2,000 per person and included a visit to monuments, a "model" farm, a kindergarten, and a railway station.

In 2000, the landmark inter-Korean summit between Kim Jong Il and South Korea's then-president Kim Dae-jung paved the way for Moon's tourism project. Its other effect was to allow for the reunions of families split by the North-South divide. More than 20,000 Korean families have been permitted brief reunions since that year. The few lucky ones had to wait more than half a century to meet their family members, and once the opportunity has passed, they probably won't see them ever again. Time, unfortunately, is short for those who haven't had a reunion yet and are in their eighties and nineties. About 4,000 people on the South Korean waiting list pass away each year.

The cross-border exchanges were cut short in 2008, when the conservative administration of Lee Myung-bak won the election and abandoned his predecessor's engagement policies. The Red Cross-brokered family reunions, too, have also been hostage to the unpredictable tussles between Seoul and Pyongyang.

PURITY

One December I got a taste of the frigid winter life near the Chinese border. In the process, I came to understand how triumphantly North Koreans hold their sense of national purity. On the train from the Chinese border town of Dandong to Pyongyang, I had to wear a thick winter coat and warm shoes, covering my feet with three layers of socks. The train was not heated, and the outside temperature had fallen far below the freezing point; there were also frequent power outages, and to top it off, the ride was delayed past the frigid midnight hour.

The North Korean passengers traveling back home huddled in the cabin with their heaps of luggage. Most of them were diplomats and businesspeople, plus a couple of children. The poor weather brought us closer together, and we started chatting away. Thanks to us hitting it off, we quickly began sharing food and drinks, an entrée that included the typical meat, fish, eggs, salad, rice, and kimchi for 6 euros. It was good entertainment that spiced up what would otherwise have been a dull journey.

The Koreans were curious about me, my family, my life in Pyong-yang, and what I was doing in their country. I told them about my wife and my little daughter. Then, thinking my wife was from Swit-zerland, they asked if it was not too difficult for my wife to adapt to North Korea. I explained, in what turned out to be a faux pas, that my wife was not Swiss but a Vietnamese woman born in Hanoi. I went on, perhaps to their discomfort, that Vietnam and North Korea were full of similarities in eating habits and culture.

The conversation came to an abrupt halt, and I wondered if I had offended my new acquaintances. Of course I did, I realized. North Koreans are proud of the purity of their race and their culture, which they believe to be untainted by decadent foreign influences. They thought that only puppet South Koreans married foreigners, who were inferior to themselves, and that these marriages were a conse-quence of Western oppression.

My friends were uneasy that a comrade from the capital of the Vietnamese socialist revolution, an event Americans call the "Viet-nam War," married a foreigner from a nonsocialist European country. The revelation must have startled them: it was the latest evidence that the DPRK's ally had betrayed its revolutionary roots.

After an awkward bout of silence, I relaunched the conversation with a joke. "It is a known fact that mixed children pick the best genes from both parents and tend, therefore, to become superior to their parents," I said. A new theory of superior races was instantly born. One fellow traveler, apparently challenged in his beliefs, responded politely, "Is that so? Interesting!" The conversation then resumed, though they didn't touch on family matters.

Historians pretty much concur that, in prehistoric times, the ancestors of present-day Koreans migrated from North Asia. But this theory would have been heresy in the eyes of my fellow travelers. North Koreans consider their nation to be one cradle of humanity, which gave birth to the ancestors of all of humankind. The North Korean government, of course, does not give much thought to the archaeological evidence that countless tongues were spoken here, all bearing little relation to today's Korean language.

To be fair, though, the idea of racial purity stretched beyond Pyong-yang and even into the so-called decadent American fiefdom of South Korea. Until 2006, biracial South Koreans were not allowed to serve in the military even if they held South Korean citizenship; neverthe-less, all other citizens were required to serve for two years in the armed forces. Discrimination against biracial South Koreans is still common in the countryside. They're often teased and bullied at school, and not a single one has held public office. North Koreans, it would appear, have more in common with their southern brethren than is usually stated.

Others have had it worse than me. My friend Eduard Meier-Lee, a Swiss senior project manager at ABB with a South Korean wife, was on the receiving end of even more racially charged questions when he visited Pyongyang in 2003. One evening I took him to a centrally located Japanese restaurant, where we sang karaoke after dinner. The charming waitresses, wearing their typical *chosŏn-ot* national dress, invited us to sing and dance with them. They were keen to learn about Edi's family life, thanks to his decision to marry a Seoulite. In their eyes, the pairing was so outrageous that they bombarded him with questions and ignored me.

Until the early 1960s, mixed marriages were allowed in the DPRK. But that permissive time was long before the waitresses, all in their twenties, were born, and they were surely not aware of this. In 1963, the party began a campaign against mixed couples, going as far as to ask interracial couples—mainly Korean and Eastern European couples—to divorce. Since then, the party storyline has been that South Korean women were forced by the brutal American occupation forces into prostitution and arranged marriages. The liberated woman in the DPRK, on the other hand, could marry the man of her choice, who was, of course, always a Korean.

Another time, a group of foreign children—mostly the kids of diplomats—were invited to play soccer and rope-pull with their North

Korean counterparts. The Korean children overwhelmingly defeated the foreigners in every game by a significant margin. North Korean parents cheered on their allegedly superior offspring, once more reassured in the natural strength of their race. They probably didn't know that their children had trained for weeks or months before the informal competition, whereas the expatriate kids arrived unprepared.

After a few years in Pyongyang, I realized that North Koreans presented themselves differently to the outside world than they did at home. North Koreans were trained to be polite to foreigners and to skirt around political talk that could antagonize these impure humans. Like many East Asians, they're pragmatic enough to subordinate their personal views to the higher calling of bringing in foreign investment and charity. They would never tell a foreigner that he is a suspected spy or troublemaker, or that his work in the country equals an expression of greatness of the Kim regime.

Yet this is exactly what they believe in, at least under the surface. My staff occasionally translated political slogans, books, newspaper articles, and even North Korean songs played in karaoke rooms. I correspondingly scoured through the English-language literature on ideology and politics, finding some differences in the way they portrayed ideas.

To cite one example, our guides told American tourists, "We love American civilians!" Kim Il Sung, however, used to call upon the Workers' Party to always prepare for war against the Americans by instilling hatred against them: "The most important thing in our war preparations is to teach all our people to hate U.S. imperialism. Otherwise, we will not be able to defeat the U.S. imperialists who boast of their technological superiority."

I also tried to spark improvised discussions that revealed their true mindsets. While this helped me understand the business environment, my inquiries destroyed the wishful thinking that I had come to adopt, as most foreigners are prone to during short visits. We can acknowledge, with a touch of humor, that the North Koreans see themselves as exceptional, and get used to it.

NOTES

1. Yonhap News Agency. Parliamentary speaker chips in to unification funding campaign. July 18, 2012. http://english.yonhapnews.co.kr/national/2012/07/18/28/0301000000AEN20120718005600315F.HTML.
2. eChinacities.com. Why is China reluctant to abandon North Korea? March 11, 2012. http://www.echinacities.com/news/Why-Is-China-Reluctant-to-Abandon-North-Korea?cmteditid=#page_cmt.

TOP: An Air Koryo flight attendant sells alcoholic beverages, ginseng tea, and souvenirs (including copies of her hat), all made in North Korea.

ABOVE: North Koreans demonstrate their reverence for soldiers. In this case, the armed forces are waving to onlookers, who shout word "Kamsahamnida" (a formal way of saying thank you). The crowd is honoring the military for defending the country against foreign aggressors. But as the new leaders shift priorities away from national security to economic development, Songun (military first) propaganda is being toned down. Kimilsungism and Kimjongilism, a mixture of socialist ideals and Juche nationalism, are being promoted instead.

TOP: The many propaganda posters, coming across in such quantity and intensity, added color to an otherwise rather white and bland city. On the posters, the colors were dramatic and included references to fire, which was the dynamic and purifying element of the socialist revolution. But to be fair to the Pyongyang authorities, both new and old buildings were soon painted with more colors from the mid-2000s onwards. That's thanks in part to a newly established paint factory set up by North Korean and Chinese businessmen. The roofs of markets, for example, became light blue, and some buildings started appearing in green and orange.

ABOVE: The grand finale of a perfectly choreographed entertainment show at the Mangyongdae Children's Palace. The children perform a loyalty song to Kim Jong Il for their parents and other visitors.

ABOVE: The slogans of this propaganda poster from 2007 reveal one priority for North Korea's government: "Let us quickly advance the modernization of the light industry. Let us produce a lot of good-quality consumer goods." It displays pharmaceuticals with the logo "PS" (PyongSu). The government picked PyongSu not for political propaganda but because it legitimately felt that we were, at the time, the country's model pharmaceutical company—and the only one acknowledged by the World Health Organization to have achieved the international industry standard called Good Manufacturing Practices (GMP).

ABOVE: Popular ice skaters perform a show on Kim Jong Il's birthday, on February 16. All sorts of sports and festivities are unveiled on this day, one of the country's most important national holidays.

ABOVE LEFT: A boy walks with his dad, who is busy on his mobile phone.
ABOVE RIGHT: Teenagers who do not yet have a mobile phone use a public phone booth.

ABOVE: Since my North Korean staff were diligent and hard-working, we compensated them with beach holidays, sports outings, countryside excursions, and evenings of karaoke and dancing. Other North Koreans were slack-jawed at our crowd, astonished that their brethren were mingling with a foreign boss.

LEFT: On the South Korean side of the DMZ, a poster at this souvenir shop illustrates a South Korean and a North Korean soldier in military police garb. The South Korean garb resembles an American armed forces uniform, while the North Korean outfit could fit in the Soviet Red Army. The juxtaposition is a reminder of who divided Korea into a socialist North and a capitalist South, and a lingering ghost of the cold war.

ABOVE: In 2004, a huge explosion of a cargo train flattened large parts of Ryongchon, a city close to the Chinese border town Dandong. Rumors and propaganda spread by defector groups claimed that it was an assassination attempt on Kim Jong Il, who happened to pass by in his train just hours before the explosion took place. But there was no hint that the explosion had anything to do with that, as the regime remained unshaken and stable on that day and thereafter. I did not see more police and military in the streets of the capital that day. I took this picture less than three months after the accident, when the newly erected raw buildings had been finished in what the government called its "speed battle" in the tradition of the Chollima. If I had not seen it, I would never have believed it. Of course, speed came at the expense of quality: a few years later I noticed that many of these buildings were already dilapidated.

LEFT: On my way to work on a main street in Pyongyang at 7:30 A.M., I took this photo from my car in March 2007. Even though the streets here aren't crammed, the capital streets witnessed a steadily swelling amount of traffic over the years.

TOP: In the North Korean equivalent of a pilgrimage, most patriots visit the "holy mountain," Paekdu, at some point during their lives. Historically it has been a site of worship for all the surrounding peoples, like the Koreans and the Manchus to the north. All of them considered it the home of their ancestral origins. On the road to Paekdu, most North Koreans make a pit stop at Samjiyon city. The town is one of the coldest places in the country, with an annual average temperature of about 1 degree below zero. Developers hoped to turn the area into a ski resort, putting up guest houses (right), as well as secondhand ski lifts imported from Switzerland. A new power station was even built to ensure the smooth operation of the resort. It was a project started in the 2000s, when "Sunshine" was at its height. The intention was to fly loads of South Korean tourists directly from Seoul to Samjiyon and to make it an important source of revenue. Much to their chagrin, South Koreans have been able to visit the holy Paekdu Mountain only on the Chinese side.

ABOVE: Kim Il Sung Square on a rainy day. The entire square, pictured, is reserved for male bicycle riders.

Every year, for several weeks between May and June, party officials issued "rice planting battle orders," a euphemism intended to push workers to work at the speed of the Chollima, the fleet Korean winged horse. Workers, students, and children who live nearby rush to the rice paddies to

plant rice all day long. The goal is to secure a good harvest with a minimal loss. The government sometimes invites diplomats and foreign residents to "help" the farmers. In 2005, one fancy guest was the former British ambassador to the DPRK, David Arthur Slinn.

No traffic crosses the imposing Rungna Bridge over the Taedong River. Public transportation was minimal, and state-owned vehicles were not allowed to be used on Sundays, to save electricity and petrol. Everybody crossed the bridge on foot on Sundays. Deceptive foreigners sometimes took pictures on Sundays, reporting back home that there are no vehicles on the streets of impoverished Pyongyang. On the other hand, tourists visiting on a weekend during an important national holiday when, exceptionally, there are plenty of buses and cars on Pyongyang's streets—in any case more than on any other day of the year—took videos of the street traffic. They uploaded them on YouTube to "prove" that Pyongyang has much more traffic than in the past.

Highways were built during North Korea's "boom years," a period before the massive economic downturn in the 1980s and 1990s. The photo shows the highway from Pyongyang heading toward Kaesong and Panmunjom, the de facto border between North and South Korea, on an ordinary weekday, quaint and free of traffic.

The entrance of a state farm guarded by an armed guard. The slogan at the entrance calls for "single-minded unity" between the Korean people, the ruling Korean labor party, and the party's leadership. Buildings always carry propaganda slogans but never or only extremely seldom do they list the name of the farm, the company, the ministry, or any other entity, as this is considered to be of importance only to those dealing with it. Those who have nothing to do with the entity would not need to know what is going on behind the building's walls. One of the few places with a name I came across was—astoundingly—a pub.

The Moranbong Hotel is Pyongyang's only boutique hotel. The room rates for both a double and a single premier "first-class" room hover around $140 a night, while a budget third-class room goes for $80. The cheapest single room costs $65 a night and includes breakfast. This is a centrally located and quiet alternative to Pyongyang's top hotels, which cost about 80 percent more per night but offer all sorts of amenities. Still, the Moranbong was one of my favorite hangouts for its quality sushi and its sauna, pool, and fitness center. Karaoke rooms are built into a cave. Western diplomats and NGO staff based in Pyongyang can be seen lounging around at this charming little spot.

South Korean lawmaker Choi Sung visits the PyongSu booth at an international trade fair in Pyongyang, a time when visits were on the rise thanks to the Sunshine Policy.

The story of the Rason economic zone—a combination of the words Rajin-Sonbong—suggests history might be repeating itself. Located near the Chinese border, Rason is a flagship center for North Korea's economic development that, to some extent, mimics a key predecessor in the 1980s: the Shenzhen Special Economic Zone, which China set up next to wealthy, British-run Hong Kong during its own reform process. From left to right, this photograph shows the former chairman of Rason, followed by Susan Chayon Kim, a Korean American scholar who has trained North Korean executives there, and finally me.

Nosotek was the first IT company with foreign investors in North Korea; the company took industry experts by surprise with its popular games discretely made for Western players. This included one popular role-playing game for the Nintendo Wii, an iPhone app that reached Apple's Top 10 list in Germany, and its award-winning medical software. (Clients want these products to stay confidential, for obvious reasons.) Pictured here is Nosotek's founding troupe from left to right: Ju Jong Chol, Vice President and Deputy CEO; Felix Abt, Vice Chairman of the Board of Directors; and Nosotek President and CEO Volker Eloesser (extreme right). Eloesser found another calling on the side, playing the role of the villainous foreigner for North Korean military flicks.

I welcomed graduate students to a seminar at the PBS (Pyongyang Business School) under the watchful eyes of the country's leaders, Kim Jong Il and Kim Il Sung. The slight downward slant in their portraits creates an illusion that their eyes follow you everywhere in the room.

In addition to my everyday business work, I became an agent for North Korea's most talented painters, helping them sell their artwork overseas as part of the country's first e-commerce project. Unfortunately, U.S. and UN sanctions impeded money transfers to Pyongyang, and hackers repeatedly took down our website. We eventually gave up on the project.

ABOVE: In 2003, I was part of a meeting over a multimillion dollar precontract memorandum of understanding between the ABB group and the North Korean government. The dignitaries present, from right to left, are the Minister of Energy production and coal industries, the Swiss foreign minister (and President of Switzerland as of 2011), and the Swedish ambassador to the DPRK, in the background. The international media broadcast details of the meeting worldwide, framing it as a subtle coup d'état against the staunch American policies of the time. The *Financial Times*, for one, wrote: "The company confirmed that a signing ceremony in Pyongyang was attended by Micheline Calmy-Rey, Switzerland's new foreign minister, and Hang Pong-Chun, North Korea's minister of power and coal industries." It further read, "Washington is planning to put pressure on Pyongyang by isolating its crumbling economy, and ABB's agreement to improve North Korea's power network could undermine this policy."

TOP: PyongSu became the only drug manufacturer in North Korea that met international quality standards, and the only North Korean company that ever won contracts in international tendering against foreign competitors. With that reputation, we set up our own "quality pharmacy" chain, focusing on providing high-quality but affordable products and customer service. This photo was taken at the opening event of PyongSu's fourth pharmacy in Pyongyang.

ABOVE: North Korea hadn't been exposed much to global business practices, so quality and service-mindedness never played an important role. I tried to instill a culture of quality into business, pushing for a good working environment, offering employee incentives, and training workers in-house and abroad. In this photo, I took my North Korean management team on an industry fact-finding mission in China, followed by a training course at a leading pharmaceutical company in Shanghai.

My North Korean friend painted this piece using a medium of colored stone powders. Basically, he took different gemstones and ground them into different-colored powders, and then put the powders on the canvas. The entire lengthy process is done by hand, and no artificial or synthetic colors are added. The colors also don't lose their strong shine over time. It's a technique common in North Korea that would be considered unique elsewhere. It takes months to finish one painting, and the style has a special meaning for the nation. Even though it was once called "powder painting," Kim Il Sung changed the name of the style to "Korean jewel painting," to point out that it was developed on the peninsula using precious Korean stones. Until some years ago, Korean jewel paintings were made on rigid panels. At my request, the painters in Pyongyang for the first time made the paintings flexible, so they could be rolled up and shipped more easily. Along with other paintings, I exhibited rollable paintings like this one for the first time at the Nha Trang Sea Festival at the coastal town in southern Vietnam in 2009.

Chapter 8

Feeding the People

All we have is guns and millet.

— Deng Xiaoping, 1974

When I traveled in summer months in the countryside, I saw the devastation of frequent heavy rain falls, which destroyed large parts of the rice harvest. The downpours even triggered landslides that upended roads and houses and washed human excrement into the mostly untreated water supply.

As the torrents came, farmers desperately scoured to collect their wet rice. Only a few trucks were available to assist them; most vehicles sat idly thanks to a lack of petroleum and spare parts, making the situation worse for those poor planters.

Floods and famine have killed thousands of people in the past, orphaning children and tearing apart families. Currently, the children are being cared for with the modest quantities of stored food and medication in orphanages in the larger provincial cities, which I saw during my own visits. Regional differences also struck me: the rugged northeastern provinces were much worse off in terms of food availability compared to provinces in the southern "cereal bowl" that produces most of the country's grains.

Everywhere I went, I saw the deeply lined faces of farmers in their forties and fifties that were proof of physical hardship. Transplanting rice by hand is tiresome and backbreaking work that requires hours in the scorching sun. Farmers without rubber boots were exposed to all kinds of nasty waterborne diseases. Visitors were often asked by farm managers, empathetic to their workers' plight, to donate boots, along with spare parts for machines and fuel to operate the machines.

In North Korea, food is closely tied to politics. For a long time the highest echelon of politicians dictated which food their citizens would eat, along with how much of it. This is because free food fit into the socialist state's role as a provider of necessities, including work, housing, health care, education, and clothing. The government, in fact, had a very particular type of food in mind for its children, a meat-based soup with rice.

This description struck me as I read a New Year's editorial published in the three, army, party, and youth, newspapers. The op-ed echoed Kim Il Sung's principle that all North Koreans should get their daily rice and meat soup for free. The most influential paper, the *Rodong Sinmun*, lamented in December 2010 that North Korea hadn't met the goal. "I'm the most heartbroken by the fact that our people are still living on corn," Kim Jong Il was quoted as saying. "What I must do now is to feed them white rice, bread, and noodles generously."

It wasn't just newspapers that played with the idea of food for all. On North Korean TV, the Dear Leader visited chicken farms, fish ponds, and food-processing companies. It was obvious from the broadcasts that food issues were a top priority to the leadership.

The shortages of food were used by adversaries in South Korea, Japan, and the West to prove that the DPRK was a failed state. Outsiders raised the question to me all the time. "Do you have enough to eat in Pyongyang?" a South Korean university professor asked me during my luncheon presentation organized by the European Chamber of Commerce in Seoul. "How can you live in such a place?"

While I was in Seoul, others raised similar questions. "You wouldn't get your favorite Italian ice cream, your Starbucks coffee, or a crispy chicken leg from KFC there, would you?" a young Samsung executive sarcastically reminded me. As a foreigner living in Pyongyang, I was privileged to be so well fed. But the situation in North Korea wasn't as bad as many outsiders perceived it. *The New York Times* and *The Guardian*, for instance, published a lot of chatter about the thousands of people starving. I feel compelled to offer a corrective. Because I was a resident businessman, my travels around the country were far less choreographed than those of others. In the mid-2000s, I did not come across starving people, though I did see scores of thin Koreans who looked malnourished. This was, of course, after the famine of the 1990s.

At times, I bluntly gave my unsolicited opinion to agriculture officials. Because I had lived in Vietnam from 1996 to 2002, I mentioned that the country provided a great example. Over there, Hanoi solved food problems within a year by giving farmers larger plots to work on, outside the collective state-run farms set up after the end of the Vietnam War in 1975. As in Vietnam, collectivized land, I argued, was demotivating farmers and giving them little reason to work hard. The poor souls had little personal incentive to "reap what they sow," to apply the proverb in a literal sense, because they couldn't make any profit off of them.

There is no doubt that North Korea's shortcomings, which the Vietnamese and the Chinese have solved since the 1980s, remain a major cause of the lack of food in North Korea. Food supplies, coming from the U.N. World Food Programme (WFP) and other organizations, helped cement the status quo. The absence of it would have obliged North Korea to undertake the necessary privatization reforms like Vietnam and China, even if changes in Pyongyang's system would not have fed its people to the extent that its neighbors were successful.

To start, here's a brief background on those countries' paths to agriculture reform, and how they're different from North Korea. Chinese leader Deng Xiaoping shifted responsibility from state farms to private household farms in the early 1980s. At the same time, the quota fixed by the state called the "iron rice bowl," meaning food formally guaranteed by the state as is still the case in North Korea, was massively decreased. The food produced above this minimum quantity could be sold in free markets at unregulated prices. Poor agricultural performance and the then-common food shortages were soon things of the past.

In 1981, Vietnam too started moving away from a collectivized agricultural production system to a household responsibility system, in which individual households could cultivate land outside of government control. As a result, after two decades of importing rice, Vietnam became a rice exporter in 1989. Today it's the world's third-largest rice exporter after India and Thailand.

From the 1980s, China and Vietnam no longer believed that collectivized land with a higher level of mechanization would produce higher yields than smaller and less mechanized private household farms. North Korea, however, has held on unwaveringly to this socialist myth to this day, refusing to follow the promising example of the more pragmatic Asian countries.

In my home country, Switzerland, only 17 percent of the land is arable, meaning most food has to be imported to feed its people. North Korea is an equally rugged country, with all its mountain ranges and hills, giving it no more arable land than my alpine republic in Western Europe. As such, North Korea depends to roughly the same extent on food imports, a fact mentioned by neither the Western media nor NGO or business reports that I have read.

While the food situation was improving during the years I lived in North Korea, it is also true that the country had just risen out of disastrous famine. In the 1990s, natural calamities, consisting of floods followed by droughts, triggered a food crisis and indeed fostered mass starvation from 1995 to 1998. I won't speculate in the actual numbers of deaths, though North Korea's strongest critics pegged higher estimates at several million.

Among them, *The Wall Street Journal* claimed that "a famine from 1995 to 1997 killed two million to three million North Koreans."[1] Professor Lankov, a better-informed and less biased North Korea expert, estimated, however, that the famine "from 1996 to 1999 killed between 600,000 and one million people."[2] On the other hand, the regime's most ardent supporters, generally left-leaning intellectuals and politicians, put forward the lowest figures, at around 100,000 dead from starvation and disease. The person who probably knew best, Christian Lemaire, was then the U.N.'s Resident Coordinator and U.N. Development Programme Resident Representative to the DPRK. He told media that the lower estimates of 600,000, while less "newsworthy," were probably most accurate.

After 1999, North Korea halted the major food shortages through a combination of food aid from foreign countries, agricultural and infrastructure repair work, and growing private business activities. Nevertheless, the Western mass media continued to rant about the supposed food debacle for years to come. In a typical year, the WFP contributed with alarming, embellished conclusions that the threat of food shortages loomed over the countryside.

The WFP persisted with these claims, even when the South Korean government and private watchdog groups documented "bumper harvests," or increased harvests during a season, which reached record levels.

Andrei Lankov, for one, has documented the conflicting interests that led to these different estimates in 2008 and 2009. "Unless the 2008 harvest was the result of incredible luck, it seems to indicate that fertilizer is far less important than previously believed," he wrote in *Asia Times Online*. "It is possible that North Korean farmers have devised strategies to deal with fertilizer shortages."

In October 2010, a headline by Agence France-Presse declared, "WFP chief says child malnutrition widespread in North Korea." The WFP claimed in a press statement that a third of North Korean children up to five years old suffer from severe malnutrition. On the other hand, UNICEF argues differently, pointing out in its report, "The State of the World's Children 2012," that under-five and neonatal mortality rates in North Korea are substantially lower than the developing country average.

The country was ranked by UNICEF at 73 out of a total of 193 countries, because of its under-five mortality rate of 33 out of 1,000. That's just over half the developing country average of 63 out of 1,000—not the best it could be, but certainly an accomplishment given its tumultuous famine. Another international charity, Save the Children, similarly released a global study on changes in the numbers of stunted children from 1990 to 2010, placing North Korea as the sixth-best country in terms of making progress in curbing this problem.

Other groups have challenged the notion that North Korea is stark and desolate. From 2000 to 2005, a couple of years after the famine, the Food and Agriculture Organization of the U.N. declared that North Korea was among the world's top ten producers of fresh fruit per year in terms of total production. Vegetable production ranked twelfth at 2.45 million metric tons, behind the production of rice, at 2.5 million metric tons. Most of this produce was not meant for domestic consumption, but for export. It generated hard currency and helped pay for imports.

For this reason, regular North Koreans didn't realize that an abundance of fruit was produced in their country. What was left in the country was not sold at a cheap price. When driving, from time to time I stopped my car at a small food stall where an older woman was selling apples. I paid 1 euro per kilogram, even though I could have pushed it down to half that. But my conscience got the better of me, since few Koreans could afford this fruit and she only sold a few kilograms a day.

The situation could be improving with greater supply and, I hope, prices in the reach of locals: in 2011, China gave North Korea millions of apple trees, giving fruit production a boost.

During a dinner with a minister, I asked him why his government had asked foreign nations and organizations to supply food instead of laying down the conditions for agricultural and industrial growth. "Our first and more short-term priority was to get as much food as possible to save lives in an emergency situation," he said, "while our second, longer-term priority was to strengthen our agricultural base to make food security more sustainable. As you know, donor countries did not support our second priority. That is, they refused development cooperation, and instead of giving us fertilizer and other requirements for agricultural development, they sent us their own surpluses of agricultural products."

Andrei Lankov wrote in Asia Times Online:

"Every year, we get reports about a looming famine in North Korea—and this year is no exception." A quick look through headlines of major newspapers can clarify that such reports surface with predictable regularity every year.

In March 2008, the *International Herald Tribune* ran a headline 'Food shortage looms in North Korea.' In March 2009, the *Washington Post* headline said 'At the Heart of North Korea's Troubles, an Intractable Hunger Crisis.' One year later, in March 2010, the *Times of London* warned: 'Catastrophe in North Korea; China must pressure Pyongyang to allow food aid to millions threatened by famine.' In March 2011, *The New York Times* wrote: 'North Korea: 6 Million Are Hungry.' The predictions of gloom come every year, but famine does not.

Actually, from around 2002–2003, we have seen a steady but clear improvement in North Korea's economic situation. North Koreans are still malnourished, and likely to remain so for the foreseeable future. Nonetheless, they are not starving anymore—at least not in significant numbers.

However, opponents of the regime cannot admit that people are not starving or report about (however marginal) improvement of the food situation, since, as I have said, from their viewpoint nothing can possibly improve in North Korea. At the same time, supporters of the regime will not admit that the North Korean people are still malnourished, and the regime itself is active in presenting exaggerated evidence of a looming famine (or perhaps, even fabricating such evidence when necessary)—as this will help it get more free food from the outside, and this is what Pyongyang needs."

I do not mean to sound like a Pollyanna on the food situation. I am merely adding nuance to the sensational reports that appear around the world.

On the flip side, I observed no abundance of food when traveling the country, and even caught occasional glimpses of villagers picking up the scarce rice grains that had fallen out of their automobiles while being transported. I also noticed the meager diversity of food that farmers and workers were eating out of their bowls when I sat with them. While the quantities didn't look small, they consumed corn mixed with rice and porridge, along with some vegetables and herbs including kimchi—not the balanced diet recommended by nutritionists. A watery soup was also often part of the menu, along with potatoes and noodles made of potato starch.

There wasn't much meat and fish, a dearth that probably added to the malnourishment. To get at least some proteins, North Koreans compensated for the lack of beef and chicken with tofu. Meat and fish were rather expensive and reserved for leaders' birthdays and other celebrations.

Some press accounts overlook these cultural factors when pointing out the diets of North Koreans. In 1999, *The New York Times* claimed, "Millions of North Koreans survive on tree bark and the husks of corn kernels and the country is getting millions of tons of emergency food aid from abroad." While the famine was dramatic, the circumstances must have improved in the meantime, as people eating edible grass, roots, and herbs never came my way—as reflected in the ranking by Save the Children.

What many outside North Korea generally ignore is that the much-quoted "foraging for food" is an age-old North and South Korean tradition, a result of the absence of arable land in the North to grow crops. For centuries Koreans from all over the peninsula have consumed wild mushrooms and edibles—long before the foundation of the DPRK—and they still love to eat them.

FOOD AND JUCHE

Before the cold war ended, North Koreans took pride in their egalitarian society, which was, in many ways, a model socialist state where cadres from around the world studied in the 1960s and 1970s. Kim

Il Sung's North Korea came closer than all other countries to Karl Marx's definition of a true communist society—one in which all property is publicly owned and each person works and is paid according to his abilities and needs.

While some may disagree with me, it's true that the DPRK, at the beginning, was better off than South Korea, with its free housing, free education, free health care, zero taxes, and demonetized society. A declassified CIA country study, later published by its author, Helen-Louise Hunter, revealed that North Korea was indeed pretty well-off compared to South Korea in the 1960s.

Before the collapse of the 1990s, North Koreans were particularly proud of their Public Distribution System (PDS), an effective food rationing system that was unmatched by other socialist countries. By the mid-1950s, most other socialist countries had abandoned their food rationing systems, but North Korea unwaveringly maintained it for another forty years.

A look at the system shows us that it truly was Marxist, aimed at different groups according to their needs. For every working adult, the PDS provided daily rations of 600 to 900 grams worth of cereals, cabbage, soy sauce, and other goods, according to the number of calories they needed. Those who were less active and burned fewer calories, such as retirees and students, received 300 to 600 grams.

The apparatus was not perfect, but it worked fairly well until the end of the 1970s. The drought and subsequent economic collapse of the mid-1990s dealt a major blow to the PDS, which had already been weakened after the end of the cold war. The once-socialist states of Eastern Europe broke away as its major markets and benefactors and deprived the DPRK from earning income, thanks to exports that would have allowed it to purchase foreign food, fertilizer, and machines.

With the PDS in tatters, and with people needing to eat to survive, they took to private and illegal black markets to get their food. As the markets gained popularity, the Korean Workers' Party reluctantly recognized their existence and started regulating them. But while the communist parties of China and Vietnam actively promoted these types of economic reforms, the North Korean authorities soon panicked. They were trying, in a very defensive way, to get private trading under as much control as possible. They didn't want privatization to hurt the planned socialist economy that was a basis of their rule.

In the mid-2000s, the party began its "correction" of the markets when it realized that merchants were veering far from the "fatherly care" of the Dear Leader. The Korean Workers' Party issued several directives in 2007 that stated that the "markets have become a place of violation of government rules and social order," a sort of infringement on its communist ethos.

They alleged that "some merchants serve food and drinks, and there are customers who get heavily drunk and fall at a bus stop or a vegetable garden. … And there are those who curse, argue, and fight. Such ugly behavior is just what the enemy is wishing for us." The markets, the directive finished, "have become a place for merchants to make money by charging a lot more than they should. We should abandon such ideas as making a big profit out of business."

Unfortunately, foreign aid gave the repressive regime the means to halt the opening of the market. Between 2002 and 2004, an influx of food aid stabilized this sector, enough to roll back the capitalist activities that were tolerated for a few years, at least to make up for the failures of state distribution. In October 2005, the government announced that it would reactivate the PDS; it then prohibited the sale of grain in markets, forcing peddlers to sell their grain to the state at a lower fixed price.

Thereafter, authorities issued an order barring men from selling goods at markets, because men were considered more able-bodied. In December 2007, women below fifty years of age were also prohibited from trading at markets, as they were seen as the second most active group. Some would say the decision was a mild form of ideological re-education: from that point on, all able-bodied men along with healthy women no older than fifty years were expected to work at government factories—not as "capitalist traders."

One day that year I read the official explanation published in a translated decree. It explained, in a euphemistic way, that the party did not generously offer these people a good university education to become nothing more than traders—an about-face that comfortably justified the crackdowns in a way that would support their political legitimacy. Though the book *Famine in North Korea: Markets, Aid, and Reform* by Stephan Haggard and Marcus Noland is not free from an anti-DPRK bias, it contains information for readers interested in learning more about this.

All this private trading gave rise to a small affluent class that I could see in my everyday life. My wife and I, like many foreigners, were happy that we could visit the Tongil (Reunification) Market in Pyongyang, the largest in town, where we could buy a wide variety of fresh meat, fish, rice, vegetables, and fruit—along with pretty much any household amenity. Here we haggled next to affluent North Koreans, like the wives and children of senior officials, cadres working for foreign-trading state companies, and the growing number of private traders enriched during the past decade. I saw many from this young consumerist class buying jewelry and clothes in expensive shops and dining out in fine restaurants.

My wife and I felt the effects of the government's rollback on trading at this market. By the end of 2005, we couldn't buy rice anymore, and the young, enthusiastic saleswomen suddenly disappeared from Tongil. Other products were still available, such as vegetables and fruit, but were less fresh and found in lower quantities. As a result, the state-run shops, which were less attractive to buyers, got more business that benefited state coffers. Contrary to the expectations that the government would make things cheaper, our household expenditures grew by about 50 percent thanks to these shops.

BURGERS, BEER, AND COLAS

Despite the attempts to rein in the bazaars, North Koreans deserve credit for trying to improve their economy in more sustainable ways. Many times I met, and came to respect, the long-serving DPRK ambassador to Switzerland in Geneva, Ri Chol (also known as Ri Su Yong). He was well connected in Pyongyang, but he gave off an aura of modesty, hard work, and complete dedication to improving the situation back home. He was particularly effective in his work because he knew Switzerland better than me—and was therefore one of the few North Korean cadres who understood how Westerners thought.

Ri Chol exerted a charismatic influence on foreign businesspeople, including the most seasoned ones. In 2000, he persuaded Swiss investors to set up PyongSu and Egyptians to set up a mobile phone company. Using his connections, the envoy bought a secondhand brewery based in England and using German equipment, a bargain that he dismantled and sent back to Pyongyang to brew the tasty Taedonggang beer. Although North Korea was home to several competing breweries, the Taedonggang brewery used not only German equipment but also the country's authentic recipes. The beverage became so popular that manager Kim proudly told me a couple of years later that the company had reached an impressive market share of two-thirds in his country.

When a global leader in cement production, the French company Lafarge, opened up shop in North Korea, Ri told its Swiss competitor, Holcim, to hurry for opportunities there as well. A few months later a Holcim delegation made a confidential trip to Pyongyang, although it found the market too small for two large competitors.

Another time, he visited a small consulting company in Switzerland specializing in power generation and grid rehabilitation. Its owner told me that he was surprised to walk into his office and find an ambassador hanging out there. He told Ri: "I never expected an ambassador to visit me and I did not even put on a tie." Ambassador Ri took his tie off and told the man: "Don't call me Ambassador; just call me Ri."

In the foreign ministry, Ri was given the nickname "businessman" thanks to his remarkable track record. Interestingly, he wasn't perceived as a threat to the party ideology. On the contrary, a senior official close to him admiringly revealed to me that he got the DPRK's most prestigious recognition of a "people's hero." But in addition to business, the ambassador was also a visionary in economic development. According to a senior Swiss official, Ri persuaded the Swiss Agency for Development and Cooperation (SDC) to help the government introduce new potato varieties that were cheap, easy to grow, and nutritious and could ease food shortages in the late 1990s.

The initiative was pretty successful: within a few years the potato harvests took off and more North Koreans had hearty meals on the table. According to the same source, he also wanted to introduce goats from Switzerland into his fatherland, because they could produce meat and dairy in a cost-effective way—helping to nourish the barren countryside.

What the Koreans call the "Potato Revolution" not only changed their diet since 1999 but put more food on the table. Like most other Asians, Koreans loved their white rice with every meal. But the acreage devoted to potatoes grew significantly, in part because of newly introduced varieties. The most recently introduced "Juwel" and "Magda" seed potatoes need only a few weeks to be ready for harvesting. A restaurant in Pyongyang's diplomatic village promoted potato dishes as "health food," a trend that I saw around the country. The party also launched a Juche information campaign that elevated potatoes from a secondary food to a primary one. Potato farming provides more calories than any other crop, in terms of area farmed, and contributes more than rice to the consumers' health. They are rich in carbohydrates, protein, and vitamin C, making them an ideal source of energy.

Something vital completely escaped the attention of Western and other foreign media obsessed with trivialities such as North Korea's leader's hairstyle, his shoe heels, and his preferred French Cognac. Amazingly, Kim Jong Il was, unlike other Asian leaders, highly enthusiastic about potatoes and soybeans and gave them a key role in agricultural development.

These crops, and potatoes in particular, were indeed more suited for North Korea's climate and more nutritious than the rice so dear to Asians. Moreover, soybeans were not only an important source of protein for the North Koreans but greatly contributed to boosting organic nitrogen levels in the soil, which is the most important element for plant development in the absence of chemical fertilizer.

Farmers didn't need to feed their goats, unlike their cows, grass and corn, the latter being a cheap staple that humans needed when food was scarce. Goats could survive on all sorts of provisions and in different environments. Most importantly, good goat species could produce 2 to 3 kilograms of milk per day or the equivalent of the minimum daily requirement of food for a family of five.

From the late 1990s to the mid-2000s, the goat population increased from an estimated few hundred thousand to an impressive two million. A few hundred thousand animals were slaughtered every year, adding a substantial amount of meat to the economy. With the increase of the goat population, culling them became more sustainable, even though the privileged saw a disproportionate benefit.

In addition to the new food sources, the skins of the slaughtered goats could have eventually been made into quality soft jackets and gloves—an asset for a growing affluent class experiencing frigid winters. But the government agreed that the products would be largely exported and that the leather-processing workshops and those who sold and/or tanned goat skins would be the main beneficiaries from the sales proceeds. My wife, who was once the right hand of the Italian manager of a luxury leather factory in Hanoi, found out about this opportunity when she was hired by the SDC as a consultant. The state tannery was ill-equipped to turn the skins into decent leather, so she traveled across the Chinese border to find shops that could handle the task at low prices. In North Korea, she hoped to help launch workshops with little investment—meaning they had sewing machines without electricity. She also planned to bring in Vietnamese leather specialists, who have built their expertise from the country's booming garment and leather industry, to train the North Korean laborers.

Then the situation changed for the worse, reflecting the inefficiency plaguing governmental aid organizations. A new director was appointed to her office in Pyongyang, who, as a farmer by trade,

A few restaurants in Pyongyang were selling goat yogurt, goat cheese, goat soup, and grilled goat, which tasted as delicious as a classic Korean dish, bulgogi, or barbecued beef. The picture shows the production of goat yogurt in a rural area in 2006.

wanted to focus on agricultural projects. To pool together a larger share of the budget for his ventures, he cancelled this meaningful endeavor that would have created many jobs and substantial earnings in hard currency.

Still, Ambassador Ri Chol wanted to make up for those inadequacies by bringing in more humanitarian organizations. He told the Salvation Army in one meeting, "You are Christians; you should help my country," according to my own conversations with those representatives. He motivated several such organizations to become active in his country. Once they set up shop in Pyongyang, he continued to help them find local contacts.

One of these organizations was the Adventist Development and Relief Agency (ADRA), created by the Seventh-day Adventist Church. It's a Christian humanitarian organization that is based in the U.S. but worked on its North Korea programs from its office in

Switzerland. Every day ADRA's flagship project, an industrial bakery, produced tens of thousands of vitamin-enriched breads for malnourished children in a large nursery. The Swiss retail chain Migros, along with ABB and others, lent support to the project with furniture, machines, and other equipment as well as training.

It made me feel good when my then-employer, ABB, agreed to offer, free of charge, electrical equipment such as transformers, switch gears, and electric cables. To help the project break even, the group opened a restaurant and bakery to sell the bread, and then used the profits to buy spare cookery parts, flour, and other items that needed to be expensively imported.

Ambassador Ri Chol, in his typical affable fashion, worked his connections to land the eatery a central and visible location in Pyongyang, a short walk from the "foreigner hub" of Hotel Koryo. Their restaurant, the Pyolmuri Café, was a favorite of mine because of its range of European dishes. A couple of times, birthday parties for North Korean children were held in a side room while I was eating. Once I was invited to greet the kids, who hoped to practice their English. I obliged with pleasure.

The North Korean manager, a gregarious and eager woman, asked me and other foreign guests how to improve the menu. I suggested that she invite an Italian chef from Beijing for a few weeks' paid holiday, who could then train the kitchen staff to make pizza and pasta the Italian way. Unfortunately, this idea never went further, and the so-called European food lost its European taste over time. I dined at this restaurant sparingly over the next few months, and regrettably, so did other guests. I believe the manager agreed with the idea, but as in other cases I came across, perhaps her superior had never eaten in the restaurant and didn't understand the request.

North Korea may be isolated, but fast food is still popular in its capital. Fast food restaurants had all the typical traits of those around the world: the frugal equipment that included small, hard plastic chairs; the way people lined up; and the speed at which I got my meal had nothing that could be considered "typically" North Korean. The only

When traveling through counties and villages, I got the impression that every square meter was cultivated. The flat agricultural land is reserved for state farms. Northwards, near the Chinese border, many sotoji, or private plots, were emerging on slopes. It was a sign that authorities were begrudgingly tolerating privatization. These plots had been pretty much deforested to make way for farming and to get firewood for cooking and for heating in winter. But the deforestation, a result of the demand for firewood, caused dangerous landslides.

noteworthy difference was the price, about a dollar for a standard meal, and a kind of excitement among the many North Korean visitors.

Though my wife and I became fond of our daily kimchi, rice with vegetables (*bibimbap*), and cold noodles (*nangmyun*), we occasionally yearned for Western dishes that the bakery couldn't live up to. But imported food was out of reach even for us "wealthy" foreigners. A liter of milk from China, for instance, cost three times as much as in China. Depending on its weight, a salami from Italy or Hungary cost between 45 and 75 dollars (35 and 55 euros). French cheese hovered around 25 dollars (20 euros).

At the diplomatic supermarket, full of foreign and North Korean customers who worked at embassies and foreign organizations, Swiss chocolates, gummy bears, French wines, and many other nonessential items were offered. When I had to travel to China on business, I took the opportunity, like other resident foreigners, to fill my suitcase with food items that were not available or much cheaper than in Pyongyang. There were no import restrictions and no import duty to be paid for food and household items.

KOREAN CUISINE

Korean cuisine has been subject to many geographic and economic influences over thousands of years of history. Harsh winters and a demanding, hilly landscape made cultivating food difficult. As such, Koreans engaged in very rigorous labor, making them consumers of hearty meals such as big bowls of soup with a side of white rice for breakfast. With a large coastline and many rivers, fish, both fresh and dried, became a regular staple.

With its unkind winters, Koreans built a tradition of drying, salting, and pickling their food to preserve it. The taste, to this day, is cherished in both North and South Korea. In the late autumn, Koreans all over prepare their winter kimchi made from Chinese cabbage. In North Korea, the entire country mobilizes its vehicles to bring enormous amounts of cabbage from the countryside to the cities. Families get their rations by turning in coupons.

From the beginning, China has also exerted an enormous influence on Korean food. More than 4,000 years ago, Chinese traders introduced rice to the peninsula, along with iron 2,500 years ago that enabled farmers to use more efficient equipment. This development gave farmers the means to more vigorously cultivate the limited arable land, and many diversified to domesticate cows and pigs alongside cabbage and the wood to make chopsticks.

After the Europeans conquered Central and South America in the 1500s, they found and began trading the sought-after chilis that were native to the region. Pepper commerce had a profound influence on Korean cuisine by way of Japan. After Japan acquired the peppers from Europeans, its warriors spread it to Korea via conquests in the sixteenth century. From the eighteenth century onwards, chilis became a main ingredient, smothered in some form or another on kimchi and used in *jjigae*, or soups.

Although North and South Korean food is remarkably similar, North Korean food has a purer, cleaner taste. It is much less salty, fishy, and spicy, even to the point of blandness for certain dishes.

That's in part, of course, because of the scarcity of some ingredients.

With the exception of the soup, all dishes are served as one meal, like in many other Asian countries. On special occasions, twelve or more dishes are served. Common flavorings include soybean sauce and paste, along with ginger, garlic, rice vinegar, sesame oil, and chili. Like other Asians, Koreans prefer to steam, stir-fry, grill, barbecue, and stew their meals.

Kimchi is the most prominent and internationally recognizable Korean dish. It can be either a side dish or the main component of every meal (such as in stews like *kimchi jjigae*), including breakfast. It consists of grated or chopped vegetables—one of the most important ones being Chinese cabbage—which are mixed with various ingredients such as chili, garlic, and ginger. Thereafter it is stored in an earthenware pot, where it is fermented. A number of tastes blend together to give kimchi its unique pungent taste: food critics have described it as raw, tangy, slightly sweet, and sometimes very spicy.

Another popular dish is *bibimbap*, a bed of rice that uses kimchi as its main ingredient. The bowl also includes vegetables, meat, and hot chilis served in a heated iron bowl. Before eating, Koreans stir it together with a spoon, turning it into a sort of "dirty rice" in Western terms.

Bulgogi (fire meat) is a prevalent Korean-styled barbecued beef, marinated in soy sauce, garlic, chili, and sesame. The concoction is grilled on a hot plate on a table for a group of two to four diners. Some restaurants add duck, short ribs, and other meats.

Pyongyang onban (cooked rice served in chicken soup) is the traditional food for Chuseok, the Korean harvest holiday on the fifteenth day of the eighth lunar month in the traditional calendar. On this day, "many people visit national food restaurants in Pyongyang to taste this food," as the governmental Korean Central News Agency once reported on a Chuseok day.

Sinsollo is the Korean version of the iconic Japanese *shabu-shabu*. Diners throw in dozens of vegetables, mushrooms, seafood pieces, noodles, and red meats into a pot and boil them.

Nokdujijim is a well-liked side dish, or a tasty snack when not part of a full meal. It consists of pickled vegetables and meat, mixed with green bean flour and pan fried.

Naeng myon (cold noodles) is another highly popular Korean specialty. The noodles are made of buckwheat and are believed to cleanse the body. South Koreans, in fact, have told me repeatedly that Pyongyang is the most famous place to try the cold noodles. A variant of this dish, known as *hamhung* cold noodles in South Korea, is known in North Korea as "potato starch noodles." These thin noodles are thrown into a mild cold broth and mixed with raw fish, pork, cucumbers, and an egg.

Tongchami kimchi, a milder form of white kimchi not smothered in chili is tasty, too, and is often mixed in with cold noodles.

Both North and South Koreans are so fond of noodles, in fact, that they're the world's top per capita noodle consumers. Even Japan, China, and Italy can't match them.

The most famous cold noodles restaurant on the Korean Peninsula is the Ongnyu Restaurant in Pyongyang, just north of the Ongnyu Bridge overlooking the Taedong River.

North Koreans are also fond of all kinds of soup, known as both *jjigae* (stew) and *kuk* (a more standard, clear-broth soup). These can vary from all sorts of kimchi stews, hot spicy fish soups, and even dog soup—all of which are lathered over a bowl of white rice and eaten.

Dog meat, or "sweet meat" as it is called in North Korea, is highly popular among men for its widely believed improvement of virility. The taste is bolder in North Korea than in South Korea, and it isn't as greasy, suggesting less use of additives and a different way the dogs are fed. There are several dog meat restaurants in Pyongyang, the most famous one being on the sometimes crowded Tongil Street, which offers only dog meat dishes. Another delicious "sweet meat" restaurant is near the Tongil Market. The meal costs about $14 per person—a price affordable for foreigners but not for average North Koreans. A bowl of dog soup at the Kaesong Folk Hotel costs $6 (5 euros).

In addition, ostrich meat can be found on the menus of Pyongyang's most prestigious restaurants. To the surprise of many, North Korea is home to ostrich farms, one of which I visited.

With their meals Koreans usually drink water or barley tea. But at other times they enjoy a wide variety of beverages made in North Korea, such as mineral water, soft drinks, and beer. The fruit waters and the weak sodas reminded me of the ones I drank in Soviet Russia. The men like hefty drinks with the high alcohol content found in soju (a strong white liquor that is sometimes compared to vodka, though it doesn't quite meet that definition). Soju is made from spring water, rice, and maize, and the strongest brands have an alcohol content of up to 45 percent.

While the soju in South Korea is often mixed with ethanol and chemical flavorings, North Koreans celebrate their soju as the real thing. Both North and South Korean men are heavy drinkers, a way of coping with long, stressful working hours.

Dry red wines, made by the Daesong Group with grape varieties imported from Switzerland, have also been on the shelves for several years. It isn't the best bottle, to be honest. Aside from Western-inspired luxuries, North Koreans sometimes turn to a lineup of exotic drinks, such as rice beer (*tongdongju*), a somewhat cloudy beverage with a sour taste and low alcohol content. Snake liquors were available as aphrodisiacs, just as in Vietnam and China. One particularly sweet drink was blueberry wine, a mauve that North Koreans enthusiastically recommended—because it supposedly came from the "holy mountain," Paekdu Mountain, the location where they believe Dear Leader Kim Jong Il was born.

NOTES

1. Evan Ramstad. North Korean leader Kim Jong Il is dead. *The Wall Street Journal*. December 19, 2011. http://online.wsj.com/article/SB10001424 052748703864204576321193199255166.html.
2. Andrei Lankov. Staying alive: why North Korea will not change. *Foreign Affairs*, March/April 2008. http://www.foreignaffairs.com/articles/63216/andrei-lankov/staying-alive#.

Chapter 9

Flowers of the Nation

Women are flowers. Flowers for life. Flowers that take care of the family.

— A popular folk song in North Korea

A young married woman, Mrs. Han, sighed to me at the buffet table after we finished an official function in 2005. "I am not so happy that my husband has little interest in our children and little time for them," she lamented. "I have observed Western fathers who have a more intense relationship with their children. Korean men are different and should change."

Both she and her husband came from politically influential families, living in an area of the central district of Pyongyang popular among senior cadres. One of their children goes to North Korea's best kindergarten, named after Kim Jong Suk, the most revered woman in the country. The older child of Mrs. Han made it to Pyongyang's elite middle school.

Because Mrs. Han and her spouse were well-to-do and were loyal to their country and the leadership, I did not misinterpret her frustration as a criticism of the socialist system. On the contrary, the North Korean regime has overseen an improvement in the rights of women. In past centuries, few women received a formal education and their social standing was low. Nowadays all boys and girls go to school.

WOMEN'S RIGHTS

Years earlier, when I was living in Cairo, Egypt, I put an ad in a newspaper for a maid who could cook and clean my house. Back then I was a bachelor and a busy country director of a multinational group, and I needed a helping hand.

All the respondents had one experience in common: they had previously worked for Arab families in Saudi Arabia and Gulf countries. They all told me horrible stories of abuse. They were regularly beaten or sexually abused, deprived of sleep and free time, and refused payment. They all managed to escape their abusive employers and ended up in Cairo as illegal immigrants. Unfortunately, given their gray status, they were vulnerable to police abuse and were desperate to look for some paid work.

I hired one Filipina maid who even had a university degree and helped her regularize her status in Egypt. She was happy because her nightmare ended in Saudi Arabia, where women are repressed, and she was well treated in my home.

The average North Korean woman is certainly better off than the average Saudi woman or Filipina migrant.

There is one relationship in North Korea, as with the rest of East Asia, that can be oppressive: that between daughter-in-law and mother-in-law. The Democratic Women's Organization, as it is called, has been using its influence to instill more respect between these two. Daughters-in-law who feel oppressed by their mothers-in-law can file a complaint with the organization, which in turn helps fix the problem, as one young married manager of a computer shop told me.

But while the socialist system has certainly improved the position of women in society, it has unintentionally made it more difficult for them in other ways. It has, for instance, let tradition clash with socialist accommodation ideals. Indeed, an old tradition, still maintained in the DPRK, obliges the groom's family to provide accommodations for the young couple, whereas the bride's relatives have to supply the furniture and household items. Since the socialist state provides housing for free or a trivial rental fee, the financial burden has fallen almost exclusively on the bride's family, which usually has to start saving for the daughter's wedding when the girl is in her early teens. It is another reason why families prefer sons to daughters.

Like other socialist countries, North Korea promotes role models with ideal socialist characteristics: model workers, model students, model families, and of course model women. Though not legally enforced, women are taught from a young age to see immorality in skirts that end above the knee, long hair that is not bound in a ponytail, and too much makeup on the face.

These morals were strictly respected by my own female employees and the many women I worked with. Not only did skirts cover knees, shirts were mostly buttoned up the neck, often to the last button. Only in the length of their hair did women seem to have some room to express their femininity, by letting it fall loose when it was no longer than shoulder-length.

The "flowers of the nation," a label for women often found in DPRK propaganda, happen to be the hardest workers of the nation. I often saw women performing heavy labor, such as erecting buildings, paving countryside roads, and carrying around heavy construction equipment. Men, on the other hand, worked as supervisors and mostly watched from a distance. *Mokran* (magnolia) is the national flower of the DPRK, which the governmental news agency called on June 10, 2002 "a beautiful, solid, and simple flower representing the stamina of the resourceful Korean people." I would call it something that represents the stamina of the resourceful Korean *women*.

One "flower of the nation" once told me half-jokingly that men are particularly good at drinking, smoking, and relaxing, whereas women are utilized for working and for taking care of the family alone. Women are holding up far more than half of North Korea's skies, to play with the old dictum of Mao Zedong.

From visiting universities, I also got the impression that the share of female students at universities is rather high, and certainly not lower than at universities in Western countries. Official figures aren't available, to my knowledge. At some schools I have met female headmasters, and at hospitals I've chatted with female department heads and hospital directors.

Women often do, by the way, a better job than their male colleagues. For example, I was once revisiting a garment factory where I met the new director, Ms. Kim. I knew her predecessor, Mr. Ri, and asked my translator what had happened to him. After inquiring with some of the factory staff, he told me that Ms. Kim is much more competent and more hardworking than her male predecessor.

The saying that old habits die hard is particularly true in Korea (both North and South), which from my experiences are much more Confucian than the less principled and more pragmatic Chinese and other East Asians. Even though the state has promoted gender equality since it was founded more than sixty years ago, most men still behave like bosses toward their families and in society, following ancient Confucian traditions.

This patriarchal system manifested itself in my workplace. One time I was in a meeting with the CEO, the sales manager, and staff of a company in Pyongyang. The CEO's secretary was not in the office that day and could therefore not serve us coffee or tea. All present were male except the sales manager. Although the sales manager on the other side of the table was second highest in rank, it was striking that none of her male subordinates would serve drinks. Rather, the task was delegated to the female sales manager herself, a move that is increasingly rare in urban China or Vietnam.

For instance, young couples still prefer to have boys instead of girls, because preserving the male line of the family is considered more meritorious. Other countries like China and Vietnam still prefer boys, but North Korea has been remarkably swift at working against gender discrimination. After World War II, as an example, the party enacted its Gender Equality Law. And in its Constitution it expressly stressed that "women hold equal social status and rights with men."

Yet women who work mostly in light industry or office jobs are paid less than the men working in heavy industry and engineering industries. I might add that wage gaps also exist in many "developed" countries, like the U.S., which are not necessarily related to Confucianism. Women usually have a full plate of office work like their

Although the state encourages couples to have several children, most choose to have only one. That's pretty much the opposite situation in China, where the government requires families to have only one child to be able to feed its huge population. North Korea has half the population of its southern neighbor, and thus needs more people to get a sustainable economy going. The main burden of raising children lies with the mothers, who juggle full-time employment as well.

husbands, but also take on the burden of housework, looking after children, and preparing meals. Thanks to the Confucian hierarchy, though, grandparents sometimes live with the couple, lending a hand to the young mother where they can.

I was impressed by the many women who go to work, clearly representing a higher percentage than that of my native country, Switzerland. Tara Walters writes in her book *North Korea*, published in 2008, that women make up an astounding 49 percent of the workforce. She also mentioned that in the 1990s more North Korean women held government positions than there were American women holding comparable positions in the U.S.—a feat considering the different sizes of their populations.

Mrs. Han is unlucky. She will have to cope with her frustrations throughout her life. But her children's generation, which many parents are bringing up differently, might not face the same frustrations as they look for jobs and meet their spouses. Another mother and employee of mine obviously agreed with that statement. She told me that she encouraged her daughter to become a master at taekwondo, the Korean martial art, as "it is good for a girl to know how to defend herself against abusive boys and men with little respect for women."

My North Korean colleagues often gave insight into the situation of women, although it didn't sound much different from that in other developing countries (and even some so-called developed ones too). Washing machines were an unaffordable item for most families in Pyongyang and an absolute luxury in the countryside. Clothing is usually washed by hand with a cheap soap instead of washing powder, though you would not realize it from the appearance of the clean and smartly dressed women. In the countryside, I watched women crouch at rivers washing clothes.

For three days in a row, to name another example, I noticed that Mrs. Kang, my employee, stumbled into the office disheveled and with sleepy raccoon eyes. She was frequently yawning at her desk. I asked her into my office and offered her a coffee to perk her up.

"Mrs. Kang, you look so tired," I said, hoping to console her. "I suggest you go home early, have a good rest, and then you will be fresh and fit when you are back tomorrow."

She quickly denied that she was tired and insisted on finishing her work normally. Koreans do not like to admit to something that does not look good, because it makes them feel ashamed and, to use the old cliché, they lose face.

"Look, anyone can get tired for some reason," I told her. "I also get tired at times, and when I do, I try to get a good rest to be fit again thereafter."

She opened up a little, explaining that she was having sleepless nights because she heard noisy neighbors yelling and crying loudly every night.

"Why can't you and others ask them to stop making noise during the night?" I asked.

"The husband beats his wife," she responded. "The neighbors don't care, and even if they complained, the man would not change."

I gave her my earplugs for sleeping and said, "I know that, unfortunately, many men all over the world beat their wives. Tell me, does it often happen here that men beat their wives?"

"Well, you know, it's not so seldom," she hesitatingly answered.

Over the next few days Mrs. Kang didn't seem tired any longer. I am not sure if the earplugs blotted out the terror next door or if she told her husband that I, her boss, had become aware of her tiredness and he did something about it.

After a business meeting, I had lunch with members of an academic society. After a good meal, a lot of beer and soju, we all became a bit more cheerful and talkative. Professor Rim, a witty, gregarious scholar who entertained us with funny jokes sat to my left.

"Professor," I inquired, "I was told wife beating is one of the favorite sports of Korean husbands, of course after soccer."

He chuckled and answered, "That is true until they get old. Then things change drastically for the husbands, and the then-stronger wives in turn will adopt this sport as their favorite one. And as you can imagine, they take revenge by beating their husbands from thereon without the risk of the husbands hitting back."

I was intrigued by his story, even if he was joking. When I brought the topic up with other men, I got the impression that older women received more respect than younger ones. The deference isn't only because old age is more respected in this Confucian society, but also because a measure of justice comes back at a later stage.

Sometimes big open-air balls, which are formal social gatherings for dancing, take place on large squares, and I saw this, by chance, a couple of times. There must have been hundreds of young people dancing to North Korean music. I found it strange that many men were dancing together while numerous women were free and talking to and dancing with other women.

I talked about what I saw to some of my staff and asked why so many free men and women were apparently not interested in dancing with one another. "Well, they surely are interested in dancing with one another but they must have been quite young and were therefore a little shy," one woman told me. "When they go to their second ball, most of them will dance."

There were many other opportunities for young people to meet. I saw young men and women flirt at bowling alleys and other places. A Korean mother told me that her daughter fell in love with her future husband during the many rehearsals for a mass spectacle, where they had enough time to observe each other.

Although numerous things are controlled in this country, the Korean Workers' Party does not legally regulate relationships between men and women. It does discourage a liberal culture of sex, but men and women make the ultimate decisions about their marital and extramarital love lives, even if they risk their reputation in the process.

When senior party members commit adultery—particularly if it is sex in exchange for favors and privileges—they're often expelled from Pyongyang to live a harsh life in the countryside. Wives are expected to make sure their powerful husbands don't stray from the "correct" path, protecting their jobs and the family's higher living standards. This doesn't mean that wives are blamed when husbands commit adultery. Rather, it emphasizes the importance of contributing to maintain the integrity of the family, which is the basic unit upon which North Korea's society is built.

Still, everyday relations between the sexes have been relaxed in recent years, a development that owes to the loosened grip of the state after the economic downturn in the 1990s crippled the old ways. Chinese and Vietnamese students studying at North Korean universities told me that they observed more North Korean boys and girls walking together and holding hands over the years, something unheard of in the past.

Mrs. Pak had to bring an important letter to a customer in Pyongyang, and I expected her to be back within an hour. When she returned after two hours, I was rather upset given our big workload that day. Before I could scold her, she quickly apologized. "I am sorry for the delay," she said. "On my way back I bumped into a school friend with whom I attended the same class at the university, and whom I have not seen since."

She went on. "She has just gone through a divorce and was sad and told me the whole story. I did not want to be rude with her, particularly given her personal circumstances, and did therefore not run away, but stayed and listened!"

I decided that this was not some petty excuse. If she wanted to get out of trouble, she could have found twenty other excuses that were less spectacular than this one. "I am sorry for your friend," I responded. "What was the reason for the divorce? Did the husband want to leave his wife for another woman? Was he unfaithful?" I asked with a grin.

She answered evasively: "I don't know exactly. It must have been something like that."

"C'mon, after talking so long with her, you must know everything by now," I replied.

She smiled and answered: "I believe in Europe they say men are no angels."

"Now that we agree that both Korean and European men do not wear wings, let's get back to work!" I answered. I knew from other Koreans that divorces were becoming more frequent as women became more financially independent.

Despite the persistence of gender roles, North Korean women can display sophisticated and self-confident demeanors not far off from their counterparts in Seoul—a trend I began noticing in 2003. As long as the skirt covers the knees and the blouse covers the breasts, there is no limit to colors and styles a woman can wear. More women started wearing their hairstyles as perms, and around 2005 they began wearing wellies with trendy, colorful patterns; high-heels; platform shoes; and attractive business suits.

On the streets of Pyongyang I saw many elegant ladies who resembled those in Shanghai or Singapore—the only difference is that they wore a pin marking their patriotism. In another sign of pragmatic realism, the laws over the last ten years that prohibited women from wearing high heels, trousers, and earrings—considered unsocialist and Western—were abolished on July 4, 2012 (although they were never truly enforced anyway).

Until then, women were supposed to wear skirts in public. They were previously allowed to wear trousers only during their factory and farming work, but not skintight ones or jeans. Miniskirts are still not allowed, but I saw women performing in miniskirts during artistic and musical shows. Yet skirts are getting shorter, and more women can be seen in Pyongyang now with high heels. The change must be shocking to people in the more conservative countryside, where high heels continue to be associated with prostitution.

In the countryside outside Pyongyang pragmatism prevails over the principles so dear to Pyongyangites. Most women in the countryside support their families by earning money through trade, buying and selling all kinds of goods and transporting them with their bicycles (a mode of transportation that, in the capital, women don't ride).

Social and political control of both men and women used to be strong, as in all socialist countries. In North Korea, however, the political power was wielded more strongly over men, because they were assumed to be politically less loyal and reliable than women. Men were supposed to work in factories and farms and to report to their work unit every day—even when the factory was idle—to make sure they got their regular political training.

Married women, however, were allowed to stay at home and be housewives. With the downturn of the state economy in the 1990s, their lower social status allowed them to engage in all sorts of trading and other business activities. In East Asia, there's a common historical thread, in this sense, that men hold political power and women hold economic power through trading—the latter activity being associated with the low rank of the merchant.

Indeed, thanks to both the low cost and number of goods that can be carried on bicycles and the introduction of mobile phones in recent years, these women (who as the families' new breadwinners acquired a higher social position than their husbands) can multiply their earnings, which is a blessing for their hitherto poor families.

It must have escaped the U.S. Committee for Human Rights in North Korea that *inbun*, or what it calls the "hereditary caste-based system," is fast losing ground. These women (and men) constitute a growing entrepreneurial middle class regardless of their "caste." But the group claimed that "every North Korean citizen is assigned a heredity-based class and socio-political rank over which the individual exercises no control but which determines all aspects of his or her life."

Mr. Pak, a senior official of a provincial government, told me jealously that when women get too much money, they also accumulate too much power within the family. Another Korean man, who had difficulty accepting women who earn more money than men, told me that this has caused family tensions and divorces. The "problem" of women bringing home an income, of course, isn't serious, and the conflict probably comes from men anxious about losing their perceived power and self-confidence.

At least once per month I took care of financial matters at the Foreign Trade Bank, the largest bank in Pyongyang. While I was standing in line, I observed that most Korean customers were women between twenty-five and fifty years old. They were all neatly dressed and carried sharp attaché cases. These ladies, most likely, were *bu gi*, or the financial managers of companies and other entities. Since women were assumed to be more loyal, the state thought they could be a pure force to get rid of financial waste and corruption.

Even my pharmaceutical company hired a young woman who was chief financial officer. She was very competent, hardworking, and trustworthy. Another software company I cofounded employed a young woman as *bu gi* for the same reason. At a cocktail party I had some small talk with a vice minister. I told him that I realized that it is the women who are the masters of the money within companies and organizations.

"You know our country well," he answered. "Women are serious, good at numbers, and trusted. That's why we like them to be in charge of finance."

But women in North Korea were not only good at finance. I came to realize that women there were generally competent and hardworking, and generally more disciplined and honest than men. Therefore, it was no small wonder that I started the sales department at the pharmaceutical company with one man—and ended up with a sales team that was 100 percent female.

At one point I began hiring only female staff for our pharmacies. They undertook good service and friendliness to customers. When hiring technical staffers to maintain a high safety standard in a new microbiological laboratory, I chose women because they were very thorough. Additionally, the quality assurance manager also had to be a trustworthy woman, because this was a key post that involved enforcing the highest international quality standards. That was a complicated task, involving everything from the purchase of raw materials to processing them to the delivery of the finished products.

This company became the country's model pharmaceutical enterprise, a recognition from the government that owed, in large part, to its great female employees. I do owe a lot to them. Without them, I, the managing director, would have failed miserably and the company would have died a swift death. I didn't mean to pursue a sort of reverse discrimination against men, but hiring women simply made more sense because they tended to be better qualified and better at this sort of work.

In the Kaesong Industrial Park, a collaborative industrial zone run by both countries on the North Korean side of the DMZ, more than a hundred South Korean factories used to produce textiles, electronics, and machinery using cheap North Korean labor. Out of the 50,000 or more North Korean workers as of the beginning of 2012, almost three-quarters were women, according to the South Korean government. Women were believed to be more productive when using their hands at work—a requirement of many of the factories in Kaesong.

The burden on women also extends back to North Korea's historical suffering. I learned this during a farm visit in a remote province where, after being shown around the stables and fields, I had lunch with a group that included an old and frail woman sitting at the head of the table. As she hunched over, I noticed that most of her teeth were gone and she ate little, giving off a worn-out aura.

I asked who she was. "She was the founder and the boss of this farm after the war in 1953," said the farm's manager. "We are indebted to her for her great work."

I asked if we could invite her to sit closer to us. The elderly woman, who went by the name of Ms. Kim, limped slowly and sat down opposite me.

Given my interest in Korean history, I wanted to learn how she witnessed the Korean War and the period of deprivation that followed. She revealed that surviving women and children not only had to suffer so much during the war but also carried the burden of postwar reconstruction. She spoke slowly and in a subdued voice: "It was very hard for us. Everything was missing, in particular the men, as many of them died during the war," she bewailed. "Our houses and fields were destroyed by American bombers that dropped bombs everywhere. Not only were many people killed but also our animals."

"How did you survive the war?" I asked.

"We dug holes, and there were always people on guard watching and listening to detect as early as possible small flying dots approaching in the skies. When the guards yelled an alarm, we all disappeared in the holes until the airplanes had passed."

She explained that women, for the most part, constructed the farm while the men were off fighting and were killed, injured, or imprisoned in the war. The work was both dangerous and grueling. Since they had few tools, they cleared out the ordnance, bombs, and land mines from the fields with their bare hands, making room for seeds that were planted and harvested. "Later," she said, inserting a patriotic clarifier, "we received seeds, tools, and building materials as a generous help from our great leader Kim Il Sung."

The prominent American historian Bruce Cumings wrote in his seminal book, *Korea's Place in the Sun*, that the atrocities of this war have largely been forgotten. American planes systematically destroyed all cities, villages, and fields. Pointing out that more than two million civilians were killed, he even called it a "Holocaust" as a measure of the sheer brutality on the peninsula.

"Do you have a family?" I asked Ms. Kim.

"No. I was busy farming and had no time to look for a husband. Besides, men were so rare in those days," she answered with a smile that was perhaps not genuine and covered up some old suffering. "The members of our farm were my family till this day and I am so happy about it."

THE MARRIAGE QUESTION

In October 2006, one young lady had put in a job application and I invited her to my office for an interview. Her facial expression and body language looked uncomfortable. She looked nervous. She'd surely never met a foreigner before.

As she peered at me furtively, I wondered what thoughts were crossing her mind. *What are his intentions?* she must have pondered. *Is he a true friend of our country, or a spy or agent?*

Since I had hired North Korean women before, the situation was familiar. Most were nervous and did not even look at me face-to-face during our first meetings. There were ways to calm their nerves: from the first working day I explained that I appreciated their good work and that I respected them. Over time I tried to be informal and caring. I regularly asked about their families over short friendly chats. The longer they worked in the company, the more often they laughed at my jokes. It sometimes took months until they relaxed and until working with me became a normal state of affairs.

This candidate sitting in front of me, Dr. Song, was a young and brilliant medical doctor who had received the highest possible marks from her university and excellent references from her employers at a university hospital. Her English proficiency was remarkable. I had never met a junior medical doctor in this country with such fine

English skills. Although she was shy, her answers to my interview questions were intelligent and concise.

We were looking for somebody who could give fair, competent medical advice, in response to questions from readers, on our company's website. The country's intranet was then accessible to households throughout the country, rather than merely to government agencies, state companies, and universities.

We hired Dr. Song and she did not disappoint us. Because she practically inhaled vast amounts of medical literature every month, we knew she brought substantial knowledge to the table. In 2007, we began our online medical advice service, receiving one or two e-mails a day. Dr. Song diligently searched the literature for the best possible advice, and only when she was certain did she respond to the questions.

Dr. Song was also a talented medical writer. She put together terse, understandable articles with tables and illustrations on our website. Her efforts paid off for all of us: after a few weeks there was an explosion in the number of incoming e-mails from North Koreans looking for health care wisdom. Dr. Song's working days became longer and longer, but she didn't complain. She must have, after all, become one of the country's most popular doctors, building our reputation as a competent pharmaceutical company. Not surprisingly, the first orders of pharmaceuticals from remote provinces reached us a few weeks after her public image took off.

Even though North Korean women are talented, lots of other pressures loom over their young lives. Miss Han, a waitress in the diplomatic village, once bemoaned to me that, at twenty-nine, she was too old to get married. Normally, waitresses would not share their sorrows with foreign guests, and it took me a few years of building confidence to get to this point.

In North Korea, young women typically hope for nuptials when they're around twenty-three to twenty-six years old. Men similarly look for potential brides in this age bracket. When young women approach their twenty-seventh birthday, they and their families often panic. A decade ago, the age of marriage for men used to range from twenty-eight to thirty years old and for women from twenty-five to twenty-eight years old. Today, unlike in the West, couples are getting married at younger ages because fewer people are entering military service.

I felt helpless as I could not help Miss Han, a pretty, intelligent, and sympathetic young lady; I could not even find the right words to console her. Still, she had a lot going for her. Women working in restaurants serving foreigners are normally in high demand among Korean men. These waitresses are highly educated and bring home a good income. But by twenty-nine, men become more concerned with their aging than with their perceived status.

For several years the restaurant closed its doors once a week but was always open on Sundays, an inconvenient day when men weren't working and when the women could court them. Thankfully, the manager then was a thirty-something woman who was not married herself. Out of sympathy for her female staff, the supervisor changed the weekly holiday to Sunday.

The decision cheered up the female cooks, waitresses, and other staff and their families. Now their parents could go on a more promising search for suitable men, whom they introduced to their daughters and sisters on Sundays. I always felt happy for these girls, whom I got to know better over the years and whom I liked. On the other hand, it was sad to see these familiar faces slowly disappear as they found spouses and had children. I wished them well.

Not all of North Korea, however, is traditional in that parents arrange marriages. I've met women who've proudly told me that they alone chose their husbands, not their parents. These women usually fell in love with significant others at their universities. Nevertheless, many parents arrange for a groom-to-be like in the olden times. In this traditional hierarchy, the man's family is expected to have a higher social ranking than the woman's family. For the women who work in restaurants and hotels filled with foreign guests, they often welcome help from parents in finding a locally bred Korean.

Sometimes, out of curiosity, I asked married women whether they chose their husbands, their husbands chose them, or the parents of either spouse arranged the marriage. Most women I dealt with, as colleagues, were university educated and exposed to the outside world (some even traveled outside North Korea). They often giggled at the question, knowing that arranged marriage is considered backward in other countries.

Most of my female customers answered that it was mostly the parents who picked a spouse, but among the younger generation it's the young people themselves who fall in love and then make the decision. When I walked in the streets of Pyongyang at night, I sometimes stumbled on young couples whispering and giggling as they walked each other home. They obviously liked the darkness, which allowed them to get to know each other intimately. It probably helped them to make the right decision when it came to marriage. Showing affection and emotions in public was not welcome. So, to get to know each other well, darkness offered the "right cover."

Unlike most so-called developing countries, North Korea is home to an aging population, because women are having on average 2.02 babies—barely enough to sustain the population numbers, according to a 2010 report by Statistics Korea. The demographic is in part because most young couples bear one child. The government, in response, has taken a pragmatic response to population growth rather than a Leninist one: it urges families to have more children, and discourages abortions and even contraceptives though they are legal.

North Korean women often use contraceptive coils, or small plastic devices inserted into the womb. Men get condoms from friends who bring them back from abroad. When I was running the pharmaceutical company, I wanted to import and distribute condoms and other contraceptives, hoping they would be a commercial success. But the government didn't hand over a permit because it needed more babies, not fewer.

My company also looked into selling Viagra and Cialis, products also popular with Korean men. The government wouldn't mind, I thought, as these aphrodisiacs would get couples heated up and create more kids. I was quickly proven wrong when denied the permit. Ms. Thak, a pharmacist, revealed the reasons to me: "The result of the greater sexual appetite of men would not have led to more children but to more abortions," she claimed.

In 2007, I was approached by the North Korean inventor of a drug he called "Natural Viagra," a gimmicky mixture of herbs. He asked me to market it within North Korea and abroad and gave me samples. I passed them on to some friends who were using the original version of Viagra, who concluded that Viagra and Cialis offered better results. Still, the North Korean government admitted Natural Viagra for sales, and now I understand its reasoning. We would not sell it, as I was keen on building the reputation of the pharmaceutical company.

North Koreans are, in fact, human beings, and like all other humans, they do have a sense of humor and sometimes tell dirty jokes. Some of these jokes were about husbands and wives who had extramarital affairs that made listeners, including myself, laugh. "When does a wife know that her husband is cheating on her? When he starts complaining about the lack of water as he wants to have two showers a week." This was one of the many popular jokes.

With this, it was implicitly acknowledged that marital unfaithfulness was not an absolute taboo, even if it was frowned upon. In fact, I knew two Korean couples who had extramarital affairs.

Does prostitution exist in North Korea? Officially, no. It is illegal and subject to severe punishment, such as a "corrective" yearlong stay in a labor camp. Street prostitution is too visible and too risky. Still, some North Korean men can afford an occasional day of massage and sauna. Often over lunch or after work I heard men gossiping about which women in the parlors offered better "services" than others. Of course, that's with the caveat that the statement leaves much room for interpretation.

By offering discreet services, women can take in a lot of money by North Korean standards, sometimes out of the sheer necessity of supporting their families. And for all the moralistic ideology, sex work isn't a completely absent phenomenon. Indeed, some "flowers of the nation" may now be for sale, as I understood the half-joking remarks of men who said they were seeking to buy the pejorative "beautiful flowers." While marketization is about to lead to more prosperity in North Korea, sex may also become just another tradable product.

On the other hand, ever since women have overwhelmingly become family breadwinners, some female traders have increasingly had to take journeys away from their husbands that lasted weeks. I was told that sometimes these women have boyfriends and lovers on the side whom they financially support. In that way, North Korean women aren't much different than some of their counterparts from around the world.

Though illegal, plastic surgery has gained popularity in recent years among females from more affluent families in Pyongyang. I met a couple of women who admitted, in a frank manner, to having undergone cosmetic surgery. One popular operation makes their eyes look larger and, in the words of some of them, more "Western," mirroring a trend among Chinese, Japanese, and South Korean women.

This is popular because North Koreans are watching prohibited South Korean dramas with beautiful actresses who themselves underwent cosmetic surgery. That the law was not enforced had nothing to do with the privileged position of these women, because the authorities are pragmatic and do what they can to survive.

NO CAREER FOR WOMEN IN KOREA?

It is true that few women make it to the top echelons of the government and business in North and South Korea. One exception, however, is Mrs. Han Kwang Bok, who graduated as an electrical engineer from Kim Chaek University of Technology, Pyongyang. She became Minister of the North Korean Ministry of Electronics Industry and was later appointed Vice-Premier of the Council of Ministers while keeping her post as Minister of the Electronics Industry. She is also a member of the Central Committee of the Korean Workers Party'.

With so few women in top leadership positions, the rise of another woman, whom I repeatedly saw at receptions, struck my attention. Hong Son Ok, as she was known, was appointed in 2013 as the Supreme People's Assembly Presidium's Secretary-General, the first female ever to hold that position.

She previously served as the SPA Vice Chairwoman and as the Vice Chairwoman for the Committee for Cultural Relations with Foreign Countries. North Korea leadership expert Michael Madden explained, "Hong's experience with foreign relations may represent a shift toward international openness of a different sort from the past." Kim Jong Un's wife, Ri Sol Ju, is another rising female star with a high profile who has greeted diplomats and other foreigners several times in Pyongyang.

I met Mrs. Han Kwang Bok, Minister of the North Korean Ministry of Electronics Industry, several times, and I was highly impressed by her extraordinary intelligence, competence, negotiating skills, charm, and fine sense of humor. This image shows Kim Sung Hyon, Minister of the Ministry of Metal and Machine-Building Industries, wearing the gray traditional suit, and Mrs. Han talking with me.

Chapter 10
Nurturing Revolutionaries

Learn from the masses, and then teach them.

— Mao Zedong

In July 2012, state television began airing a video of five young singers dancing in skimpy miniskirts. The female troupe dressed more conservatively than their southern counterparts, famous worldwide for the salacious dance moves of "K-Pop." But these girls were North Korean, and their message was a sort of "old meets new" in this hermit kingdom.

North Korea, despite its communist system, is fundamentally not distinct from other East Asian countries like South Korea and Japan. North Korean culture has, just like that of its neighbors, been influenced by Master Kong, known today by his popular Latin name, Confucius. More than 2,500 years ago Confucius wrote about the importance of a good education as the key to social advancement, an idea that spread all over East Asia.

During the communist upheavals in China, Vietnam, and Korea in the past century, young revolutionaries tried to eliminate the social hierarchies associated with Confucianism, which they perceived to be part of a repressive feudal order. But even in communist North Korea, Confucianism has survived and today prospers as the glue that holds society together.

North Koreans are the pride of their parents when they reach high levels of education, especially at the doctorate level or higher. In this sense, South and North Korea have much in common: south of the DMZ, parents pressure their children to achieve near-perfect school results and gain entrance to top universities, the three most sought after being Seoul National University, Yonsei University, and Korea University. It is common for teenagers to study every day until midnight, in part because they join extracurricular "cram schools" that help them prepare for university entrance exams. This scholastic achievement opens the door to prosperity, a powerful network, and thus is the springboard for an impressive career.

With that sort of intensity of schooling, capitalist South Korea almost always achieves a top rank among countries evaluated for their school performance, measured by an annual exam called the Programme for International Student Assessment (PISA). North Korea is not listed among this elite tranche. But for South Korea (along with China and Japan), the prestige comes with a high price tag: it correspondingly tops the list of the countries with the highest suicide rate, owing in part to the relentless demands of schools and parents.

North Korea, on the other hand, does not gather data, and if it did, it would not publish suicide statistics that would be unsuitable for the workers' paradise image the country is promoting. I heard the reasons firsthand at a conference in 2008. "Why should we have one?" Mr. Bang, a senior party cadre in charge of educational matters asked me. "Our people are among the happiest on earth."

Even if Mr. Bang was overstating the happiness of the North Korean people, it is true that North Koreans continue to be under less pressure to achieve than their southern neighbors. First, shortages of electricity and winter heating push families to relax during their evenings and go to bed early. Second, the strict socialist environment doesn't offer a terrible number of rewards for capitalist-style competition. This lifts the potential for intense stress off the shoulders of North Korean students.

Indeed, socialist North Korea has perhaps proven that Confucian faith in education does not need to lead to inhumane pressure on pupils, as it does in Seoul. Headmaster Lim, whom I talked with when I visited his elite middle school, was aware and extremely critical of excesses in Confucian countries. He explained to me that "learning through coercion and drilling, relentless competition between individual students combined with punishment as widely practiced in countries in our neighborhood, is bad for the health of the kids and has therefore been replaced in our country by a method preferring persuasion and explanation combined with encouragement for all, not a few to achieve success."

In my agency office, my staff loved to chatter about their children's performance in school. Mothers cheered when their sons and daughters passed the rigorous university entrance exams that opened doors to the prestigious Kim Il Sung University. Other moms, I noticed, cried when their children failed to meet these goals. One time an employee brought cakes to the office to celebrate her daughter's passing the exam, whereas another coincidentally fell "sick" when her child repeatedly failed the entrance exams.

In that case, there was no other option but to leave Pyongyang for a faraway province. The universities out in the countryside were less prestigious and offered few opportunities for families to visit. On the other hand, all my staffers admired one colleague whose son entered the top Pyongyang middle school, where only the brightest children (along with the children of the brightest parents) were admitted.

Although examination subjects vary according to the school level, most exams are based on primary subjects such as Korean language, math, and science. They also cover political topics like socialist morality, the life and thought of Kim Il Sung, Juche, and the like.

The North Korean education system faces similar problems to those of other developing countries. The country is full of underpaid teachers, overcrowded classrooms, and a shortage of textbooks, notepads, and pens. The aftereffects of the economic downturn in the 1980s and 1990s was clear; aid workers who visited schools outside Pyongyang explained to me that school buildings have started crumbling and many textbooks look old and overused. Pupils have to write in tiny letters on notepads, since paper is scarce.

But in some ways, North Korean schools outperform even those of the developing world. From my own observations, it seemed that the pupils were much better at math and science than their counterparts in my native country, Switzerland. And I got the impression that even computer literacy, at least in the capital Pyongyang, was higher than in Western Europe.

This is because North Koreans attend two years of kindergarten education, four years of primary school, and six years of high school, all of which is compulsory and free under the socialist system. University education is not compulsory and lasts four to six years, while postgraduate studies last three to four years. A doctorate degree requires another two years. Higher education is divided into "general education," which includes universities, colleges, specialized senior schools, and special colleges for full-time students. The other category is "adult education," comprising factory colleges, farm colleges, fishery colleges, evening sessions of ordinary colleges, and open universities for working students without formal academic qualifications.

For a country with about 24 million inhabitants, the education figures are pretty impressive. Officials from the Ministry of Education explained to me that about 700,000 children are enrolled in more than 30,000 kindergartens throughout the country, which in theory should equal 100 percent enrollment for that age group. For working parents, the government has built about 20,000 day care centers for more than 1.3 million children between the ages of one and three. For every *dong*, or administrative district in a city, there are one to two primary schools, also called "people's schools." In every *ri*, or rural district, students can attend one elementary school.

Adding it together, about 50,000 people's schools across the country enroll more than 1.5 million students. At the middle school level, about 5,000 schools host around 2 million students. More than 400 specialized senior schools and more than 250 universities and colleges have enrolled 300,000 students, a more elite contingent but one that is nonetheless large for a developing country.

Of course, statistical figures from both North Korean authorities and international organizations have to be taken with a grain of salt as they are notoriously unreliable. But even if we downgrade our estimates, the figures are nevertheless impressive for this developing country.

It's fair to say that the government legitimately wants high standards at its universities and adult schools. In 2009, I saw the slogan "Intellectualization of the whole society" at the entrance of North Korea's leading science and technology university, Kim Chaek University. It expresses a very demanding educational objective dear to party and government and repeated over the years. In the words of Kim Il Sung, expressed in his "Theses on Socialist Education" in 1977, this means "comprehensive educational programs, eliminating the need for private educational institutions."

This is in stark contrast to other developing countries, like China and Vietnam, where education has been largely privatized over the last two decades, with mixed results. Those decentralization projects have given rise to dubious "diploma mills" that churn out students holding pieces of paper rather than real knowledge.

Though the DPRK is a socialist country that is supposed to promote equality, the education system is not entirely egalitarian. The party has set up a more selective and nepotistic tier of schools tailored to the children of political elites. In addition, the authorities systematically search for talent among children from when they're toddlers, a tendency common in centralized systems of rule like the old Soviet Union and China. A tiny swath of exceptional pupils get access to specialized schools that train them in one or two topics, such as foreign languages, science, music, the arts, and sports.

Only the offspring of high-ranking cadres are admitted to the prestigious Pyongyang Mangyongdae Revolutionary School, which over eleven years trains 900 students to become the next generation of decision makers. Graduates of this school typically enter Kim Il Sung University or quickly land jobs in their twenties as junior cadres of the party, administration, and military.

The Kang Ban Seok Revolutionary School and the Haeju Revolutionary School, both of which obtained the top qualification known as "Chollima school," serve another 700 students for an eleven-year

Schoolchildren gather from the elite kindergarten named after Kim Jong Suk, wife of the founder president Kim Il Sung and mother of former leader Kim Jong Il. She was nicknamed the "Heroine of the anti-Japanese Revolution."

education. "Elite" schools that maintain social class are not limited to communist countries, but are also common in the U.K. (with Harrow and Oxbridge) and the U.S. (with Andover and the Ivy League).

Far from being completely closed off to the outside world, the North Korean government places a huge emphasis on teaching foreign languages to its future elites. The country's best foreign language school is the Pyongyang Foreign Languages High School, with a six-year curriculum with more than 1,800 students, which feeds them into the privileged Pyongyang University of Foreign Studies. The school has twenty classes including English, Japanese, German, Russian, Chinese, Arabic, and Spanish.

Most of the students go on to become diplomats or work for the Foreign Trade Ministry. Others take up posts in companies that deal with the outside world. The school teaches not only languages but at the same time history, culture, philosophy, ideology, and of course, the way to deal with foreigners, as patriotic Koreans, in the best interest of the country.

Some of my company's staff graduated from the Pyongyang Foreign Studies University, and they were eager to take up work with a foreign-run business. I also hired professors from this university as translators for the Pyongyang Business School, and always found them well trained. To ensure that the benefits of these schools aren't limited to Pyongyang, the government has set up an additional foreign language school in each province. Each school enrolls about 400 to 500 students.

North Korea's education system, as you might realize, does not follow the stereotypical, ultra-socialist, "one-size-fits-all" approach, shuffling in ideological zombies and teaching them to drone away at the edicts of the Great Leader. Even more has been done to foster the future elites. One important move in this direction was the founding of the Pyongyang First Senior Middle School in the 1980s, together with twelve first senior middle schools named after the seats of provincial governments. After that development, the government established a number of schools that were in accordance with the "model school" in Pyongyang. Countrywide, the number of first senior middle schools grew to 210 by the mid-2000s, although the number probably remains the same today.

THE NEXT GENERATION

The regime has also undertaken enormous efforts to nurture future generations of scientists, making it a top priority to the survival of the nation. A multitude of schools train gifted students in sciences and technology, a prospect that has been bolstered with a new six-year curriculum adopted by the Pyongyang First Senior Middle School and the Pyongsung Science College. Both have enrolled about 4,000 students.

Art (including music and dance) and sports schools, too, select

Education officials try to discover and foster talents among students at a very young age, an important trait of North Korea's educational system. One schoolgirl is learning embroidery, while the other one is specializing in calligraphy.

students first and foremost in accordance with their social background. Within the core class, families are divided even further into a hierarchy: their admissions prospects are helped enormously if a grandparent fought against the Japanese, for instance.

Today this social class is well trained in the revolutionary history of Kim Il Sung, Kim Jong Il, and Kim Jong Un, and uses its talents to inspire the masses to support the people's paradise. The most visible artistic expression, which idolizes Juche and includes thousands of students, is the Arirang Mass Games.

According to the country's constitution, schools are required to educate children and youth to become faithful revolutionaries with unwavering loyalty to the party and its leadership. Article 43 of the constitution stipulates: "The state implements the principles of socialist pedagogy and brings up the rising generation to be steadfast revolutionaries who fight for the society and the people, and to be new communist men who are knowledgeable, virtuous, and healthy." On trips around Pyongyang and the countryside, teachers and officials explained to me the characteristics of the education system, which were quite similar to those of formerly socialist countries such as in Eastern Europe and the Soviet Union. Educators, for example, combined a more book-based, theoretical education alongside field labor. It's normal for students to spend their days in a classroom and library, but during other weeks to help farmers with their harvests or prepare for the mass show, Arirang.

When the Supreme People's Assembly decided in September 2012 to increase compulsory education from eleven to twelve years and promised more classrooms, it also vowed to stop the abuse of randomly "mobilizing students for purposes other than state mobilization."

Another aspect of this system was the integration of both school and social education, the guidance by the ruling party, the socialist conjunction of general and technological education, and the preferential treatment of children of late revolutionary heroes. At least, that's what a group of East European and Russian diplomats told me in an informal assessment.

Even though the party kindles the talents of its elite children, ordinary workers don't go entirely neglected. Factory colleges offer five-year courses where laborers can learn to use sophisticated technologies needed at work. As graduates they are given a diploma that the government recognizes as equivalent to one from an ordinary college.

The same goes for farm workers who finish secondary education. They learn farming techniques such as agriculture, stock farming, agricultural mechanics, and the study of vegetables and fruits. For fishermen, the coastline is dotted with fishery colleges that offer five-year courses on fish breeding, fish catching, boat mechanics, and other subjects.

Additionally, the party has opened a number of special institutes, as in any socialist country, that don't quite fit under the label of "university" or a regular "school," such as the Kim Il Sung Higher Party School. The party and government sends its cadres there every so often to invigorate their ideological knowledge on Juche as well as Songun, the policy that places the military before all else.

While we tend to look at the worship of Kim Il Sung as cult-like, North Koreans have their own reasons for seeing it as perfectly normal. They are taught from an early age to be proud of being Koreans rather than coming from a "less fortunate" race such as the Japanese. They are taught to see themselves as privileged compared to their southern kin, who they believe are oppressed by American imperialism.

As such, North Koreans consistently told me they hold their leaders in high esteem in exchange for earning their freedom from foreign aggression. With this mindset, indoctrination through songs and dances that revere the leadership is considered a normal thing and starts as early as nursery school. Four-year-old children are taught songs and dances praising the revolutionary leaders.

Around 40 percent of elementary school classes are on the childhood of Kim Il Sung and Kim Jong Il. In my visits around primary schools, I saw posters covering the walls that exclaimed "Our General Kim Jong Il is the best!" At the high school level, about a third of the curriculum teaches subjects such as the "History of Kim Il Sung's anti-imperialist and anti-colonialist struggles," "Kim Jong Il's revolutionary activities," and "Kim Il Sung's thoughts on reunification." Memorizing large parts of these histories is considered normal.

North Koreans proudly show this off to foreign visitors. To the very Confucian and hierarchically thinking North Koreans, it is natural and desirable to follow the path of their great idols. This is a cultural gap, revealed in the differences in the perceptions of Westerners raised in more liberal and egalitarian societies.

A book for the fourth grade explained that in industrial districts of Seoul, the capital of "South Korea, colonized and suppressed by the U.S. imperialists, factories are just subcontractors processing imported raw materials and assembling under contracts with capitalist countries such as the U.S. and Japan." It quoted Kim Jong Il as saying, "Relying on others for raw materials and fuel is like leaving your economic fate in their hands." This is intended to illustrate the superiority of the North, following Juche, often translated in the West as self-reliance, to the non-Juche, capitalist South Korea.

Kim Jong Il went so far as to predict that dependence on foreign powers would lead to the failure of the socialist revolution in Korea. There appears to be some irony to the fact that North Korea received subsidies and other economic packages from Soviet Russia. But pragmatic Kim Il Sung found a way out of this apparent contradiction by declaring that countries he considered socialist allies such as the Soviet Union, the People's Republic of China, and Cuba should engage in cooperation and mutual support and accept limited dependence.

For the children of foreign diplomats, aid workers, and businesspeople, there is a Korean International School with a kindergarten in Pyongyang's diplomatic village. The teachers are North Koreans who speak English fairly well. The curriculum for foreign students isn't the same as North Korean ones. Teachers leave out the ideological bent.

Still, those tutors made a few entertaining gaffes in the classroom. One day a teacher must have forgotten that he was not standing in front of Korean kids but lecturing to foreign youngsters. He said that Kim Il Sung is the father of all children in Korea, a statement that's part of the curriculum but is usually self-censored so as not to upset foreigners. The two children of Romanian diplomats said they were shocked: they thought that their father was the man whom they saw every day at home and not some portly Korean guy whom they'd never met.

In the end, the parents decided to send them to the Russian school at the Russian embassy. For them, that was a safer bet. Half a century has already passed since the Soviet Russians decided not to worship their "Dear Father Stalin" any longer and to abandon any form of personality cult.

University students frequently study Juche and Songun, but the ideological erudition doesn't end there. Every Saturday my staff studied these subjects in the office like all other adults in North Korea. It was common to come to the office on Saturdays to take part in political study and training, but also to do the work that needed to be finished by the end of the week. "What's the study topic right now?" I once asked one of my staff. "It's about Juche. We are preparing for an exam on this. I like it." She smiled and sounded enthusiastic and authentic. The trade union cells and the party cells in the company were responsible for holding regular sessions for our staff, including exams.

All kids are members of the Pioneers, a party-led movement. They are required to join the organization in elementary school and remain there until their early teenage years. As in many socialist countries, the movement's leaders try to make the children revolutionaries who are completely faithful to the Juche values they are taught at school.

On important occasions, like the birthdays of the leaders, I saw groups of young Pioneers wearing red kerchiefs around their necks, bowing in front of murals of Kim Il Sung and Kim Jong Il. After paying their respects, they laid flowers in front of the murals. However, I also watched Pioneers roaming the streets behaving like kids anywhere else in the world—playing around and causing childlike mischief.

PYONGYANG GOES DIGITAL

Belying the image that North Koreans are technologically backwards, Pyongyang actually boasts plenty of computer specialists with a remarkable level of knowledge. This development may be credited partly to the fact that in 2001 Kim Jong Il declared the twenty-first century to be "the century of information technology." When I lived in Pyongyang in the mid-2000s, I noticed a subsequent rush among youth to take computer training classes. Knowing how to work a computer offered something magical to the Korean youngsters, as if it was a window to the outside world.

Computers were a regular topic of discussion by state leaders, factory managers, and pupils. They were even included as a subject at the Arirang Mass Games. The authorities consider technology the recipe for a prosperous future, in line with China's emphasis on the matter. In many ways this technological push is exposing North

Koreans to the outside world. Professor Han from the Academy of Sciences, for instance, once explained to me that experts study foreign technologies and then apply them to North Korea's development.

Some boys were selected to work on computers for their innate talents, and during my meetings with them they outdid even my knowledge of computers. They were able to answer literally any complicated question of mine regarding the hardware and software they were using. In one middle school in the capital, I saw a ten-year-old boy practice English by putting together an English-language PowerPoint presentation in front of his class, speaking in complicated audiovisual terms that only specialists would know. In another classroom, I watched a fourteen-year-old boy write algorithms in Linux—quite an exertion of brainpower for someone at that age.

Only when I asked questions about the Internet did they appear somewhat puzzled and overwhelmed. My inquiries, as a matter of fact, were sensitive. The teacher quickly intervened and answered that they use the Korean "intranet," a countrywide network. It "includes the good parts of the Internet and excludes the parts aimed at infiltrating reactionary ideas and poisonous culture into our country," he said.

We were proven wrong in our original expectations that North Koreans would be backwards. When a German owner of an information technology (IT) business, a French IT entrepreneur, and I were setting up the first foreign-invested IT joint venture company in North Korea, we were concerned about the availability and technical competence of the country's workforce. The Frenchman, a mathematician by training, chatted with a number of software engineers from universities and other companies. He quickly realized that their mathematical skills were, for the most part, better than those of colleagues in France and the rest of Europe. This was because of the party's system of picking the best students and harnessing their talents, giving them the privilege of migrating to Pyongyang and living a more comfortable life.

From a military standpoint, North Korea had a strong rationale for cultivating its best computer minds. I once asked Professor Kim, a leading IT expert at the respected Kim Chaek University of Technology, what future role IT would play in national defense. He answered that wars without a cyber element are increasingly unthinkable, and that the Internet would not be spared from battle. North Korea, he added, would build up the needed IT capabilities to make its enemies pay dearly for their aggressions.

Given the enormous cost of maintaining a military, the approach actually made sense given North Korea's limited resources. Purchasing software and investing in computer education costs far less than buying fighter jets and nuclear-powered submarines. North Korea was cushioned from cyberattacks because it ran an intranet cut off from the outside world and didn't have to fear Internet retaliation. It could easily infiltrate foreign computer systems, perhaps by cracking passwords, with the mathematical skills that are abundant in this country.

FROM MARX TO MARKETING

In 2005, the *Financial Times* wrote[1]:

> In a business world overrun with MBAs, it can be difficult to stand out from the crowd. But one new qualification is guaranteed to jump off the CV: a degree from the Pyongyang Business School.
>
> As North Korea's economic reforms trickle through to the factory level, company managers in this communist stronghold are now learning about market research, buyer behavior, and even e-commerce.
>
> With its first graduates having just received their diplomas, the privately-run Pyongyang Business School is setting its sights on offering a Master of Business Administration. ...
>
> ... Kang Chun-il, one of the graduates, told a state publication the course had helped him set high aims for the high-technology service center he manages, which offers

a digital imaging facility and electronic reading room.

"Our aim is to raise the country's economy and technology to a world-leading level as soon as possible and, with this in mind, we welcome all partners who want true and practical co-operation with us," Mr. Kang said.

This mindset, that education was key, was a potential panacea for the black hole in North Korea's economic development. With no end in sight, North Korea had since the 1990s been dependent on a massive wave of foreign humanitarian aid. This problem motivated me to think up a cost-effective way to make food security more reliable and sustainable. I wanted to accomplish this by trying to reactivate the idle enterprises that were supposed to feed millions of employees and their families through the public distribution system.

North Korean authorities, too, quickly became aware that a healthy economy would ease the chronic shortages. They, like me, did not want to drag along with what they called a culture of aid dependence.

Solving the problem was easier said than done. We could not help these enterprises purchase badly needed spare parts for their machines, or raw materials, for that matter. No investor or sponsor would put up millions of dollars to pay for those operations, especially in what they considered to be a risky market like North Korea. We could, however, train their managers to make the best of the resources they already had.

The dilemma was that executives were familiar with receiving and executing orders in this centrally planned economy. To get their operations up to speed, they'd have to abandon much of the old model and become familiar with basic skills like accounting and controlling, marketing, supply chain management, and strategy. With that in mind, I drew up a concept for a course geared at managers and containing the elements of most MBA degrees in other countries. I sent the idea to some future sponsors: the Swiss government, a handful of multinational corporations, and the North Korean government.

Having worked in lots of sectors in North Korea, I had a strong sense as to how local managers worked and the skills they possessed. With that in mind, I rid the seminar of topics that would have been more suitable for twenty-three-year-old MBA students, focusing instead on know-how tailored for senior executives. Our goal was never to foster an economic elite. We simply wanted to see North Korean managers optimize their practices, make hard currency earnings, and raise their businesses to a level fit for international competition.

The North Korean government, on the other hand, was indeed wary that we had a political agenda. We put together pilot seminars to show that we, the Swiss initiators, had no strategic interest in overthrowing the system. We wanted to demonstrate to the authorities that this was purely a business school, a provider of the hard skills that both private and state-run bodies needed in both capitalist and socialist societies.

As the organizer and soon-to-be director, I made the opening speech for the first pilot seminar, a several-day course called "Strategy and Strategic Management." I stepped into our first classroom, looking around at the faces of the officials who attended. I was nervous that with one small misspeak the project would be canceled and my reputation as a politically neutral businessman called into question.

Yet the students were listening attentively. I soon realized that they were pleased with the seminar topic I had chosen.

My talk was short, but Professor Peter Abplanalp, an outstanding Swiss expert on business strategies, had to shoulder the heavy burden of a several-day talk. That was enough time to commit plenty of blunders. But Peter had been working with Chinese educational institutions for many years and was sensitive to the political minefield. This was perhaps not surprising, as the communist Chinese central government had awarded him the Dunhuang Award and the Friendship Award, which is the highest honor awarded to foreign experts in China. It was thanks to him that we passed our first test and were able to get the school going.

I handed the participants a questionnaire in which they had to rate the seminar contents and the lecturer. Both got surprisingly encouraging remarks. But I still had to do more explaining and convincing with the committee dispatched by the cabinet. In a meeting, a handful of men and women in their fifties eyed me in a slightly doubtful, perhaps suspicious way, and wanted to know more about the role of business schools elsewhere, especially in China and Vietnam.

One of my topics that day showed that the world's then-best airline, Singapore Airlines, was state-owned. *Euromoney*, a finance magazine, called it in 2004 "the best managed airline" and *Travel & Leisure* labeled it "the world's best international airline." The managers running that airline applied the same business administration know-how we wanted to impart in North Korea.

This anecdote may have motivated Air Koryo to enroll a senior manager in the business school. Another lure may have been my own activities representing a number of first-class multinationals in North Korea. Local businesspeople perhaps saw a networking opportunity and were interested in doing business with these groups. I planned to draw partly on their huge resources, which the North Koreans were pleased with.

Unfortunately, the raucous and cacophonous world of international politics threw a number of wrenches in our plans. After the first nuclear and missile tests in 2006, a number of multinationals and wealthy individuals changed their minds about sponsorship. They feared getting caught in the middle of tightened sanctions and the bitter controversy that could ensue if they were perceived to be working with a "pariah" regime.

The project was in jeopardy, so I took extra pains to carefully select the lecturers. I mostly took on those with an academic teaching background plus long-running business experience in Asia and elsewhere. I briefed them thoroughly on the sensitive political nature of their lectures, urging them, for instance, not to talk about the South Korean *chaebol* like Samsung and Hyundai. I revised and sometimes censored their lectures and teaching materials.

Many of the lecturers were high achievers in their respective industries. Most came from Hong Kong, but others came from all over the world. For example, one teacher of international marketing was a vice president at ABB and a pioneer in developing new markets around the world. Other lecturers came from business backgrounds in Europe and Asia, with long careers at ABB, Siemens, Sony, and Apple. Yet another was a Singaporean who was the head of SKF's logistics center in Asia and is one of the world's foremost experts on supply chain management.

I also invited a Swedish ambassador (and, by training, economist) to talk about the European Union and its markets, business, and investors. With this colorful blend of nationalities and backgrounds coming and going on short lecturing trips, it was clear that we carried no political agenda. We were very pragmatic, not following a single ideology—as were our North Korean partners.

In the mid-2000s, one joint New Year's editorial in the country's leading newspapers—where the next year's priorities were outlined for the country—mentioned that companies needed a strategy. It was the first instance, to my knowledge, that the concepts of a corporate strategy along with strategic management had been raised in a North Korean editorial. The party, it seemed, had learned about our strategy seminar and recommended it through its press mouthpieces. This seminar, and others, had indeed been translated into Korean and then published in English and Korean. We had them widely distributed to ministries, academies, universities, and enterprises.

The newspaper was surely right that students were shifting toward the marketized mode of thinking. But in a country that abandoned the rarefied version of socialism decades ago, how could it possibly move away from Marx this late in the game?

Perhaps the statement is deceiving. I have visited libraries and bookshops throughout the country but have never come across a single book by Marx or Lenin. Yet for some strange reason, portraits of both of them were then still hanging on the walls of the Foreign Trade Ministry in Pyongyang, the one body you'd think would be more forward-minded.

I sometimes happened to bump into former students who, mostly

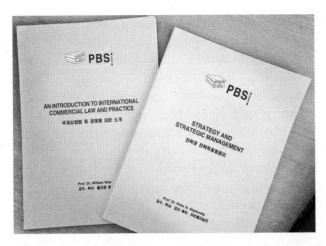

Seminar booklets spread management and business expertise across the country. The pages on the left were always written in English, while the pages on the right contained the Korean translation. This layout was highly popular among readers who were keen on improving their English-language skills. It was common to see North Koreans reading these booklets at bus stops, in libraries, and in restaurants.

with a broad smile, happily told me that they had applied this or that which they had learned at the Pyongyang Business School, which enabled them to increase productivity, reduce customer complaints, or raise profitability. They and their companies seemed to have been energized thanks to the school, which was a good omen for the economy, as there were millions of jobless workers in the terrible crisis years of the 1990s.

My involvement with the Pyongyang Business School ended at the end of 2010, when the business school was about to be closed. By the following year, the market-driven idealism of those earlier years had withered. Seminars ceased to be held on a regular schedule after the only remaining sponsor, the Swiss government, halted all its development cooperation at the end of that year following a decision by the Swiss parliament.

That was because a right-wing parliamentarian from the countryside came into the picture. He persuaded the majority of the Swiss parliament that the country should abandon working "with a totalitarian dictatorship which does neither respect human rights nor agreements regarding nuclear weapons programs and which is destabilizing the region."

From then on Switzerland limited its activities to humanitarian help such as supplying food. Basically, this meant that the government fell back into the convention of unoriginality that plagued the rest of the Western aid organizations, a stance that was creating a "culture of dependence" for the North Korean people. It was a huge swing from 1997, the year the Swiss Agency for Development and Cooperation opened an office in Pyongyang. It had publicly declared that its mission was to encourage reform. But the promising experiment was buried.

CAN NORTH KOREA BUILD A KNOWLEDGE-BASED STATE?

It's true that Confucius promoted inequality in social relations, with the exception of relations among friends. According to him, subjects should be subordinate to rulers, children subordinate to parents, younger people subordinate to elder, wives subordinate to husbands, and even mothers subordinate to the eldest son if the father has died. When the revolutionaries who once challenged Confucianism grew older, they and their successors started embracing Confucian authoritarianism.

But Confucius was also one of the first great men in history to demand education for all. He would have strongly disliked the fact that nowadays in Confucian countries, high-quality education is a privilege for an elite who can afford private school. He would also have been very critical of relentless competition and school drills, which includes learning entire books by heart without understanding and assimilating the contents. "Studying without thinking leads to confusion; thinking without studying leads to laziness," he wrote.[2]

Confucius traveled to all sorts of city-states during his time and was an open-minded person who was eager to learn from anyone. He constitutes one of the strongest symbols for North Korea in its hopes to open up and prosper in a new world of knowledge and creativity.

NOTES

1. http://pasttense7.xanga.com/337520619/item/.
2. http://wenku.baidu.com/view/7a2a63d728ea81c758f578b4.html.

Coming and Going

An ant on the move does more than a dozing ox.

— Lao Tzu

Traffic control in the revolutionary capital was a serious matter. You could tell just by peering at the omnipresent traffic police, who were young women with stern and angry faces. They directed cars with Robocop-like movements.

One time I wanted to cheer up one of the grimacing androids. I regularly stopped at a crossroads where one beauty queen stood, and on that day I offered her a lengthy smile. When she saw me, her face instantly became angrier. I did not give up. In a battle of wits and patience, I kept smirking at her over the next few weeks, and she kept on playing her game as a lifeless automaton.

It was time to reverse my tactics so I pulled up in my car, and instead of beaming at her, I mirrored her livid face. This time I won, as she could not control herself and burst into laughter, then tried to recover her earlier serious demeanor. From then on every time she saw my car approaching she started smiling, and of course I smiled back. Obviously she realized that being a good policewoman does not exclude a friendly smile. After that, I found driving in Pyongyang to be better than ever before.

To my chagrin, the policewomen didn't hang around for the muggy summer. When the weather became too hot, they took a break for a few weeks and the local authorities switched on the traffic lights. It gave me an uncomfortable feeling when nobody was there. I would stop in front of the red lights, all alone and surrounded by no other vehicles, patiently waiting until they turned green. I missed the policewomen, regardless of whether they scowled or smirked.

After finishing their shifts, male and female police officers randomly stopped cars to ask for a lift home. Drivers always obeyed out of respect and sympathy for the people's traffic officers. I stopped a few times at night when young policewomen waved. They usually quickly walked to the car, opened the door, and were about to sit down. But they were surprised to see me, a white-skinned foreigner smiling back at them. They glanced at me, politely shut the door, and walked away. Under North Korean regulations, they weren't supposed to be driving in a foreigner's car.

Only under special circumstances did North Koreans not follow the state rules on driving with outsiders. One particularly frigid night a policeman stopped me and jumped into my car, but at first he did not recognize my face. We turned toward each other and were both surprised. But neither of us made a fuss. As I drove away, we communicated with hand signs. After a couple of kilometers he made an abrupt sign to stop, and then leaped out of the car and disappeared into the darkness.

I worried that a colleague or a stranger could have seen him getting into my car, giving the wrong impression that I was recruiting spies. The next morning I informed my staff about the rendezvous. In front of all of them, I blamed myself for not kicking him out of the car and expressed sorrow over the situation. Above all, I hoped that he would not be punished for the incident.

My staff quieted down and looked serious when I talked to them. A case as serious as this had to be reported by them to the government. I repeatedly asked them in the coming days if they had heard anything about the case, knowing they could tap into their contacts in the police. After some days I was told that the policeman could continue his work but that he would certainly be more careful when stopping cars in the future. It's highly likely that he underwent some very unpleasant scrutiny and self-criticism sessions. For him, it was certainly a lesson learned.

Unplanned encounters like this gave a lot of insight into what North Koreans must deal with, and it was rare for foreigners to witness how this society truly operated. For instance, in another encounter, a concealed police car pulled me over when I, foolishly in a hurry, made a U-turn on a highway where there was no traffic. The patroller immediately asked for my passport and my driving license. I realized what this meant: a hefty penalty of $200, in lieu of which the authorities would never have returned these documents to me. Thankfully, I had changed my suit at lunchtime and left these documents in the old suit. It must have been the language barrier and the mutual embarrassment that made the policeman let me leave without a fine.

Another time I sped down a street in Pyongyang. A policeman stopped me. Even though I thought he would have difficulties proving that I was driving 50 miles (80 kilometers) per hour, instead of the allowed 35 (60 km), he insisted that I was driving too fast. After chatting for a few more minutes, he began shouting in Korean. I could hardly understand what he was saying, so I called my office on my mobile phone. I told my secretary that the policeman was correct to stop me and that I wanted to apologize.

I then passed my mobile phone to the policeman. For a moment he was slightly bewildered, because this must have been his first time talking into a mobile phone. At that time, in 2006, mobile phones were limited to foreigners and a handful of senior cadres. Only two years later, when the Egyptian company Orascom set up a telecom joint venture company, the first few lucky traffic policemen could be seen with mobile phones in the street.

After a few minutes of chatting, he ended the call with my secretary. He handed me the mobile phone and nodded to show he accepted my apologies. We said good-bye in Korean with a smile and went on our ways.

GETTING IN, GETTING OUT

When SARS and bird flu broke out in Asia, North Korea sealed off its borders. Vehicles, trains, and passenger aircraft could no longer cross. Some months after I settled in Pyongyang, the outbreak of SARS in 2002 was bad timing for me, as I had to attend a number of business meetings in Europe that set the direction and pace for my future work in North Korea.

Luckily for me, a couple of friendly North Korean business contacts with close ties to Air Koryo helped me secure one of the few seats on a cargo plane. Influential connections, as I had learned in the years of doing business in other Asian countries, are crucial in getting things done and problems solved in North Korea. Around me in this plane, a handful of North Koreans and foreigners wondered whether there would be a flight back. Another concern with the epidemic was whether we would be quarantined after our return. Indeed, some people stayed abroad longer when the epidemic got worse, and for a week upon their return were confined to an isolated guesthouse outside Pyongyang with no Internet, e-mail, or international phone. What was remarkable about this cargo plane was that a flight attendant served the handful of passengers a meal with free beverage. I thought to myself, *This is cargo flying with style!*

I was lucky again when I returned from Europe to be allowed to fly back from Beijing to Pyongyang, this time even in a passenger plane. More importantly, I was not asked to spend the following ten days in complete isolation in a deserted and dilapidated guesthouse. Had I returned a couple of days later, when this became a general rule for all new arrivals, I would have run into a severe headache. The problem was that I brought back from Europe a long to-do list that I would not have been able to tackle.

For several years China Northern Airlines had an office in the diplomatic village in the same building as the Russian airline Aeroflot. Both airlines had one, or at best two, weekly flights to China and Khabarovsk, Russia, respectively, and at times none at all. I was happy to see more choice and industry competition.

Sadly, after a few years both companies closed their offices due to lack of business. Good news was the arrival of Air China with two weekly flights with modern aircraft. But Air China is a commercial airline, not a politically backed one, which meant that it flew only during those months when it could carry sufficient Chinese tourists to Pyongyang; otherwise the airline canceled the flights.

Air China opened an office that set new standards: I was able to book flights not only to Beijing but beyond, and it even delivered tickets to the customer at no extra charge. My staff, outstanding Korean patriots, urged me to fly Air Koryo instead of Air China. I answered, "Out of sympathy with you I can do without Air China's higher quality and safety standards and the ticket delivery service. But only if Air Koryo refunds me the price difference, as Air China is much cheaper." That argument was accepted without reply and with a smile. For them, it was a practical lesson about the market economy.

Even though much of the country is agrarian and underdeveloped, North Korea was full of small domestic airports that offered a fixed time schedule as well as chartered propeller-driven planes. Flying was convenient when I wanted to visit remote areas like Paekdu Mountain but didn't have the time or energy to drive there and back over three days. These smaller airplanes flew relatively slowly and at a lower altitude, offering dazzling panoramas of North Korea's mountains and valleys.

Since the authorities feared espionage, they didn't allow photographs from above. I retorted that satellites and U.S. spy planes were hovering overhead anyway and could take better pictures than my meager camera. I didn't make much leeway with that argument at a time when Google Earth was unknown (as it still is) to many North Koreans.

THE PEOPLE'S LICENSE PLATES

For practical reasons, I had to soon learn to identify some of the government number plates. On the road, it was wise to identify cars belonging to security and military agencies and to keep a safe distance from them. A traffic accident with a powerful figure could have made life in North Korea hard and ruined any chance of business success.

Driving around, I could easily spot cars with number plates representing categories 15, 16, and 17, signifying that they belonged to the People's Safety Agency. Policemen in blue uniforms were driving these. After staying in North Korea longer, I learned that a few numbers above category 17 marked cars owned by the National Security Agency, the elite body charged with intelligence gathering and investigating "political" crimes. These drivers did not wear uniforms.

In general, the lower the category of a white government license plate, the higher its car owner in the party and government hierarchy. Categories 01 and 02 belong to powerful party secretaries and department directors. Cars driven by NGOs and diplomats had blue number plates. There was even a hierarchy determining which country they represented: Russian embassy cars were at the top, the blue number plate starting with 1-. Chinese diplomats followed with number plates starting with 2-, and so on.

There were a wide range of exceptions. Cars with category 2.16 were given to their owners in recognition of outstanding achievements. Cars with ★-XXX were special events' vehicles, and there were even cars with no plate numbers at all. South Korean vehicles crossing the DMZ into the Kaesong Industrial Zone, for example, hid their license plates.

I did not reveal my knowledge to the gossipy expatriate community, which chattered daily at cocktail parties in embassies and homes. The chairman of one of North Korea's largest industrial groups once told me candidly, "We highly appreciate discreet business partners even though the business with them is legal and not subject to foreign embargoes. But given the fact that our enemies want to shut down our economy, talkative foreigners, no matter how friendly and effective they are, may unintentionally seriously harm our business interests."

I realized that other, more extroverted foreign businesspeople were offered fewer business opportunities. I was tight-lipped. But among expatriates, I didn't make it to the top of the popularity list.

Around 2004, rumors even began spreading that I was suspect. I heard some stories falsely alleging that I harbored close ties to the leadership, while a few blabbermouths claimed I was possibly involved in drug trafficking, cash counterfeiting, and the country's nuclear weapons program. The rumors intensified with the growing hysteria over the nuclear program in the mid-2000s.

But one European diplomat, frustrated with the policy of Western countries, sympathized with me. He thought that doing business was a promising way to open and change the hitherto isolated country and the course of things for the better. He kept me informed and regretted that more than a few people working in NGOs and embassies considered me a "rogue businessman."

To avoid intrusive questions from diplomats and NGOs, I minimized my participation at cocktail parties and the like. And I always gave a true excuse for not talking about my business projects. "It would take too long to explain this rather demanding project and my possible involvement," I would say. At times I felt like I was mimicking the ways diplomats expressed themselves so well without disclosing any substance.

Diplomats and representatives of international organizations, on the other hand, received comfortable salaries and didn't have to worry about the day-to-day stresses of pleasing clients. They were also typically awarded substantial "hardship" bonuses simply for the inconvenience of living in North Korea, and lucrative promotion prospects after a few years abroad. NGO employees at German Agro Action or French Première Urgence were paid much less, but still lived a cozy life. For the most part, they hung around for up to a year and then headed out, satisfying their taste for a quick adventure in North Korea.

I quickly found that expatriates were given venerated status on the roads. For instance, I was told by my North Korean staff that I would not need a North Korean driving license. I asked the officials to let me take the driving tests anyway so I would be in conformance with the law and not dependent on arbitrary circumstances. I probably didn't correctly answer a number of questions on the questionnaire and I thought I had failed the test, but the officials nevertheless passed me, possibly out of sympathy.

I asked the officials what would happen if I caused a traffic accident. I got a surprising, and somewhat patriotic, answer: "The traffic police will ask you which organization you are working for, and when you answer that you're the head of the ABB representation, they will let you go." The government, as a matter of fact, considered my employer to be an organization legitimately helping the DPRK. The opening of the ABB office, a year before I arrived, was widely reported by the North Korean media because it was trying to alleviate the electricity shortages.

On Sundays expatriates were masters of the streets, while North Koreans tended to stay inside. Only a few cars drove around the streets on weekends, and rarely were they government vehicles, because petroleum was rationed on the weekends. Korean drivers needed a special permit on Sundays, which was almost impossible to obtain, as the government wanted to save on gas expenses. Every Sunday I went on pleasant trips around the quiet and empty streets of the capital.

THE AUTO INDUSTRY EXPANDS

Throughout the course of my stay, which ended in 2009, more cars and a wider variety of vehicles took to the streets of Pyongyang. Within the first four years I got the impression that traffic may have even doubled. But the government didn't publish official vehicle statistics. Recently I read in a foreign newspaper that the total number of cars was less than 30,000, a number that could very well be an understatement given the DPRK's economic improvement over the past decade.

More interesting was the involvement of the internationally known and anticommunist South Korean reverend Sun Myung Moon, who headed the Unification Church and passed away in September 2012. In 2003, the first few hundred Hwiparam cars, with 1,580-cc engines, hit the roads of Pyongyang. To construct them, knock-down kits from Fiat were imported and assembled at a car factory near Nampo, a small industrial city about 30 miles (50 kilometers) southwest of Pyongyang. The company that became the country's second car manufacturer and dealer was a joint venture belonging to the North Korean state-run firm Korea Ryongbong General Corp. and to the Seoul-based car manufacturer Pyeonghwa. The latter group is a subsidiary of Moon's church. His family today holds 70 percent of the shares, and Moon, because of all his holdings, was a billionaire.

The company had an annual production capacity of 10,000 units, but in 2003 it sold only 314 cars. With more models hitting the streets, it gradually increased sales over the following years, earning a profit for the first time in 2009. Companies and state agencies became obliged to purchase new cars from Pyeongwha instead of buying imported cars.

A billboard for a new car assembled in North Korea refers to it as "Whistle" and a "strong and beautiful car." Pyeongwha (Peace) Joint Venture Company's first car, called Hwiparam ("Whistle"), is an updated version of Fiat's Siena. The imported complete knock-down set was assembled in its factory in the port city of Nampo. Ordinary North Koreans believed it was a car designed by North Korean engineers and entirely made in North Korea, a notion that is not entirely true. The successful young North Korean athlete on the advertising billboard is being rewarded with a car, as is usual in North Korea. Boys and young men dream of driving or even owning a car someday when the country becomes "prosperous and strong," as predicted by the Korean Workers' Party. They too are expected to work equally hard as the young sports champion to achieve that goal.

For a while it was a sign that North Korea was truly on a path of self-sustenance. But the firm was hardly profitable, making just $700,000 profit in 2009 from the sale of 650 cars; $500,000 was remitted to its parent group in South Korea. According to the Spanish-language Chilean newspaper *La Tercera*, the Unification Church may have wanted to close the company in exchange for other rights in North Korea, such as setting up a hotel supply trading company.

In 2006, a pickup truck and an SUV were added to the range of cars assembled in Nampo, again using knock-down kits from Chinese manufacturer Dandong Shugang. In 2006, the company announced it would build the new Junma, a luxury car that resembled the South Korean Ssangyong Chairman car (which itself resembles a Mercedes-Benz). That same year the company agreed to cooperate with Brilliance China Auto, and from 2007 Brilliance's Junjie car was made under the name Hwiparam II.

When I departed Pyongyang in May 2009, the venture for the first time transferred a profit to the South Korean majority owner. A few months later I traveled to Pyongyang, this time as a visitor and nonresident businessman. Nothing had changed in the meantime except that it seemed there were more cars on the streets and more propaganda posters hung up in the city promoting the 150-day speed campaigns launched in May 2009. Those were two slightly conflicting signs of forward and backward movements at the same time, or, as they say, one step forward and two steps back. *That's North Korea, living and surviving with contradictions!* I thought.

The poor quality of North Korea's power generation, transmission, and distribution was a consequence of the erratic movements. Hugely fluctuating voltage and frequency became an enormous problem for automobile and other factories.

When Pyeongwha started using spray booths to paint cars, the company was shocked at the uneven patches of paint that stood out due to this "flicker effect." Only after installing our stabilizers could the car painting be resumed, and the promising car venture was finally on track.

It was ironic that, at the time, the George W. Bush administration was strangling the North Korean economy with sanctions. Yet despite the setbacks, I noticed that more Malaysian Proton sedans, German Volkswagen Passats made in China, and other elegant cars were hitting the roads. With the shortages of fuel since the end of the cold war, I was likewise surprised to come across one American Hummer SUV—the notorious gas guzzler—with the number plate of a state agency!

As I drove around, I frequently observed policemen stopping North Korean drivers to check their papers. They were looking for any infraction, such as incorrect information, that would allow them to extort a fee from the driver. In the end, I actually felt some sympathy for these police officers. I drove around in nice cars while policemen could barely make it by with their salaries. They needed the extra income.

Most foreigners, despite being well paid, were let off. Normally, when the policemen at control checkpoints saw me in a company vehicle driven by a company driver, they waved us through without stopping us. Obviously, my "long nose," as many Asians jokingly called this Western stereotype, enjoyed some respect on the streets. The police were afraid of a foreigner witnessing their dubious practices and telling the world.

Pyongyang boasted three major highways that were well maintained compared to those in other countries I've lived in. And the dozens of tunnels and bridges that in some places cut a straight path through mountainous terrain are truly engineering masterpieces. One 125-mile (200-kilometer) expressway stretched from the capital to the major city Wonsan on the east coast, while another 25-mile (45-kilometer) expressway continued from Pyongyang to the port city Nampo on the west coast. Finally, a 60-mile (100-kilometer) motorway from Pyongyang pointed southwards to Kaesong. North Korea at least has some excellent infrastructure for a country that is considered poor.

However, leaving aside these impressive highways, I saw a crumbling infrastructure that, in all likelihood, worsened the country's food shortages—because trucks faced constant challenges transporting agricultural produce to the cities. The majority of the road network was left unpaved. The various pathways were neatly laid piles of crushed stone, gravel, or dirt that went unmaintained. During one of my car trips around the countryside, the constant tremor of driving over the street made me vomit. Heavy rains in the summer months triggered landslides that further damaged the fragile road infrastructure, further aggravating supply shortages.

As in the old socialist days in China and Vietnam, foreign residents of North Korea needed a permit to leave the capital (I had no problem getting these in a couple of days). However, they were allowed to travel 20 miles (35 kilometers) out of central Pyongyang or up to the first round of military checkpoints without such a permit.

RELAXING THE TOTALITARIAN RULES

Though the state-guided travel system was more prominent before the economic collapse, North Koreans who want to travel within the country continue, by law, to need a document noting their destination, purpose, and period of travel. These permits were issued based on the recommendation of the work unit's party secretary. But since the breakdown of government services in the 1990s famine, more North Koreans are traveling without authorization. Local businesspeople told me that traders, along with anyone else with some extra cash, could easily buy themselves out of trouble when caught without a travel permit. Even so, this rarely became an issue.

As I drove farther out of the cities and into the countryside abyss, with its rolling hills and parched wheat fields, I saw more and more people walking instead of using cars. It was a sign of the true remoteness and poverty of these areas, which included the sight of undernourished animals and farmers working the fields with their bare hands. Some farmers rode around in small carts, and when they sat in larger carts, they were pulled along by oxen. I felt I had landed in a previous, more prelapsarian decade.

To my amusement, a traffic sign prohibited ox carts from passing by revolutionary sites, out of fear that the oxen would defecate close to these venerated monuments. These strong, resilient, and patient animals weren't merely shuffling goods along roads, but because of the limited mechanization and shortage of fuel they also plowed rice paddy fields. I got the impression that, unlike in China and Vietnam where every year is the year of a different animal, in North Korea every year was the Year of the Oxen.

TAKEOVER OF THE BICYCLE

To be fair, North Korea did not remain dirt poor forever, as I witnessed a gradual change over time. In my rural travels I saw more locals mounted on bicycles, suggesting that more people were doing better financially and could now afford this simple but, by the living standards of most North Koreans, expensive vehicle. The rising supply of bicycles made prices drop rapidly from more than $50 to between $10 and $30. It was an enormous contribution that put bicycles in the hands of regular people.

Most North Koreans who earned some money purchased a bicycle, because it was considered a somewhat prestigious marker of wealth—similar to how the nouveau riche Chinese view cars.

Secondhand bicycles imported from Japan used to be by far the most popular ones. Mr. Pang, a repairman who came to my house when something needed to be fixed, told me that although his used Japanese bicycle cost much more than a new Chinese bicycle, it was still more economical because, unlike Chinese bikes, it hardly needed any repair and replacement parts. But the dream of many North Koreans to become happy owners of Japanese bicycles was shattered when Japan ratcheted up its embargo in 2006 by denying port entry to the North Korean ferry *Mangyongbong-92*, which made twenty to thirty trips per annum between the ports of Niigata, Japan, and Wonsan, North Korea, always carrying secondhand bikes among many other equally popular products from Japan.

It's a little-known story that bicycles played a big role in propping up North Korea's informal and privatized economy, because they helped small traders shuffle goods between the manufacturers and markets. These bicycle riders, in turn, became an informal merchant class.

Chinese investors, in particular, jumped on the huge potential of bicycles. These outsiders were familiar with bikes' economic value in their home country, where they facilitated trade in cities and towns that were heavily populated and had little room for cars. In October 2005, one Chinese businessman set up a bicycle factory near the port city of Nampo, which was praised by two visiting premiers, Kim Jong Il and the Chinese president, Hu Jintao.

Despite the resulting improvements over poverty, women are still not allowed to use bicycles in Pyongyang. In the countryside, though, the ratio of men to women bicycle riders was about even. This was not the result of laxer law enforcement in the countryside but because Pyongyang was supposed to be the developed capital of the revolution with a perfect public transportation system. Bicycles, considered low-tech, did not fit well into the picture and were completely banned until 1992.

When I asked a senior official of the Pyongyang People's Committee, the official name for the city government, to explain this ban, he answered that a senior female party official had been killed in a traffic accident while riding a bicycle. Since then, he said, bicycles were considered "too dangerous for the precious lives of our female comrades."

This law isn't necessarily sexist, but has more to do with the low quality of the roads. On Pyongyang's main roads and few paved streets, cycling is also banned for men. The story was a lovely excuse in response to an embarrassing question. In the future, when more economic pragmatism will prevail, it is highly likely that the ban will also be lifted for women.

A PROLETARIAT SUBWAY

Pyongyangites without their bicycles had access to the well-developed public transportation system. The Pyongyang bus service was both accessible and cheap, costing 10 chon, or 1/10 of a Korean won. With an average monthly salary of 5,000 won (or about $34 at the officially fixed exchange rate, but less than $1 at the black market rate), taking the bus therefore took up less than 1 percent of the budget of, say, a family of four that used it twice every working weekday.

When I first arrived, it was rare to find a bus that traveled between cities; most of the public transportation served mainly Pyongyang. But over the years this scarcity was lifted. Mr. Pang, a trade official of a state company whom I met to hammer out a business deal, did not show up to a planned meeting one day. Just over a week later, when I asked him why he didn't come to the meeting, he answered that he had to go to a funeral in a remote province.

"How did you get there, as I understand there are no buses or trains serving this destination?" I asked.

"If you have a friend who happens to go there, you can go with him," he answered. "If the company happens to send a vehicle there, you may ride in the vehicle. If not, you look for somebody who will bring you there."

"But then you have to pay for the trip?"

"Of course. Many who have a car are willing to bring you anywhere provided it is, moneywise, worthwhile for them."

In my later years in North Korea, I noticed that cars, buses, and trucks in the countryside were becoming even more packed with passengers. The trend was part of a marketing tactic. Drivers and company bosses were looking out for their customers, using their company cars as informal taxis to generate an extra income for themselves and their employer. Government cadres, hoping to make some cash on the side, bought secondhand or even new cars that they registered in the name of their state agency for protection. Some of their profits went to their employer, while they kept the rest for themselves.

Adding to the positive effects of bicycles on the economy, these informal taxi services allowed businesses to expand: they could move bigger loads and bulkier goods from wholesalers and importers to the retail sellers. A small but increasingly potent entrepreneurial middle class emerged. Despite this development, the U.N. World Food Programme and various NGOs kept renewing their annual warnings of looming food crises, claiming that millions of Koreans faced the threat of starvation (see chapter 8).

While foreigners are for the most part not allowed to use public transportation, they are allowed to take the metro, or subway, for a short distance if they bring along state-sanctioned North Korean guides. That said, I couldn't hop on the subway to work every morning, but did hear fascinating things about it from my friends. They believed it was the pride and joy of the capital.

Mr. Kang, an engineer who helped build and maintain the Pyongyang Metro, was sent abroad to observe the subways of other countries. I met him one day at a business meeting. He told me that the Pyongyang Metro is the world's deepest metro, "which we Koreans built with our own techniques, our own materials, and our own efforts under the guidance of our Great Leader. Natural marble and stone of high quality, which one can find in abundant quantities in our country, were used." He added that he had seen no other place where such high-quality building materials and beautiful designs were used.

"Our president said that we were building a metro not for making money, but to help our people to live a civilized and convenient life," he explained, "and that to this end we should not spare money, and thus we constructed the metro in a very solid and modern way, and designed and decorated its inside in a perfect way."

At present there are two operating lines, which is impressive compared to, for instance, Singapore's metro, which has the same number of lines. The first one is the Hyŏksin (Renovation) Line, which spans about 6 miles (10 kilometers) from East to West Pyongyang. The Pyongyang Metro is the only one in the world where stations have names that refer not to nearby geographical locations but to important pillars of the socialist revolution such as renovation, victory, and unity.

The station Samhung (Three Origins), for example, stands for Kim Il Sung's three goals of education—knowledge, morality, and sport—which the governmental Korean Central News Agency explained as follows: "A country can thrive when pupils grow up to be knowledgeable, morally impeccable, and physically strong." In a country full of political symbolism, the Hyŏksin Line wasn't commissioned by chance in 1975. That year was the thirtieth anniversary of the founding of the Korean Workers' Party.

The second one, the Chollima Line, was named after a mythically fast horse from ancient Korean mythology. It is about 7 miles (12 kilometers) long, stretching from North to South Pyongyang. Its construction started in 1968, and the line was opened in 1973, which at the time was a far shorter time than in most countries. It took the capital of Thailand, Bangkok, with resources multiple times those of Pyongyang, seven years to build its 13-mile (21-kilometer)-long underground metro, which opened in 2004.

There was another reason for the sophisticated but highly labor-intensive construction, which benefited from little mechanization, according to the engineer Pang. "Last but not least, and as you are well aware," he proclaimed, "our country has been besieged for decades by hostile foreign forces. If these warmongers launch war on us again, the Pyongyang Metro provides a good shelter for the population of Pyongyang."

I have repeatedly visited the Pyongyang Metro. But like all other foreigners, I was allowed to travel only between Puhŭng station, on the banks of the Taedong River near the Pyongyang Cosmetics Factory, toward Mangyongdae, Kim Il Sung's birthplace, and the next station, called Yonggwang. I couldn't embark alone, but rather had to be accompanied by one or two staff members. For me, a well-off expatriate, a one-way metro ride cost nothing, as my staff paid for the ticket and refused to be refunded by me, because, in their words, "it costs just peanuts."

They were right. For North Koreans, the trip cost a mere $0.003, making it affordable even on the country's lowest salaries. Foreign students studying in Pyongyang were the luckiest of all groups. They were granted access to the whole metro free of charge because they, unlike me and other expatriates, did not have cars for transportation, and taxis would have been out of reach given their tight budgets. It was a show of international solidarity with fraternal socialist or developing countries, where most students came from.

When foreign tourists visited the two permitted stations of the Pyongyang Metro, they sometimes reported North Koreans as being better dressed in those areas than elsewhere in the city—as if a show was being staged for them. This could be a mistaken impression based on their stereotypes of traveling in North Korea. For example, I sometimes gave employees a lift in my car and dropped them at stations that were off limits to outsiders; I never observed that passengers there were dressed any less nicely than at those stops visited by tourists. Neither did my employees change their clothing when they arrived at certain stations.

It's understandable why foreigners (with the exception of foreign students, who are seen as having solidarity), who may be suspected of being spies, cannot travel to most stations. The Pyongyang Metro is an object of national security, subject to the utmost level of secretiveness imposed by the government. The subway gets this veil because it is considered important for the defense of the country, a bomb shelter for Pyongyang residents in case of war. The state fears that foreigners will report this information back to hostile governments such as Japan and the U.S. The metro is even left off maps of Pyongyang.

At the bottom of the Puhŭng station, which is the terminus of the Chollima Line toward the city's south, the end of a corridor reveals thick, steel blast doors—confirming that the metro serves a dual purpose as a bomb shelter. Newspapers are prominently displayed, in particular the *Rodong Sinmun*, and all advertising is absent.

The metro is not only a war refuge, but also a haven where the party portrays the glorious history of the country and the exploits of its leaders; this is because the metro itself is considered an outstanding exploit. The impressive mosaic "The Great Leader Kim Il Sung among Workers," a title that pretty much describes what's happening in the picture, always grabbed my attention, along with the lavish chandeliers hanging from the ceiling.

At the Yonggwang (Glory) station, the architecture gives off a similar totalitarian but awe-striking aura. Huge pillars line the area, displaying what looks like revolutionary victory torches and flames. The torch is a common motif in North Korea, from the torch of Pochonbo, commemorating Kim Il Sung's 1937 guerrilla raid on a town with that name, to the torch of Kangson, symbolizing rapid industrialization and forced collectivization. Most familiar, though, is the torch of Juche, for the victory of Kim Il Sung's independent stand and self-reliance ideology.

A mosaic reveals a panorama of Chonji, or the Lake of Heaven on Paektu Mountain, the mountain near the Chinese border considered to be the mythical cradle of the Korean people (Kim Jong Il was also said to be born there). In another area, a mural depicts the Tower of the Juche Idea in central Pyongyang.

In 2004, I met by chance a railway engineer from the German company Siemens at the bar of a hotel in Pyongyang. He explained to me that the first rolling stock was new and made in China. He said that secondhand train sets were later mainly supplied by the formerly socialist German Democratic Republic (East Germany) as part of a countertrade deal.

Pyongyang also runs a tram system that covers most areas where the metro doesn't venture, such as the western and southern parts of the city. The standard-gauge lines, the classic style around the world, run along Pyongyang's wide streets, including Tongil (Reunification) Boulevard and Kwangbok (Independence) Street. Kim Il Sung presented the first tram line, about 12 miles (20 kilometers) long, on his seventy-ninth birthday in 1991. As with most important construction projects, the Korean People's Army took care of the construction.

Needless to say, the tram lines were finished in a massive effort

Locomotives made in North Korea on display at an exhibition hall in Pyongyang. "We are looking for investors to build a modern factory for 1,000 locomotives," Mr. Lee, a senior official from the railways ministry, told me. "Is that figure not too high?" I inquired. "If there are locomotives left, we can export and sell them abroad!" Mr. Lee answered. It wasn't clear to me how he did the math: to handle a passenger and cargo traffic volume multiple times larger than the total volume of North Korea's in the world's largest railway tunnel beneath the Swiss Alps, called Gotthard Base Tunnel (due to open in 2016), only 29 trains with locomotives were ordered.

by thousands of soldier-builders who worked at what the government called "Chollima speed," a reference to the lightning speed of the Chollima, the fleet horse from Korean mythology. The second tram line, 6 miles (10 kilometers) long, was also finished in a timely manner and put into service a year later on Kim Il Sung's eightieth birthday. He died two years later at the age of eighty-two. The Great Leader always attached great importance to public transport, at least in Pyongyang.

TRAMS IN NEED OF REPAIR

As for all the pomp and circumstance displayed on trams and subways, I realized from watching television what it all meant. On TV shows, public transportation was a recurring motif, a symbol of progress of the socialist civilization. The regime used it to prove to the

A streetcar moves in front of the Pyongyang Maternity Hospital. One January, when the streets were covered by snow and ice, I drove by car every day and at all hours, once even at midnight, to this hospital, where my pregnant wife had to stay for a health problem. It was an impressive place in a country that, surprisingly, has good medical facilities, depending on where you go. Doctors and nurses took care of her extremely well. Her room was heated so well that she had to open the window from time to time. As the shower had only ice-cold water, I brought thermos bottles every day so she could mix cold and hot water and have a warm shower.

Koreans that the workers' paradise had become reality and that they could rely on the party for such efficient and cheap technologies that benefited all.

The first trams had been purchased in 1990 in what was then communist Czechoslovakia, a set of forty-five double-articulated ČKD/Tatra trams. Several hundred more followed in 1991, and then used cars from East Germany were commissioned. After the German reunification, the trams in the formerly socialist East Germany were systematically replaced by new, modern trams. The used trams were meant to be sold to the highest bidder or to be disposed of.

There was considerable interest in these trams. But the German subsidiary of my first employer, the ABB group, lobbied hard against strong competition and successfully got hold of them free of charge. The German government figured it was cheaper to give the rolling stock away for free than to properly dismantle the cars. Therefore,

ABB did not need to convince the German government to give them away, but rather the company had to show authorities it had a better purpose for these trams in a country that desperately needed them.

An ABB division that specialized in producing locomotives, train motors, and drives for trains launched a sort of public relations offensive to get a foothold in this isolated market, a strategy explained to me by Dr. Klaus Wilhelm, a senior executive at ABB Germany in charge of business development. Before dispatching the trams, he ordered the company logo to be prominently displayed in their interiors. The strategy, unfortunately, didn't work: ABB was disappointed to learn that all logos were removed when they arrived in Pyongyang.

Pyongyang's trolley buses were definitely aging and sometimes didn't operate well. But North Koreans don't loathe this inevitable process. The constant scarcity of resources made North Koreans frugal people who cultivated the long working life of their tools. Stars were painted on buses, trucks, and trolley buses to mark every 30,000 miles (50,000 kilometers) of service, a sort of award for longevity. Occasionally I saw buses with fifty stars—signifying a superb 1,550,00 miles (2.5 million kilometers) of service, or sixty-three times the distance around the globe.

Thanks to the rapid development of North Korea's neighbor, China, the city's public transportation became brighter and more colorful. Pyongyang saw the benefits in 2005, when it was granted dozens of used Chinese single- and double-decker buses, free of charge, in a wide range of colors including pink, green, tangerine, and dark blue.

At PyongSu, our resources were extremely tight, but I could afford to purchase a bus in China at a low price. With the low cost came a caveat: the bus didn't offer sufficient heating during harsh winters, and there was no air-conditioning for the very hot summer days. Nevertheless, it was a step forward, making our staff less tired and allowing them to spend a few hours more with their families. Still, I regret not buying a bus with these modern amenities that are considered "normal" anywhere else. My staff deserved these perks.

For the sales team, which had to travel to hospitals, clinics, and pharmacies, I intended to buy motorbikes. But all of these employees were females, and were not allowed to ride motorbikes just as they couldn't ride bicycles. I abandoned the idea and instead made a tightly coordinated travel schedule for them. I hired a minibus to pick them up and drop them off at the visiting points.

Finding good transportation was demanding and a headache. We had to take into account many parameters, such as proximity to hospitals and density of the population in a targeted area. When our then-new company became known to the most sought-after doctors and pharmacists, I freed up resources by reducing promotions in hospitals and shifting the marketing side predominantly to pharmacies. From then on a salesperson—who was usually a trained medical doctor or a pharmacist—could stay in one pharmacy for several hours observing customers, training pharmacy staff, and helping them sell products.

Our transportation and logistics became more straightforward as we became familiar with these pharmaceutical practices. In addition, the health authorities and our staff were relieved when we gave up on the state-owned hospitals. We were the only company—and, to complicate matters, a foreign and North Korean joint venture—that promoted new therapies and pharmaceuticals.

In 2006, the state closed a Chinese-run pharmacy that sold medicine at the entrance of a hospital. It was threatened by the challenge of a privately run pharmacy to the socialist public health system. We considered the move a clear warning to limit our activities, and our readjustment did not come too late.

Chapter 12

Partying, Pyongyang-Style

Great ideology creates great times.

— Kim Jong Il

While living in Africa in the early 1990s, I traveled extensively throughout the west and center of the continent as regional director of a multinational group. I witnessed all sorts of famine, civil war, ethnic violence, violence against women, and street crimes. My house in Abidjan, Ivory Coast, where the company had its regional headquarters, was surrounded by high walls and armed guards.

I was advised by the local police to wake up at a different hour every morning and to take different routes to my office for safety reasons. But one night at 8 P.M., when I dropped a customer off at a lively street on my way home, three thugs forced their way into my car and forced me at gunpoint to drive out of Abidjan. Driving down the streets, we passed civilian and military police commandos, heavily armed with machine guns.

I was afraid of the police more than the gangsters, because if law enforcement saw any criminals, they could shoot indiscriminately regardless of my presence. We finally arrived at a forest where I had to leave my car, wallet, watch, glasses, and clothes, except for my underpants. I was happy they let me go without shooting me. Others haven't been so lucky.

Because of experiences like these, I understand that the problems that afflict North Korea are nothing compared to the misery in other parts of the world. Therefore, I cannot credit the declaration by the prestigious British magazine *The Economist*, in August 2012, of North

Korea as "the worst place on earth." The country toughed its way through serious conundrums in the 1990s, but this judgment is unfair and patronizing to the North Korean people, who have been stone-walled by the international community. North Koreans have learned to make do with what they have, and many of them are happy despite their meager lives.

HIGH TIMES IN PYONGYANG

At a young age North Koreans learn to sing, and they love to do so their entire lives. They even greet foreigners at farms and factories by singing national themes as a choir. This can be quite embarrass-ing for foreigners, who aren't trained to sing as well, when they are asked to sing in turn. Restaurants are also full of highly popular kara-oke rooms. Of course, there are a number of good restaurants besides the many dysfunctional ones that lack funding. Despite the electric-ity blackouts, they're open until 10 or 11 P.M. or sometimes as long as guests are wining and dining.

In high-end North Korean restaurants in Pyongyang and overseas in China, Thailand, Russia, and the United Arab Emirates, the main attractions are the waitresses, who are graduates from the rigorous Pyongyang University of Music and Dance. They are selected for their beauty, grace, and singing skills and usually master at least one musi-cal instrument. Looking splendid in their traditional Korean dresses, "they seem to hover as they glide between tables, effortlessly serving customers or serenading them from the stage or floor," as a foreign journalist described them.

When the first Western-placed North Korean restaurant opened in the Netherlands in 2012, Human Rights Watch (HRW) was quick to condemn it with the usual cliché of famine at home. HRW repre-sentative Wenzel Michalski was quoted in the German news maga-zine *Der Spiegel* as claiming that "while one can enjoy these specialties in Amsterdam, the people in North Korea are starving to death."[1] HRW prefers to exploit the mirage of the total isolation of North

For a holiday, a pair of masked dancers entertain visitors in a public park. Masked dance dramas have a long history in East Asia, and the Korean form is known as talch'um.

Korea rather than admit that the country does have openings to the outside world. Usually, not only are North Korean employees decently treated by foreign restaurant owners during their stay of three years, but they also get a glimpse into the outside world. It is an eye-opening experience for them, and the sort of international exchange that North Korea needs.

North Koreans also love to go on picnics. Family and friends gather at parks on their free days, usually on Sundays, where they lounge around and eat on the grass. Amid laughter, people take part in informal sports competitions and play musical instruments that they bring with them. The locals, it would seem, are not so much different than their southern counterparts after all.

In the capital, the locals have one favorite spot, the Moranbong Park, which is the country's most famous and picturesque one—its name stemming from the peony flower. The landscape is well-known for the Moran and Chongnyu waterfalls, which cascade gently down to the nearby Taedong River. The park is also home to historic relics, including vestiges of the old Pyongyang Castle walls and various ornamental pavilions, in addition to a small zoo and an open-air theater. The pavilions were restored in the recent past and the area was turned into a "workers' park."

Foreign journalists are usually surprised when they visit parks like this one on Sundays, which don't meet with their expectations that the country is full of suffering. Even Jill Dougherty, a seasoned journalist at CNN who was experienced in socialist countries, having studied in the former Soviet Union and worked as the Moscow bureau chief, was taken aback when she arrived. She asked expatriates whether the dancing and singing in the Moranbong Park was a specially staged show for CNN. They responded that the theater can be seen every Sunday regardless of the presence of foreign journalists.

Workplaces regularly organize picnics in parks, just like reasonable companies around the world do to take care of their employees. The PyongSu clique went on picnics from time to time. The gifted musicians among our staff strummed at their guitars and accordions behind the talented singers and dancers, who all entertained us after a good pork and beef barbecue. The rest of the staff merrily danced to the tunes.

Music education is an important part of the school curriculum for Korean children, which is why so many are good at playing an instrument. Playing music after work is another popular pastime for Koreans. In the case of our staff, they regularly remained a little longer at the office to play the guitar and sing together. We also had a ping-pong table inside the company building and a volleyball court outside, which were frequently used after work. Although I often lost, I enjoyed playing ping-pong with my staff from time to time.

At parks and along rivers, men line up to play cards with each other. They also go fishing, and some of them use a primitive fishing setup that has an underwater marker attached to the line, which falls to indicate fish biting. These older fellows enjoy meeting each other to play *janggi*, or Korean chess, a board game widely thought to be derived from the Chinese version, *xiangqi*. The Korean Central News Agency disagreed when it explained that "The origin of the game is still unknown, but it has a long history."[2] These informal games can draw large crowds, enthusiastically following and loudly commenting on the games. While the men pursue competitive endeavors, the women love signing up for dancing courses in which, among other styles, they learn salsa and Latin American moves.

Since the early 2000s, North Korea has been reviving traditional Korean holidays like the Lunar New Year, along with the more contemporary revolutionary holidays. The state is also trying to popularize long-forgotten traditional games such as *yut*, seesaw, and kite flying, a promotional strategy that's meant to block out the alien influences that it fears are a threat.

One of these new national holidays, the Chuseok Festival, takes place on September 12, marking the Korean harvest. Ancestor worship is common on these dates, similar to practices in the south. Groups of family members bring bundles of food to the hills, where they bow to graves and place offerings before them.

Chuseok was banned until 2003, and then it was turned into a one-day holiday rather than a longer festivity: the communist party originally considered the practice to be a feudal tradition incompatible with its utopian ideology, although it allowed visits to ancestors' graveyards starting in 1972. On Chuseok Day, kids fly kites and play a top-spinning game, two other revivals that have become more popular recently.

Neolttwigi, a traditional outdoor game popular with women and girls, is played during this festival, as well as on the Lunar New Year and other dates. Women stand on each side of a seesaw-like board, called a *neol*, and jump, propelling the opposite person into the air. The hobby can be quite a spectacle, because the experienced jumpers do flips and jump rope while in the air. The game was invented by women from Yangban in feudal Korea, who first used it as a method for seeing over the walls that surrounded their homes. During the Choson Dynasty, they were not allowed out of their living compounds.

Korean wrestling, known as *ssireum*, has become popular too, thanks to the government's initiative to start the regularly held National Ssireum Tournament. The winner has for the last decade become a national celebrity after three days of competition every August. The hundred best wrestlers from Pyongyang and each province meet to compete in their weight classes, and the winner is awarded a "grand bull," a gold bull bell, and a diploma.

Soccer is a popular pursuit in North Korea, where the national soccer team became world famous after defeating Italy at the World Cup in 1966. The women's national team became one of Asia's strongest teams after it took home the championship of the Women's Asian Cup twice in the last decade. It's not uncommon to come across youths, inspired by their soccer idols, playing soccer in the numerous parks and sports facilities across the country. For most North Koreans, though, volleyball is a more accessible game because of the courts that dot so many factories and schools. One reason it is probably so popular is because both sexes can play together.

Weightlifting and taekwondo, the Korean martial art, are two other popular sports that give North Korea, contrary to stereotypes, its international prowess. The roots of the martial art go back more than 2000 years, although its modern form has been called taekwondo ("the way of the foot and the fist") since 1955. It is equally popular in North and South Korea, which harbor rival associations. Today, foreign enthusiasts even travel to the country to take taekwondo lessons with some of the country's elite masters. The World Taekwondo Championships, held by the International Taekwon-do Federation in Pyongyang, attract some 800 competitors from more than eighty countries and include corporate sponsors like the Egyptian-invested North Korean telecom Koryolink.

Pyongyang is also home to a beautiful ice rink that from the out-

The Taekwondo building in Pyongyang is designed in a shape symbolic of its sport. I would interpret the architecture to be a reflection of bricks that are supposed to be broken in the sport with a knife-hand strike. In 2012, a much larger modern Taekwondo center was constructed, covering 107,640 square feet (10,000 square meters) and housing a training center, library, conference hall, and history museum.

side looks like an alien spaceship, and its roof is shaped to mimic an ice skating hat. Outside Pyongyang, residents take advantage of their natural environment rather than relying on these creatively designed monoliths. When the wintertime comes, children who cannot afford ice skates build their own by improvising blocks of wood with knife blades stuck into them. They propel themselves along frozen lakes and rivers with sticks.

Unlike adults, the children of Pyongyang did not restrain themselves when approaching foreigners to practice English. They would ask simple questions learned in the classroom, such as "How old are you? What's your name? Where do you come from? Good-bye!" They would then run off.

At the shooting range in Pyongyang, we could fire rifles and pistols with real ammunition, or the more cautious among us could use electronic shooting gear and electronic targets. But contrary to the impression from the Western press, American figures were not the targets. Even though average North Koreans have heard a lot about the supposedly evil Yankees who deserve to be shot, Americans

239

remain an abstract concept for them. Most have never met one. A few times I brought foreign visitors to this place for some shooting practice, all in good fun.

As far as attractions go, the rifle range would ironically be considered less patriotic than the other options. Foreigners cannot visit the cinema and theater located in every city, which show homemade films only. (International films are banned because they could undermine socialist morals and foster decadence.)

Even more spirited is the Museum of the Revolutionary Activities of Comrade Kim Il Sung, a generic museum located in every provincial capital. The exhibits depict the country's revolutionary history, framed along the lines of the exploits of father and son Kim. And finally, revolutionary operas and musicals are commonly performed at the theaters, spectacles that foreigners attend. I watched a couple of revolutionary operas where the heroic Korean people, fighting off Japanese oppressors, were cheered.

BEING CULTURED

Occasionally the government invited foreign musicians to perform their work for North Koreans in the myriad of concert halls and theaters. The Pyongyang Spring Festival, to name one example, was the first of its kind and is today held every other year, allowing North Koreans a glimpse into the outside world of foreign film, theater, and art. The cost was affordable, at 25 to 45 dollars (20 to 30 euros) per performance for foreigners and a smaller amount for locals. Festivities like these show that the regime isn't entirely isolated after all.

On the leaders' birthdays and in particular on important round anniversaries, such as the sixtieth anniversary of the Korean Workers' Party in 2005, there was an atmosphere of festivity. Around town, partygoers sat in front of open-air band concerts, men threw darts at balloons in festival games, and people cheerfully dawdled around food stalls, nibbling away at pancakes, fritters, pizza, and cotton candy.

On Sunday afternoons during the winter, Pyongyangites shuffle

Schoolchildren and students make their way to the Grand People's Study House, which houses millions of books. It also has an extraordinary conveyor belt, a futuristic-looking contraption that brings their choice of patriotic tome straight to their reading table.

Children splash around in central Pyongyang, with a department store on the left. Koreans are called upon in propaganda posters and in training courses to behave with a "revolutionary soldier spirit." Still, the adults passing by did not scold the children for their gamboling. They probably remembered that Kim Il Sung said that "children are the future and we should treat them as kings."

around the roads clearing snow from a ten-lane motorway by hand. During the spring clearing, they clear the Pothong River of silt. It was nothing extraordinary to see schoolboys with brooms and other cleaning implements returning home from another "voluntary" activity, such as, for example, cleaning revolutionary monuments.

Plastered around city walls, propaganda posters heralded the arrival of what they then called "the greatest national holiday: February 16." It was a reference to Kim Jong Il's birthday, and preparations started months in advance. Schoolchildren learned poems and workers learned patriotic songs and dances, all leading up to the festivity. In 2008, for example, the second National Pencil Drawing Festival for schoolchildren was held to celebrate Kim Jong Il's birthday. Even kindergartners participated, and some made drawings entitled "Let's cut the throat of U.S. imperialism!" When the day itself approaches, everybody takes a day off for a picnic and relaxation.

After a selection process, children as young as nine years old can become members of the Young Pioneers. The ceremony takes place on February 16 (Kim Jong Il's birthday), on April 15 (Kim Il Sung's birthday), and on other important national holidays such as National Day on September 9, when the DPRK was founded. Army Day, February 8, signifying the founding of the army, is also a popular day. The awarding of membership is a great event for the child and the family. During a gala celebration at school in the presence of their families, the new Young Pioneers receive their red tie and pin. It is a Korean's first step toward becoming a member of the Korean Workers' Party.

For businesses profitable enough to send their employees on several-day vacations, the Songdowon beach in Wonsan and the Myohyang Mountains are common destinations. The trips usually end with a visit to the International Friendship Palace. This is a large museum displaying gifts presented to the leaders from foreign dignitaries. The Songdowon beach is quaint and charming, although strangely it segregates Koreans from foreigners. Koreans pay a 100 won entrance fee, while foreigners pay the equivalent of about $2.50.

When the beach designated for foreigners is empty, Koreans can loiter there.

In August 2008, the *Pyongyang Times* published a patriotic eulogy to the beach: "Holiday makers cultivate their body and mind there, hardening their resolve to work harder for the socialist country that provides every condition for them to lead a happy life." That statement basically sums up how my colleagues approached the trip, as a chance to relax and reflect so that their resolve was hardened when they returned to the workplace.

In the Myohyang Mountains, the International Friendship Exhibition is the country's elite showcase. It's a large museum with 150 rooms, covering an exhibition area of around 753,475 square feet (70,000 square meters), almost the size of the legendary Greek city-state Troy. The curators proudly display hundreds of thousands of gifts from global leaders, especially prime ministers and presidents from countries of the former Soviet Union and nonaligned countries.

Some of the most entertaining objects? Josef Stalin donated his bullet-proof limousine, Mao Zedong handed over his armored train car, and the U.S. secretary of state Madeleine Albright offered a basketball signed by Michael Jordan. Of course, the museum skews the diplomatic custom of exchanging, rather than only receiving, gifts. The official explanation reads that the lavish souvenirs are "proof of the endless love and respect toward the leaders Kim Il Sung and Kim Jong Il."

ENJOYING THE EXPAT LIFE

At the end of the nineteenth century, Pyongyang, with its many churches and believers, was nicknamed "Jerusalem of the Far East." Even though on paper the North Korean state espouses atheism, the authorities have put up Protestant, Catholic, and Orthodox churches over the past decade for the spiritual needs of expatriates. North Koreans aren't supposed to attend, although they can be spotted there as well.

However, a true Christian believer in today's North Korea would be branded a traitor of the worst kind. During the century before the DPRK was founded, white American Protestants from the Bible belt promoted Christianity as the religion of a superior foreign race, making it today antithetical to the revolution.

Resident foreigners may make use of the services the leading hotels have to offer. The Koryo, Yangak, Changwangsan, and Sosan Hotels all house indoor swimming pools, and some of them even offer massages. The Koryo Hotel, in particular, is known for brewing

The Pyongyang Golf Course is large enough to host an international golf tournament, and will probably do so sometime in the future. With eighteen holes at par 72, it covers 300 acres with 110 acres of green—twice the size of the typical Western course. It can service up to one hundred competitors at a time and is home to many shops, restaurants, conference rooms, and even a sauna—in short, the course looks like an exceptionally large Western country club. When players take breaks, they can take advantage of the angling and boating facilities. In 1987, the ribbon on the course was cut in celebration of Kim Il Sung's seventy-fifth birthday by the pro-DPRK association of Korean residents in Japan known as Chongryon. Tourists can also check out a few mini-courses, such as Yangakdo golf course (recently turned into a new health complex), the Pyongyang golf practice range, the Mount Kumgang course, and the nine-hole Nampo Wawoodo golf course.

beer on site and, along with the Yangak, is home to a revolving restaurant at the top—offering a good view of the Pyongyang skyline.

Since fewer than a third of hotel rooms are occupied during most weeks, foreigners don't need to worry about the hassles of booking a room. In *The Guardian*, a journalist wrote on her 2010 visit that the British Lawnmower Museum has several thousand more visitors than the country of North Korea, which brings in an average of 1,500 Western tourists and up to 10,000 Asian tourists each year.

TOURIST ATTRACTIONS

Following is a brief guide for visiting foreigners and tourists in North Korea.

- Mansudae Grand Monument, usually the first monument a foreigner must visit. Tourists are expected to bow to the 65-feet (20-meter)-tall bronze statue of the eternal president, Kim Il Sung, and the late leader Kim Jong Il. Tens of thousands of North Koreans visit the statues on special occasions to pay their respects.

- Mangyongdae, the birthplace of Kim Il Sung. It is a central pilgrimage site for North Koreans.

- The Arch of Triumph, which is 30 feet (10 meters) higher than the Arc de Triomphe in Paris. This is where Kim Il Sung addressed the Koreans for the first time in 1945 after the liberation from the Japanese occupation.

- Kumsusan Memorial Palace, the former official residence and office of Kim Il Sung. It was transformed into a mausoleum where the embalmed bodies of Kim Il Sung and Kim Jong Il are lying in state inside a clear glass sarcophagus. The mausoleum is much larger than those of Lenin, Mao Zedong, and Ho Chi Minh. Unlike the other mausoleums, it can be visited only with an invitation.

    - Fountain Park
    - Mass games (Arirang)
    - Local park (Moranbong)
    - Amusement park
    - Grand People's Study House
    - Korean Central Art Gallery

- Pyongyang Metro
- Three Revolution Exhibition
- Historic Pyongyang
- Drive to Kaesong, visit Koryo Museum and Panmunjom/DMZ

- Monument to Party Foundation, which consists of a hammer, a sickle, and a writing brush representing workers, farmers, and intellectuals. It is 165 feet (50 meters high), symbolic of its purpose when it was built to mark the fiftieth anniversary of the founding of the ruling Korean Workers' Party.

  - Juche Tower
  - Pyongyang Film Studios
  - Pyongyang Zoo
  - Kim Il Sung Square
  - Tomb of King Kongmin
  - Rotating restaurants on top of Yangak and Koryo Hotels
  - Bar/restaurant on top of TV tower
  - Korean War Museum and the U.S.S. *Pueblo*
  - Pyongyang Golden Lane Bowling Alley
  - Revolutionary Martyrs' Cemetery (where more than one hundred revolutionary martyrs are buried in graves topped by their busts)

- Drive to Myohyangsan, literally meaning "mountain of mysterious fragrance." The pristine surrounding area of hills, mountain trails, and waterfalls is untouched by mass tourism and offers light hiking and barbecue facilities.

  - International Friendship Exhibition
  - Tour on an old steam train
  - Kumgang (Diamond) Mountain at the border with South Korea

- The Chilbosan ("Seven Treasures") mountain, located in North Hamgyong province and popular for its scenic views. One attraction is the Kaesim Temple, dating from the ninth century. Tourists may wander freely in the hills without tour guides, as there is nobody else there.

- Paekdu Mountain, the sacred site for all Koreans. The "Son of the Lord of Heaven" descended to earth and the first Korean kingdom was planted, according to Korean mythology.

- Swimming at the beach of Wonsan or Nampo
- Visit to the West Sea Barrage in Nampo, a huge 5-mile (8-kilo-meter)-long dam with three lock chambers and thirty-six sluices, allowing the passage of ships up to 50,000 tons. North Korea considers this a major accomplishment.
  - Chollima Steelworks, the country's major heavy industry site where the "Juche steel" is made. It was the birthplace of the Chollima movement that continues to drive the economy.
  - Tae'an Heavy Machine Tool Complex, another showcase heavy industry complex where workers can be seen manufacturing shaped steel, turbine components, and other products
  - Tae'an Glass Factory, a state-of-the-art factory set up with Chinese help that produces windows and other glass products for the domestic market. The factory was opened in 2005 in the presence of China's president and North Korea's leader.
  - Ryonggang Hot Spa Guesthouse, 6 miles (10 kilometers) from the port city of Nampo. There is a big main house with restaurant and various rooms and a bath house with large spa bath with very hot salt water gushing out.

Visits to cities like Hamhung and Chongjin, the second- and third-largest cities of North Korea, are now also possible. Visits to Sinuju, Taehungdan county, and Samjiyon, Musan, and Rajin-Song-bong may also be arranged, particularly if the visitors have a professional reason to go there.

Visitors who would like to change their program by adding, for example, a dog meat restaurant or a school, should ask the Korean tour guides immediately upon arrival in Pyongyang so that they can make arrangements with the authorities.

Don't forget to bring your medicine with you, as well as basic items such as tampons, condoms, batteries, and memory sticks for your camera.

Popular shopping spots:

- Stamp shops near Koryo Hotel in Pyongyang and at the Koryo Museum in Kaesong. Prices range from 75 cents to 13 dollars (0.5 to 10 euros) for a collection.

- Postcards can also be bought at the stamp shops. Most book shops also have postcards on sale. Some have a large collection of interesting postcards. A postcard costs 75 cents (0.5 euros) and postage costs from $1.35 (1 euro), although stores take all major worldwide currency. The cards can be sent all over the world. 3-D postcards are particularly popular.

- Posters: some hotels sell posters and the Foreign Languages Bookstore has one of the best selections of posters. Paekho Art Studio also has an excellent selection of posters.

- Artwork can be bought at the Mansudae Art Studio or the Handicraft Exhibition (Min Ye Exhibition Center) and the Paekho Art Studio.

- T-shirts with "Welcome to Pyongyang," etc., can be bought at the Wol Hyang Exhibition Center near the Arch of Triumph and the gift shop at the Grand People's Study House for about 20 dollars (15 euros).

- Books: The Foreign Languages Bookstore in Pyongyang has the best and widest-ranging selection of books. Hotels may have a small choice of books as well.

- Films: The Foreign Languages Bookstore also sells a selection of DPRK movies.

- Ceramics: Mansudae Art Studio and Paekho Art Studio have the best selection of beautiful Korean celadon. Quality pieces are signed by the artist. Handicrafts can also be found at the Kumgangsan Exhibition Center (near the Arch of Triumph), which also sells traditional Korean food.

- Ginseng: Kaesong is famous for growing the country's best ginseng (insam). Ginseng in various forms including in cosmetics can be bought in Kaesong and in souvenir shops in Pyongyang. The best choice can be found at the Daesong Exhibition Hall, run by the company that is the largest ginseng manufacturer.

Another sight is the gigantic mausoleum built for Tangun, the mythical king of the first Kingdom of Korea during the Gojeseon Dynasty from c. 2333 to 237 BCE. It's in a convenient location near

The U.S.S. Pueblo, a lightly armed American ship that was captured in 1968 for, as North Korea claimed, spying in North Korean territorial waters, though others argued the ship was on the high seas. President Lyndon B. Johnson, already dealing with the Vietnam War, immediately denied the charge. After his administration apologized and then admitted in writing that the Pueblo had been spying, Pyongyang released the crew of eighty-two sailors. It was a major propaganda victory for Kim Il Sung: the North Koreans proudly display what they consider to be a symbol of Yankee aggression, and proof of the hostile attitude of the U.S. against them. Today, though, North Korea remains one of the most heavily spied-upon countries. Most of the operations are led by the Pentagon and CIA, which send reconnaissance satellites and aircraft over the country every day.

Pyongyang at the foot of Mount Taebak, where his remains were supposedly found by archaeologists in 1993. Politics and nationalism may overshadow the truth, and as long as no independent scientists can analyze the evidence, we may never know. Koreans believe that the "grandson of heaven," as Tangun is referred to in their mythology, founded the kingdom in 2333 BCE, and that all Koreans can trace their lineage to him. In North Korea, the communist regime at first considered Tangun to be a superstition but later promulgated his story as a historical fact.

Another popular attraction is the Kaeson Youth Park amusement park, which underwent renovation after I first visited it. In 2010, I returned to see six new rides, including the iconic Viking ship, a vertical drop, and a swing carousel like those common at Western carnivals. Every foreigner has an incentive to visit this place: a single roller coaster ride costs 50 won, or a few cents when exchanged at the black market rate. Since my visit, the theme park has set up a Western-style fast food restaurant that sells, to name a few comfort foods, hamburgers and Mexican burritos. The Western meals certainly don't hinder the massive popularity of this place: every day some 5,000 visitors, mainly children, young people, and military personnel, visit it.

There were two more amusement parks in Pyongyang, both more Soviet-style and several decades old. At one of them, open on important holidays only, known as the Mangyongdae Fun Fair, I didn't have the courage, unlike the Koreans, to go on the looping roller coaster. But other foreigners braver than me have tried. Even diplomats know how to have a good time. Because of a photograph that was spread around the Internet, Western journalists chided a British diplomat in 2012 for riding with North Korean officials on a roller coaster at the opening of a new amusement park.

Despite the fun and laughter, Kim Jong Un scolded the groundskeepers at the Mangyongdae Fun Fair in 2012 for poor maintenance, a violation that, predictably, was published by the Korean Central News Agency. "Seeing the weeds grown in between pavement blocks in the compound of the funfair, he, with an irritated look, plucked them up one by one," the mouthpiece wrote. Lately, in addition to declaring that he will bring more food to the people, the young reformer has been moving his country into new festive endeavors. A little more than half a year after taking over, Kim Jong Un inaugurated the newly completed Rungra People's Resort, which includes a water amusement park on Rungra, an islet in the middle of the Taedong River. In the tradition of SeaWorld, the area boasts a dolphinarium.

Westerners tend to assume that as far as hot springs go, Japan is the ultimate place to be. But North Korea is also home to some won-

In summertime, it's common for Koreans to go boating on the Taedong River; dignitaries, tourists, and businesspeople can even enjoy a meal and wine along the waterway. Pictured here, the Indonesian ambassador (far right), the Vietnamese ambassador (second from left), another diplomat, and I enjoy a restaurant cruise.

derful relaxing springs in Onchon, a town on the western coast. The Ryonggang hot springs, as they're called, are a one-hour car drive from Pyongyang and have been a soothing meeting point for a century. Japanese colonial administrators were already relaxing there in the early twentieth century, and today it is a special resort reserved for government officials, foreign guests, and tourists.

Around the area, a welter of villas offers indoor tubs, a restaurant, a karaoke room, and a billiard room. North Korean doctors recommended the place for a visit and explained to me that "the hot water is rich in bromine and radon, two elements that act as therapy for hypertension, arthritis, gastrointestinal disorders, neuralgia, and other diseases."

In the absence of a surfeit of nightclubs and bars, foreigners in Pyongyang can enjoy bonding among the small number of fellow expatriates. One popular hangout was the RAC, the Random Access Club, a sort of tavern based at the World Food Programme (WFP). It got its nickname because it was the only place in North Korea that WFP staff and other aid workers could "randomly" access without much government oversight. And, in a claim to fame, it was the only place in North Korea where foreigners could dance on the tables. In 2012, some French aid workers and a young Belgian employee of a foreign-invested business had the glorious idea of staging a "workers' party" at the RAC. Those participating at this party were asked to dress as North Korean workers. Making fun of laborers, who are a cornerstone of North Korean revolutionary ideology, and the ruling Workers' Party was not amusing to the authorities. The party decided to teach the misguided youths a lesson: visas were not extended for the French aid workers and the young Belgian, who had a residence in Beijing, got a stern warning. More annoying for other expats was the shutdown of the popular RAC. Of course, foreigners do get bored, and many of them leave after a year or so.

North Korean art is indeed regime art, derived from the socialist realism of Stalin's Soviet Union in the 1930s. But the individual character of each piece of artwork is reflected by the artist's skill and sensitivity. The acclaimed "People's Artist" Kim explained to me: "We want to show the positive side of life to make people happy and enjoy our works." His paintings indeed showed merrily dancing kids or a smiling farmer on a tractor in the fields, who he explained was a "hero of daily life." Another of his subjects was a beautiful young woman, who represented the "glorious future of Korea."

You wouldn't find avant-garde paintings here as you would in South Korea; abstract expressionism would clash with socialist realism. Yet North Korean painters do not want to be limited by political reality. They use an impressive traditional repertoire, inspired by traditional Chinese paintings but with their own unique characteristics. The motifs often entail flowers and birds in the countryside, as well as the so-called four gentlemen: bamboo, plum, chrysanthemum, and orchid.

The "Merited Painter" Han showed me his paintings, which included beautiful mountains with high peaks, a popular theme in rugged North Korea. He said, "We would love to show the beauty of our country to people all over the world. I would be happy if you could help us in doing so. If people abroad fall in love with our landscapes, they may desire to visit our country and we could make friends with them."

I had found the dazzling aesthetics I was looking for—the talented North Korean artists who deserved to show their work to the world.

NOTES

1. Von Benjamin Dürr. Nordkorea-Restaurant in Amsterdam: Ein bitterer Beigeschmack. *Der Spiegel*. March 24, 2012. http://www.spiegel.de/reise/europa/erstes-nordkoreanisches-restaurant-in-amsterdam-a-823278.html.
2. Korean Central News Agency. Korean chess. May 23, 2001. http://www.kcna.co.jp/item/2001/200105/news05/23.htm.

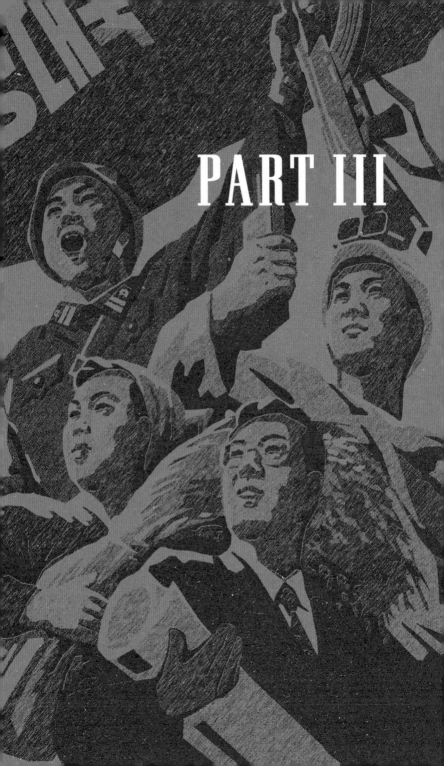

PART III

Chapter 13

The Price of Glory

The Age of Northeast Asia is fast approaching.

— Roh Moo-hyun,
former South Korean president

North Korean and foreign companies constantly feel the pressure of political accusations and sanctions directed at their businesses, even if the evidence is lacking. I remember how this hurt European fund managers who ran the Daedong Credit Bank joint venture, with their 70 percent share ownership.

I knew and worked with the bank's manager, Nigel Cowie, whom I appreciated for his competence and seriousness. The bank offered normal "high street" commercial bank transfers, savings, and credit opportunitites in hard currency, and only to foreign groups and individuals doing business in the DPRK. It was also the first North Korean bank to introduce strict procedures against money laundering and counterfeiting.

In February 2005, $25 million, a substantial part of which belonged to Daedong Credit Bank's commercial customers such as British-American Tobacco (BAT), was frozen. About $2.6 million of that amount belonged to BAT. The U.S. Treasury Department called the Macau-based Banco Delta Asia, where the amount was deposited, a "primary money laundering concern" under the 2002 USA Patriot Act. Under the law, passed after the September 11 attacks, the government could cut off funding to groups that constitute a security risk.[1]

Absurdly, the accusers did not have to substantiate the accusations; the onus, rather, fell on the Daedong Credit Bank to prove its innocence. It did, and the money was released more than a year later. But the economic and reputational damage had already been done.

In August 2011, Nigel Cowie and his foreign colleagues looked like they were fed up with the screws getting so tight. They sold their shares to the Chinese Nice Group, and Cowie resigned as general manager. They declared in a press release that "the decision has been made easier by the general sanctions-laden environment in which financial business here is framed these days."

Unfortunately, Western embargoes did not target illegal activities, but hurt legitimate businesses and drove them underground. The sanctions were misguided, because the real criminals would have been using black market tricks on which sanctions had little effect. Even then, I am not aware of any instance in which the accusers produced any evidence of malfeasance.

As merely one consequence of U.S. policies, large Western banks refuse to carry out any payment transfers from and to North Korea. This creates difficulties for a lawful business to receive money from foreign customers and to send money to overseas suppliers. Small banks in Macau, Mongolia, and Vietnam, for example, were visited by U.S. Treasury officials, who pressured them into ending their business relationships with North Korea. In 2012, one Vietnamese newspaper even reported that Vietnamese diplomats in Pyongyang had to fly to Beijing to receive their regular salary.

Since all U.S. dollar transfers pass through the United States, any payment in that currency from or to Pyongyang can be confiscated in the U.S. Therefore, banks dealing in U.S. dollars refrain from doing business with North Korea, afraid of getting into even the slightest dispute with the U.S. treasury.

Another round of U.N. sanctions, passed in March 2013 in response to North Korea's third nuclear test, targeted the Foreign Trade Bank. It dealt another blow to legitimate businesses as well as the emerging entrepreneurial middle class, who depended on the financial sector to carry out their trade operations.

Legitimate businesses will now have to resort to unconventional business methods to survive. They'll depend on cash couriers, bartering, and an "underground banking" system that the Arab world calls *hawala* and that the Chinese call "chop," "chit," or "flying money." These gray financial markets debit the sellers and credit the buyers living in different countries—without physically moving any money.

Foreign banks are only a slice of the entire population of at-risk businesses. Under the sanction system, pretty much any luxury or high-tech item—mobile phones, alcoholic drinks, and French cheese— are affected. If the international community had exhaustively enforced the measures, all sorts of small shops and restaurants would have had to close during my time there.

Another area of concern is "dual use" products, or anything that is used for both civilian and military purposes. These include chemicals needed for the processing of food items and of pharmaceuticals that can also be used in chemical weapons. Around the world, most motorbikes and cars are made of aluminum alloy. But that compound is banned since it can also be used in ballistic missiles and gas centrifuges. Thankfully, most manufacturers continue to use technologies and materials from the 1960s, so that element of the sanctions hasn't taken a toll. Nonprivileged North Koreans would have to walk instead.

Let's take some more examples of allegations that were completely ungrounded in fact—and were even refuted by other governments. The U.S. has launched a broadside attack on North Korea for supposedly faking U.S. dollar notes and producing illegal drugs. Even if the allegations are to the slightest degree true, the supposed drug trade would probably make up only a few dozen million dollars. Even with that caveat, the allegation makes little logical sense. Compare this amount with the trillions of dollars in wealth packed into the metals and minerals this small country possesses. North Korea could easily exploit these vast natural resources with Chinese help, and doesn't need drug money.

The renowned German bank note expert Klaus Bender, who is no friend of the North Korean regime, has explained why North Korea was not in a position to make fake superdollar notes. Such an operation requires vast technological prowess. Pyongyang lacked the specific type of paper, chemicals, colors, and machines to get the job done. More than 95 percent of currency printing machines are made in Switzerland, and their whereabouts are closely tracked by the Swiss federal police force. This organization has the best experts in the world on bank note forgery, and it unmistakably rejected the U.S. allegations.[2]

In July 2012, the U.N. Security Council released a report on sanctions, according to the AP news agency, which wrote: "No violations involving nuclear, chemical, or biological weapons or ballistic missiles were mentioned in the 74-page report to the Security Council committee monitoring sanctions, published Friday."[3] On the other hand, the document highlighted North Korea's responsibility for illegally imported luxury goods including tobacco, bottles of sake, secondhand pianos, and several secondhand Mercedes Benz cars. It is stunning that these would be considered serious crimes which the Security Council had to urgently address.

I wondered why pianos are illegal. I visited a modern piano factory in Pyongyang, operated by a joint venture established in 1988 between North Korean and Austrian piano builders. The pianos have been exhibited at musical instruments exhibitions in Europe, and the Austrians have even been importing larger quantities of high-quality pianos made in Pyongyang for sale in Europe. They complained that the North Korean-made pianos were subject to 4 percent import taxes by the European Union, whereas pianos from other countries were not subject to any such taxes.[4]

In October 2012, *Bloomberg Businessweek* ran a piece called "Sanctions: How the U.S. Is Hurting Innocent People in Iran." It could teach us a lot about North Korea. It read, "Sometimes the obvious needs to be said: The U.S. is hurting innocent people in Iran. American-led sanctions aimed at stopping Iran's nuclear weapons program are badly damaging the economy of a nation of 75 million people. Prices are climbing so fast that the price of milk jumped 9 percent in a single day last week." "Chicken has become so scarce that when scant supplies become available they prompt riots," it added, quoting *The Economist.*

The reality in Iran is also true in North Korea—or any other country strangled by sanctions.

Pyongyang is not a mafia state, and cornering a country is ethically more questionable than engagement. Foreigners engaging with North Koreans are change agents. The North Koreans are confronted with new ideas that they will observe and test, reject or adopt. As the French economist and writer Frédéric Bastiat once said: "When goods do not cross borders, armies will."

MARKET DEARTH

Every so often I visited factories, cooperative farms, hospitals, and power plants all over North Korea. They were usually in a dilapidated condition. The factories had outdated technology from the 1960s and 1970s and didn't receive enough electricity, spare parts, and raw materials. They also didn't have much-needed working capital, which was not allocated by the state nor sufficiently built up through earnings from direct sales.

Here was the problem, I found. Customers who placed processing orders, because they didn't have cash and materials to process, did not only supply their own, for example, cloth, thread, buttons, and zippers, but even had to pay for all electricity and fuel costs up front. That's a stark contrast to industry practices in, say, Sri Lanka and Vietnam, where a large part of the payment comes after the project is finished. By having to pay up front, most businesspeople would assume they were taking on too much risk for these products in a lightly tested market.

Yet the engineers from foreign companies whom I represented as an agent were amazed by the relatively good quality of the products. It was even more dazzling that they were manufactured under the crushing weight of poverty and sanctions. We were also impressed by how clean and neatly kept the factories were, and how well-maintained and functional the equipment was. Even when factories went idle because of power cuts or material shortages, workers scurried to take care of repair work and cleaning. In short, everyone seemed eager to do their duties.

The North Koreans, like their southern brethren, are hard workers—and it showed. Laborers sometimes stayed overnight and worked weekends without resting, sometimes even for weeks if an urgent project needed to be finished. Workers didn't complain around us about long working hours. I observed this in my North Korean business partners as well as in the factory I was running myself. I must admit, though, that our workers were remunerated substantially better in cash and food.

David Woods, the manager of the Eermel cashmere garment factory in Mongolia, which employs 80 North Korean workers, told the media: "They are hard workers, they don't complain." Approximately 3,000 North Korean workers are already employed in Mongolia, 20,000 in Russia, and about three to four times as many in China, and the numbers are rising, generating dozens of millions of U.S. dollars income for their country. The Pyongyang-based General Corporation for External Construction (GENCO) has built lots of dwellings and public buildings in Kuwait and recently completed the sixty-four-story Al-Fardan Tower in Qatar. The Mansudae and Paekho Art Studios have built numerous monuments and panoramas in more than a dozen countries. They have become renowned for their extremely fast construction time and very competitive low prices.

I always wondered how North Korean workers could pull off these feats with their minuscule salaries. Their monthly salaries were the equivalent of $3 to $4 per month—even less than the minimum hourly wage for South Koreans. Living conditions were anything but luxurious.

Average salaries used to hover at around 70 to 80 won in the 1970s and 1980s and 100 won by the early 2000s. Since 2002, they have remained around 3,000 to 6,000 won. Until the early 1990s there was comprehensive rationing unmatched by other socialist countries, and only one employer, the state. The government distributed food, produced by a then-functional state-controlled agricultural sector, and many other consumer products free of charge to its employees.

Education and health care, accommodations, and transportation were free of charge or cost next to nothing. Salaries constituted mere pocket money to buy things like cigarettes or movie tickets. However, when the socialist rationing system collapsed during the 1990s and the agricultural sector was not able to produce enough food, most people turned to technically illegal free market activities to earn real salaries to pay for food and all other daily necessities—or to barter—for the first time in their lives. That's when a market economy started emerging.

Unfortunately, power outages and other shortages proved to be beyond the control of workers, a hindrance that would block their ability to produce goods. But even if a worker did, in exceptional circumstances, exceed his target and earn 8,000 won, or around $7, thanks to his effort, the income never compensated for the rising living costs. In the mid-2000s, the price of rice fluctuated but generally was about 2,000 won per kilogram, and corn stood at about half the price of rice during the years I lived in North Korea. Compare that to a typical monthly salary of 4,000 to 5,000 won.

Think about it this way: a pair of imported Chinese socks went for 1,000 won, or one-eighth of the typical laborer's monthly salary with added bonuses. How would the average American office clerk, for a comparison, feel about paying $250 for a pair of socks out of a $2,000 monthly salary?

Perhaps this was balanced out by the fact that North Koreans received rice and grain free of charge through the Public Distribution System (PDS). In a rationing of calories, housewives received 300 grams of rice per day, while heavy-duty construction workers and miners were awarded 900 grams. However, the PDS followed through with its promises irregularly, because it depended so heavily on good harvests, food donations, and logistical resources. At times, the state simply did not have enough grain to hand out, especially in rural areas. When it did, the rations were far below the promised quantities. Much of the food aid, contrary to popular belief, was not stolen because it was handed out in the presence of WFP staff.

Koreans simply learned to make do with the situation. In the 1990s, they developed extraordinary skills to get by, such as by opening informal private businesses on the side. Petty trading among the masses led to a quasi-marketization in the world's hitherto most centrally planned economy, according to North Korea historian Andrei Lankov.

Women, in a North Korean socialist tradition, were engaging in trade and countertrade and, with the support of husbands and other family members, ran small-scale household productions that included sewing garments, making furniture and shoes, doing repair work, gathering wild foods for themselves and others, preparing food for sale, running food stalls, doing hairdressing, and growing vegetables on balconies and in gardens and plots elsewhere for their own consumption and for sale in markets. In that sense, to quote Chairman Mao, women really did hold up "half the sky"—or even more!

Even North Korean households became subject to market supply and demand, even if it not on a large scale. Local people made use of every bit of space in their rural households, which typically consisted of 1,075 square feet (100 square meters) on average. Every plot of land was cultivated with vegetables and fruit as well as small livestock such as chickens, rabbits, and pigs, and the much larger private plots on slopes were also exploited as much as possible (because flat, accessible land was reserved for state enterprises). Unlike state-collectivized farms, which were subject to currency exchange and import restrictions, private households could get what they needed with the Korean won.

The prices for these items were not state-pegged, so families could take a profit and reinvest it in more baby animals and feed. It was the state farms that were tied down by these measures, which made them unable to compete in markets and to produce more. Having recognized this, Kim Jong Un worked out a new agricultural policy in 2012 addressing some of these problems. Indeed, farmers were told in July 2012 that the state would henceforth take only 70 percent instead of 100 percent from their entire harvest.

Even the most ardent of state companies turned to the markets and private traders for raw materials and other items. Almost everybody seemed to be involved in some private business, not only the neediest families but also wives of party and government officials, who combined entrepreneurship with knowledge from their state connections. It is an East Asian route of economic development in which elites unavoidably enrich themselves while at the same time allowing a middle class to develop and poverty to decline.

As in many parts of Asia, a lot of men are heavy smokers, a pastime that cuts into their seemingly small salaries. But maybe they're not *that* small: the most popular cigarette brand in North Korea is Craven A, made by a joint venture factory, a pack of which sold in markets for 1,500 won. How could they afford packs of cigarettes costing half their monthly salary if they did not have a substantial extra "private" income? If we assume that at least three quarters of the population lives on income from private economic activities, the actual GDP could be more than double the official one.

AID DEPENDENCY

In spite of the rapid changes under way in North Korea, the community of humanitarian do-gooders that played an important role during the famine was not open to market thinking. I began representing ABB every Friday morning at the WFP building's interagency meeting, where representatives of U.N. organizations, EU aid programs, and NGOs discussed their activities and plans of action. The Swedish ambassador introduced me there; it therefore seemed reasonable that we could get involved in some meaningful smaller, decentralized infrastructure projects like supplying solar power and pumping clean water.

I went to the next few meetings, listening to the discussions without saying anything. At the end of one meeting, the presiding U.N.

official took me aside to tell me that he and others felt uncomfortable in the presence of the representative of a for-profit company. My presence, he claimed, set a precedent for other companies to come to the meetings, which were intended for nonprofits. His concern was frivolous. With so few foreign companies operating in North Korea, there was a minuscule risk that the private sector would overwhelm them—and among that group, I was the only one who expressed interest in these meetings.

The real dilemma was that the aid community was holed up in an intellectual silo. Humanitarian organizations, for all the help they offer, thrive on human misery. They also considered our interests to be at odds with theirs. As has happened in Cambodia and parts of Africa, the organizations would have preferred to create a "culture of dependence," a point that the North Korean government was correct about in its statements. After all, many well-paid jobs depended on their continued presence.

Businesspeople, on the other hand, pursued a different strategy, what the French sociologist Alexis de Tocqueville called "enlightened self-interest." In this case, it was the tendency of businesses to want to inject true, sustainable reforms in North Korea, creating a feedback loop in which profits return to them later. But the aid organizations had every interest in doing the opposite: they originally intended to offer emergency assistance to a country at rock bottom and then leave when no longer needed. But they were cementing the status quo to make themselves indispensable. And that's why we were serious competitors.

There may have been other reasons that businesspeople were unwelcome in their eyes. Neither I, as the ABB representative, nor any other Western company representatives were ever in a position to sell anything to them, as far as I know. Although I could compete in terms of quality and price with Chinese suppliers, my competitive disadvantage in the eyes of aid workers busily traveling back and forth to China must have been my signature on an ABB compliance paper. This prohibited me from paying kickbacks to my customers in exchange for contracts. Resident aid workers, on the other hand, had funds from their donors to buy water pumps, generators, tractors, and the like. They preferred to buy all this from suppliers in China, who generously entertained them.

The aid industry, moreover, distinguished itself from commercial industries in its inefficient allocation of resources. For example, PyongSu had been visited three times over one and a half years by WHO inspectors, demanding to see evidence of changes in accordance with the GMP standards. When after two years the WHO at long last confirmed that we were fully GMP compliant, I asked UNICEF to purchase from us on competitive terms. But UNICEF refused, and wanted to send its own inspectors to start the whole procedure anew, possibly to maintain the cozy relationship with its existing suppliers. Such costly exercises ate away at donated funds, which were being diverted from the needy.

Another time, the country director of the Swiss Agency for Development and Cooperation, which sponsored the Pyongyang Business School, told me to reduce the small budget for paper and pencils given to students. He then cut the budget for the publication and distribution of seminar texts for North Korean companies, government agencies, and universities. The same year he bought at least six new vehicles, mostly Toyota Land Cruisers, for the staff—at a cost exceeding by far the total budget of the Pyongyang Business School. Our annual budget was less than $250,000, while the new cars must have cost far more. In this case, Swiss taxpayer money did not reach the intended beneficiaries, but was once again spent on comfortably maintaining an organization for the sake of itself.

My experience in North Korea convinced me that I would never again donate money to a U.N.-affiliated bureaucracy. Rather, I'd be generous with the Bill and Melinda Gates Foundation and George Soros's foundations, in which I believe bureaucracy is kept to a minimum and effectiveness is high; their founders, who are private businesspeople, built their careers on cost-effectiveness and efficiency and won't tolerate waste.

A few specialists have observed this tendency. "The foundation has brought a new vigour," said Michael Edwards, a veteran charity commentator, in *The Guardian* in 2010. Seth Berkley, head of the International Aids Vaccine Initiative [IAVI], agreed, stating, "The foundation has the advantage of speed and flexibility. When they want to, they can move quickly, unlike many other large bureaucracies."

I also came to know that smaller religious NGOs were far more efficient than the big organizations. They gave me insight by comparing their budgets with those of larger organizations. Every dollar spent by one particular religious NGO, for example, yielded 2.5 times the results of a dollar spent by larger organizations, although I promised I would not quote their names.

From the viewpoint of the Workers' Party, the days of humanitarian aid are numbered. Unlike the parties of the former Soviet bloc, the Korean Workers' Party developed an unmatched ability to instill a sense of security—a fervor for national unity, if you will—despite the enormous affliction of shortages and famine. Its general secretary was legitimately considered a wise, fatherly leader and protector. Astoundingly, I never came across people who would have criticized or even challenged the system, nor did I meet expatriates who had heard about such cases. When North Koreans did talk shyly about minor shortcomings, they did not tie their opinion into a more grandiose hope for political change.

Put yourself in the shoes of the average North Korean, and the unity behind the party seems even more remarkable. Low incomes did not offer villagers and laborers an incentive to work hard. Workers were motivated by having their patriotic feelings called upon and having them work for lofty goals such the construction of a "socialist workers' paradise" or a *gangseong daeguk*, meaning a "strong and prosperous nation."

Interestingly, the South Korean president and strongman Park Chung-hee wanted his country to become a strong and prosperous nation too, when in 1970 he launched the New Community Movement. Diligence, self-help, and cooperation were then popular propaganda slogans, which sounded similar to those in the North. There was not just a geographical proximity between northerners and southerners but also one in spirit.

TECHNO-FETISH

In 2003, I traveled with a North Korean delegation to the Kiruna mine in Sweden, the largest iron ore mine in the world. Accompanying me was the director of North Korea's Musan Mine, which is Asia's largest iron ore mine. He was impressed not so much by the sheer size of the place but by its technological savvy. In a scene that would be appropriate in *2001: A Space Odyssey*, the miners sat in air-conditioned rooms looking at monitors, from which they directed unmanned excavators and trains.

North Koreans are "techno-fetishists." They believe that advanced technology can help solve any problem, regardless of whether the technology makes sense economically. Chinese investors and buyers of mining products, on the other hand, usually wanted to buy cheap secondhand equipment for the mines they wanted to exploit. From an economic point of view this made perfect sense, ensuring a relatively faster and lower-risk return on investment.

In short, the two positions were not reconcilable: North Korean techno-fetishists were interested in high-tech gadgets, while the Chinese businesspeople placed profits at the forefront. Since the North Koreans had the last word, cheap, at times secondhand and non-state-of-the-art equipment was rejected.

As the representative of mining equipment manufacturers like Sandvik, I urged the North Koreans to equip the mines with technologies that would outlast the short term, during which the Chinese investors would exploit the mine and then leave. If the Chinese had their way, after the contract expired the North Koreans would not be able to work the mine for much longer, thanks to wear and tear of the cheaper equipment. The Chinese miners, in the end, begrudgingly bought our equipment.

THE SOPHISTICATION OF NORTH KOREAN BUSINESSES

Contrary to popular belief, not everything in North Korea is ordered top-down, an assertion that critics argue makes private business competition impossible. Many North Korean companies pursued their own opportunities regardless of what their supperiors in the government wanted. For example, I drank cola drinks from bottles that looked like and tasted similar to Coke. At least two North Korean beverage producers were in that market, and they were indeed competing for the loyalty of their customers.

A senior official at the State Planning Commission told me that "a healthy competition between manufacturers within the socialist planned economy is not unwelcome." Competition among them was lively. In rural towns and villages one could see "compost competition production charts" showing the results of competing neighborhood units racing to collect kitchen waste, mud, and even human excrement to produce compost.

Although they were not supposed to reveal "unhealthy" rivalry in front of foreigners, enterprises had difficulty hiding how fiercely they were competing for foreign customers.

And of course, most if not all North Korean companies were interested in selling products to foreign companies. In April 2012, Kim Jong Un acknowledged in a landmark speech that he would make sure that North Koreans "will never have to tighten their belts again." Indeed, ever since his succession, a number of economically oriented policy advisors have risen to power. This will lead to more streamlining of the bureaucracy and the creation of a more investor-friendly environment.

I have met some of these new bureaucrats, whom I consider to be clearly pro-business and pro-growth. A few small changes have already been made in market policy: more flexible opening hours are allowed for markets, and more companies are permitted to interact with businesses abroad. These have led to changes in light industry and economic development in the broader sense.

In an interview in Pyongyang with the Associated Press's new Pyongyang bureau, Yang Hyong Sop, vice president of the Presidium of the Supreme People's Assembly, said that "Kim Jong Un is focusing on building a knowledge-based economy and looking into cases of other countries' economic reform, including China's."

It's telling that the taboo word "reform" was used by a top official just a few weeks after Kim Jong Un took power. Later, Kim Jong Un also stressed the importance of using the Internet to "find more data on international trends and advanced science and technology from other countries." He went on to proclaim, "We need to send delegations to other countries to learn more about what we need and have them gather a lot of references."

Over the years, I always found army-run enterprises to be most efficient at getting things done. Especially in the area of mining, they were resourceful: one major cost in those operations is the transport of extracted products from mine to ports. But in some instances the transportation infrastructure was crumbling. Only the military had the resources and manpower to swiftly construct tunnels, bridges, and ports—a financially extravagant undertaking. With non-army enterprises as partners, getting anything done took longer, and hiring construction companies was too expensive.

At other times, though, this compartmentalization of the economy was a drawback. On behalf of PyongSu, I once opened a foreign currency bank account with the Daedong Credit Bank, but one day the cabinet, which consisted of ministers who reported to the prime minister, decided to consolidate the scarce foreign currency from various banks into its Foreign Trade Bank. While I understood that this measure was intended to give the government a more efficient command over scarce hard currencies, I still opposed it because it had too much potential to hurt PyongSu.

Here was the problem. The bank exchanged all foreign hard currency at the official rate for won, pledging that it would transfer the cash back into foreign currency again at the same exchange rate when needed. The dictum sounded good on paper, but the official exchange rate was significantly worse for PyongSu than the more lucrative black market rate—and the dollar-to-won gap widened almost every day. It was only a matter of time before a massive depreciation would be ordered, with the risk that my business would lose most of the value originally deposited in the foreign currency.

The government's order applied to its own companies, but not to companies and banks under the party and the army. This was because there were three self-contained economies: the civilian economy under the civilian government, the army's economy under the National Defense Commission, and the party economy under the Central Committee. This has led to unproductive frictions, and Kim Jong Un has started shifting economic decision making away from the party and army and to the cabinet headed by the prime minister. And that's not all: even a number of military companies were recently moved away from the army and are now under civilian government control—an amazing move for a country with an "army first" policy.

All foreign groups operating under the cabinet, which reported directly to the prime minister, obeyed and closed their bank accounts with the Daedong Credit Bank. But all other entities not operating under the cabinet could keep their bank accounts with the Daedong Credit Bank, which was operating under the purview of the party.

PyongSu, which reported partially to the Ministry of Public Health under the cabinet, was the last one to move its account to the Foreign Trade Bank. That was more than a year after I sent a letter to the Minister of Finance explaining my reasons for objecting, including my argument that the measure dealt a blow to this foreign-invested bank and would discourage potential investors in North Korea.

WHY NORTH KOREA IS NOT YET AN "EMERGING MARKET"

For a foreign business, North Korea is home to a limited domestic market, with a similarly small growth potential. So the domestic market is not attractive for foreign companies in the way Vietnam and China are—at least not in the foreseeable future.

On the other hand, North Korea is competitive for its processing activities in garments, shoes, and bags. Investors supply the cloth, leather, and any accessories, and the North Korean contractor returns finished products. The effect of power shortages is, strangely, not the foremost problem in this industry: to sidestep this problem, smart Chinese investors have brought in, for example, manual sewing machines.

The same goes for the extraction of minerals and metals, which are abundant in North Korea. The financier supplies the equipment, and mining products are sent back in return. Low- to medium-technology items, encompassing artificial flowers, dentures, furniture, and toys, can be a good investment as well. Indeed, such items are already being produced on behalf of foreign investors.

North Korea also harbors an extraordinary number of untapped mathematicians and engineers, making IT a particularly promising industry. The country's first and only software joint venture, Nosotek, of which I was a cofounder, churned out windfall profits shortly after it was founded in July 2007. Less than one year later one of its iPhone games even made it to the peak of Apple's top 10 best-selling iPhone games list in Germany. Of course, stating the name of that application could bring disrepute to the company, so it will remain anonymous.

The most significant overhead cost for any North Korean operation is foreign managers and technicians. But North Koreans are quick learners, meaning this high cost can be minimized quickly. When I left PyongSu, the local managers and staff were able to run the show alone—through the entire process of manufacturing, importing, wholesaling, and setting up new retail outlets. A thirty-year-old man with a degree in Oriental language studies followed me to act as the "economic conscience" of the foreign investors, a sort of messenger from the inside of North Korea. Neither a pharmaceutical background nor industry and management experience nor even a basic business education was a prerequisite any longer.

A HISTORY OF THE NORTH KOREAN ECONOMY

In 1984, the first law on foreign investment was passed, allowing foreigners to set up factories with majority ownership. The change was prompted by the decline of the economy and of Soviet subsidies. In 1992, the Supreme People's Assembly adopted three laws allowing and regulating foreign investment: the Foreign Investment Law, the Foreign Enterprise Law, and the Joint Venture Law. More relevant laws and regulations including special provisions for trade zones and tax breaks and reductions, several dozen in total, were added over the years, and existing laws have been adjusted and refined, usually in favor of foreign businesses. The laws provide the legal framework within which foreign investors can operate, and define the allowed areas of investment, along with the rights and the obligations of the foreign investors.

What's interesting is that, going against the grain of stereotypes, a few companies and NGOs have won court cases against politically connected North Korean groups.

The North Korean website Naenara used to publish the most important laws related to foreign business and investment, but was closed. Foreign investors can get an updated CD with the relevant laws and regulations from the DPRK Chamber of Commerce, which has its office at the Ministry of Foreign Trade. Businesspeople may write there and ask how to get the CD. They may also ask to be invited to visit the chamber of commerce for a briefing. Alternatively, they may ask the DPRK embassy in their resident country to get the CD on their behalf against payment.

How difficult is it to do business in North Korea? It depends on the expectations, industry, and choices of the investor. First, you need a North Korean partner for your business, as you cannot practically conduct business without one. Second, you have to be meticulous in finding the right one for success.

When you first visit Pyongyang on a fact-finding mission, you will come across people who want to introduce you to a specific busi-

A Chinese-invested shopping mall with its name in red Korean letters and underneath in gray Chinese letters.

ness partner, and in some cases that person will be themselves. Of course, they almost always have a vested interest and most likely will not introduce you to more suitable business partners.

But you need to know that in every industry there are companies of different sizes and competence levels and with different ranges of products, distribution networks, and levels of competitiveness. Therefore, you have to insist on having a reasonable choice from where you select a partner, or else there's a risk that your investment will turn sour. You should also know your joint venture partner and his thinking before pouring money into any venture. The expatriate manager you will send to North Korea should not only be professionally competent but should be able to cope with a highly demanding and exotic business environment.

Some marketers have, perhaps unfairly, exploited the "Made in North Korea" label in a twisted way. For example, North Korean factories produce millions of trousers, including jeans, for export every year. But since this North Korean industry is hardly known to the outside world, three young, clever Swedish advertising executives were able to achieve a gimmicky kind of glory. They placed a small order for 1,000 pairs of jeans, which filled one tenth of a 20-foot (6-meter) container, and sold them in Europe. International news media like Reuters and BBC eagerly broadcast the story around the globe. No regular repeat orders ensued from it. But that was not the intention in the first place.

While I met a number of risk-averse leaders of socialist bureaucracies, I also met young company heads with sharp business acumen. One bright fellow was Dr. Jon Sung Hun, the president of Pugang, one of the country's largest state-run corporations. His group, founded in 1979, had capital of $20 million and eight business divisions spread across many industries, such as mining, electronics, pharmaceuticals, coins, glassware, machinery, and drinking water factories. Collectively, Pugang realized annual revenue from sales of more than $150 million.

The group had sales offices or agents all over the world, in Germany, Bulgaria, Egypt, Ethiopia, and Malaysia, to name some of its prime markets. In parts of China it was able to build a strong brand for its mineral water, Hwangchiryong, which it sold at twice the price of France's Evian. In its marketing it emphasized North Korea's peerless clean natural environment, which was the source of the water.

When companies made good products, like natural perfumes, they were sometimes not aware of the importance of design and packaging. Over time, younger, better-trained, and more dynamic and competitive managers designed new and more attractive products better suited to the tastes of an international clientele, like these alcoholic beverages.

Pugang also promoted its interestingly named "Royal Blood-Fresh," which, for $39 per 160-tablet bottle, claimed to be a traditional health formula created "from fermented soybeans of the old royal palace" that would "make you younger and cleverer. Students' results are better on exams." The way the product was marketed impressed even old Chinese marketers, regardless of whether all the claims can be scientifically proven.

Dr. Jon was indeed gifted at salesmanship. At Pugang's booth at the yearly Pyongyang International Trade Fair, he attracted the most visitors, and he himself regularly manned the booth to fire up his sales team. Once I met him and his wife on a Sunday by chance in the "Argentina shop," a retail outlet that got its nickname from the fact that a former Swiss Nestle executive supplied it with goods from Argentina.

He pointed out that Pugang's products were on sale there, and the company's advertisements were plastered on the shelves. The man was on a mission: he was visiting in person—a rarity for large corporations—to check the sales of his company's products and to compare them with those of his competitors.

Perhaps Dr. Jon's charisma owes to his upbringing and career background. Before turning to business, Dr. Jon was an English professor at the Kim Il Sung University. He speaks not only perfect English but also Chinese. He grew up with his family in Beijing because his father was the ambassador to China. He comes from a family of thriving sales pitchmen: his brother, whom I also met, was nicknamed in North Korean business circles "Rockefeller of Pyongyang," in reference to his slick skill at running his oil business.

THE DEBT DILEMMA

At ABB, our biggest challenge was the lack of funds for infrastructure and industry rehabilitation projects. Unfortunately, the DPRK could not fund these projects by itself. The government was already struggling with chronic trade and payment deficits and foreign debts exceeding $10 billion, according to a 2001 estimate by the CIA *World Factbook*. I saw the need to minimize any sort of external funding and make the business sustainable, so I negotiated several joint ventures for low-tech items, like electrical cables, power capacitors, and transformers. My idea was that North Korea could have produced them more cheaply than in ABB factories in other "emerging markets."

To release ourselves from the need for outside financing, we had to quickly find potential customers with the rare luxury of a hard currency income—an amenity usually reserved for export-oriented industries like mining. North Korea's maritime fleet became such a customer, buying equipment and spare parts for between $500,000 and $1 million a year.

The fleet, which earned revenue in hard currency from foreign customers for their transportation services, had bank accounts in foreign currency abroad. When we sold products, like ABB turbochargers for example, the North Korean vessels would pay us against a simple invoice from these foreign bank accounts. The profit margin on sales of spare parts, in particular, sometimes reflected a markup of 100 percent, meaning it was so high that it exceeded the entire cost of running the ABB representative office, including my salary. The shipping revenues were extraordinary because the fleet, comprising a few dozen vessels, sailed around the world picking up all kinds of products at different destinations and shipping them to other destinations. Customers could be Chinese, other Asian, Arab, or Western companies.

Our company, however, later turned out to have a desperate financial situation that I didn't know about at first. It turned out that the group was not able to outsource some of its products to low-cost North Korea nor to help prefinance and supply, in the North Korean tradition, some smaller "reference" infrastructure projects in the form of supplier credits to get an edge over our competitors. In the absence of a cover for our export risk, commercial banks in industrial countries where ABB had factories, such as in Germany, Switzerland, and Poland, refused to give export credits to our shipments.

Of course, ABB wanted to sell products and services in North Korea as it did in dozens of other countries, regardless of whether it had a factory there or not. Even for the planned joint venture factories, we were interested in exporting some products made by ABB factories elsewhere. Only a few low-technology products could have been made in North Korea, and the rest would have to be procured from ABB factories in other countries. My idea was that the planned joint venture factories could partly have paid for the imports from ABB factories abroad, using their exports.

INFRASTRUCTURE WOES

When Pyongyang's Russian-built water supply and drainage system had to be overhauled, as it suffered from leakage and water losses of around 50 percent, according to the government, the state made an international tender call for a project that would turn out to be ill-fated. The Kuwait Fund offered $20 million to fund the undertaking—an ironic donor, considering the country was (as it is today) a close ally of the U.S.

In fact, it was the only institution prepared to lend money to the North Koreans. Perhaps Kuwait had only a charitable agenda, but its ally may well have had a burning interest in getting to know North Korea's capital better. What would have been better than a large infrastructure project across the city? Kuwait, of course, still owes its friend and ally a few favors since it was liberated from Saddam's army.

At ABB, we were familiar with the Australian consulting firm that managed the project on behalf of the Kuwait Fund and the Pyongyang People's Committee. In an attempt to get that contract, my Korean staff tapped into their contacts who would lead us to the government decision makers. We fed the People's Committee with technical information on the project's centerpiece, our supervisory control and data acquisition (SCADA) system for the water purification system, which I was hoping they would agree to use. My staff and I were sure that we would win this tender.

But once again, trade embargoes got in the way. The SCADA system runs on PCs with Microsoft software, causing our company's head of this division to get nervous about participating in the tender competition with an offer. The consequences could be disastrous for his portfolio in the U.S. if the government chose to enforce sanctions.

I argued that the American software constituted only a minuscule portion of the whole scope of supply, and that they should ask for a formal permit to get U.S. approval. This move would have likely been no problem, as Microsoft software didn't constitute technology that could be used for military purposes. They replied that it would take a long time for the request to move through the cumbersome bureaucracy in Washington. It was a loss for us and for North Korea, and one that made my staff furious after all their long hours that went into marketing our idea.

In 2003, ABB and British-American Tobacco were the only multinationals with expatriate staff active in the country. But at the same time, ABB got into deeper financial troubles and had to cut costs so it could save $800 million in expenses. The company immediately closed down dozens of factories and offices around the globe. Our North Korean office covered costs just fine, but apparently this market wasn't a priority: headquarters shut down our office. The corporation also signed a cost-effective agency agreement with me that ABB cancelled after five years.

Like other multinational groups, it was afraid of getting into trouble with the U.S. government. The sharply rising rhetoric and the pressure on the "axis of evil" that included Iran, Saddam's Iraq, and North Korea had become too strong for a company with a very large business in the U.S.

The large majority of foreigners doing business with North Korea were Chinese, often of Korean origin. There was hardly any business field where not at least one Chinese company was active. Together with North Koreans, they were running shops, restaurants, gas stations, fish ponds, furniture factories, garment production, greenhouses, bicycle manufacturing, mining, and just about anything else possible.

In a survey carried out by the U.S. scholars Stephan Haggard and Marcus Noland in 2007, of 250 Chinese businesses operating in North Korea, 88 percent said they were turning out profits. The majority also admitted to paying bribes. Although Chinese businesses routinely face difficulties, most said they would persist and hope for economic liberalization.

This level of profitable enterprises is indeed surprisingly high, and certainly higher than that of non-Chinese foreign as well as South Korean companies doing business in North Korea. From time to time I bumped into my friend Joe (a Chinese businessman from the Chinese border city Dandung and then a resident of Pyongyang, who had been running a large garment operation in North Korea for more than a decade) at the dancing hall of the Health Club restaurant, which was one of the few places expats went for eating and meeting.

Later in the evening, after Joe's blood alcohol level had sharply risen, he used to complain about quality and reliability problems he faced. He said that he would like to give up and start another business in another country, particularly when a customer from a foreign country had just returned containers with finished goods. Obviously Joe could somehow cope with these worries, as I heard his story again and again for several years until he was finally gone. I missed him, and his departure made me question if I myself would be able to successfully run a business over a longer time if such a smart and experienced Chinese businessman found it necessary to quit. There were some Chinese businesspeople even less fortunate than Joe, who told me that their North Korean counterparts were exploiters and cheaters.

I met a large number of other Chinese businesspeople—often of Korean descent—who all had their grievances, for example, not being paid on time or not being paid at all by their customers, but were mostly happy with the way they did business. From time to time I saw new faces, and some familiar faces disappeared.

I rejected most North Korean business proposals. I was not sure if the buyers would ever pay me. Much to my surprise, my Chinese competitors often took risks, based on the naïve assumption that state-owned companies would pay them at some point. They realized greater sales but with less overall profit. Sometimes that came with a big loss.

Still, I met both honest and dishonest North Korean business-people and officials, just as in other countries where I have worked. But there is no doubt that honesty and integrity are much more decisive factors for success in North Korea than in industrialized Western countries, where it is easier to legally pursue wrongdoings.

To help sort out the black from the white sheep, I hired a younger North Korean man. He worked as a "scout" who identified business opportunities, along with the profiles and shortcomings of potential business partners. He was well connected and could avoid the risk of being suspected as a spy. He himself was a sincere person, who once told me that not only are the competence and resources of a North Korean business partner important, but that "it is even more important in our country to find honest business partners. Korean companies, too, are wary of other Korean companies not respecting contracts."

It's perhaps the inexperience, boldness, and lack of due diligence that brought the Xiyang Group Co., from China's Liaoning province, into deep trouble.[5] The privately owned company produces and distributes magnetite products and steel in its own steel mills, as well as fertilizer. In 2007, the company became North Korea's largest foreign investor, putting forth $37 million for an ore processing plant, which corresponded to 70 percent of the total investment. Its North Korean joint venture partner supplied the land, which with the iron ore corresponded to the remaining 30 percent.

In 2011, a few months after the plant started processing iron ore, the North Korean partner demanded sixteen modifications to the contract. The new scheme included 4 to 10 percent of sales revenues for the finished products for the raw materials, $1.24 for every square meter of land leased, and $0.17 for every cubic meter of the seawater used in production. Xiyang refused to compromise and its Chinese workers were deported to the Chinese border. Xiyang publicly accused North Korea of stealing its ore dressing facility.

From the ensuing public debate between the North Korean Central News Agency and the company, it appeared as if the Chinese company may not have fully respected its contractual obligations either, since the North Korean side accused it of having implemented only half the agreed investment. Whatever the truth is, the precautions I took for my much smaller ventures must have prevented me from getting into similar trouble.

NOTES

1. Kevin G. Hall. U.S. counterfeiting charges against N. Korea based on shaky evidence. McClatchyDC. January 10, 2008. http://www. mcclatchydc.com/2008/01/10/24521/us-counterfeiting-charges-against. html.

2. Kevin G. Hall. Swiss authorities question U.S. counterfeiting charges against North Korea. McClatchyDC. May 22, 2007. http://www. mcclatchydc.com/2007/05/22/16472/swiss-authorities-question-us.html.

3. Associated Press. UN report: NKorea violating sanctions. 7News WSVN. July 2, 2012. http://www.wsvn.com/news/articles/world/ 21007894897051/un-report-nkorea-violating-sanctions/.

4. Pyongyang Square. Economy: US consultants for Kaesong. February 2004. http://www.pyongyangsquare.com/updates.html.

5. Pakistan Defence Forum. http://www.defence.pk/forums/world-affairs/201069-north-korea-kicks-out-chinese-company-after-completion-factory.html.

The Loss of Innocence

I came here because I wanted to see you.

— South Korean president Kim Dae-jung, in a statement
to the North Korean people upon arriving in Pyongyang
in June 2000 for the first inter-Korean summit.

Throughout the history of the peninsula, South Koreans born in the north, along with wealthy businesspeople, have attempted numerous pet projects to bring both sides together. The first North Korea-born engagement leader was Chung Ju Yung, the founder of the Hyundai business conglomerate and the most famous businessman in Korean history, who passed away in 2001.

The second was Sun Myung Moon, a businessman who founded the Unification Church and passed away in September 2012. Both were able to make use of their North Korean connections, and their heritage, by propping up sizable investments in North Korea worth somewhere between $1 billion and $2 billion (although the exact figures haven't been made public).

In 1998, Chung made worldwide headlines when he sent 1,001 cows from the South over the DMZ to the North. He hoped to make up for a single cow he had stolen from his father decades ago and to repay the debt as a gesture of Confucian-style deference. The animal indirectly created his fortune: after selling the cow, the young and poor Chung had the money to buy a train ticket south and escape poverty in the North. "I was repaying North Korea 1,000 times over for the 'loan' of a cow I had 'borrowed' from my father to pay for my ticket south," he told *The New York Times*.

Chung founded Hyundai in 1946 in anticipation of the enormous need to reconstruct and industrialize Korea after World War II. In 1989, he correctly foresaw another important business opportunity: Mount Kumgang, or Diamond Mountain, with its 12,000 sparkling peaks, was considered the most beautiful mountain on the entire Korean Peninsula. Due to the division of Korea, the highly popular mountain just north of the DMZ was no longer accessible to South Koreans. Chung sensed a pent-up desire by South Koreans to visit this mountain, and the development plan was in a good location for tourism. Just south of the border in this area, South Korea's Sokcho city was renowned for its well-preserved Buddhist temples and the serene Yeongrangho Lake nearby. In addition to the travel venture, in 2000 Hyundai set up the joint business area in Kaesong, North Korea, close to the DMZ.

Starting in 1998, South Korean tourists could travel by cruise ship to Kumgang Mountain; five years later Hyundai started using a land route for bus travel to the special zone. In June 2005, the millionth visitor arrived on the mountain, according to the company. With so much success, the conglomerate hoped to expand the site to include a ski resort and golf courses. Unfortunately, the project ceased on July 11, 2008, when a South Korean tourist crossed into a military sector after wandering over a sand dune and was shot dead by a North Korean patrol.

The debacle became a national incident that added to the South's worries over the North Korean nuclear program. Seoul demanded an immediate explanation, to which North Korean officials responded that the sentries had had no choice but to shoot the South Korean woman. She did not obey an order to stop, and instead fled, they claimed. South Korea temporarily suspended all tours to the mountain until an on-the-spot survey could be carried out. North Korea rejected the demand, arguing that the facts were clear and the victim was fully responsible for the incident.

In 2010, North Korea seized properties belonging to Hyundai "to compensate for the damage suffered by the northern side due to the suspension of the tours for a long time," said a government statement.

There is no doubt that North Korea did suffer from the suspension of the tours, although the consequences were probably worse for Hyundai. The seizure was also a result of the generally declining relations between the countries from 2008 to 2010. The left-leaning South Korean newspaper *Hankyoreh* wrote on July 26, 2011, that the "resumption of Mount Kumgang tourism remains suspended due to the Lee administration's hard-line North Korea policy," rather than a provocation on the part of the North.

As the dispute escalated, North Korea offered tours to Chinese and foreign tour operators from its side, as well as cruises that embarked from Rason, a city northeast of the port of Kumgangsan. Sadly, Hyundai's huge investment—a boon for the North Korean economy—became a victim of another inter-Korean political conflict.

On the other hand, the Hyundai division (Hyundai Asan) that oversaw the Kaesong Industrial Park had been lucky at the economic zone for about five years until political misfortune struck. The zone is located 5 miles (10 kilometers) north of the DMZ—about an hour's drive from Seoul—and is connected by rail and road to South Korea. Its first 3 South Korean companies started production in 2005, and five years later 110 factories had opened shop with some 42,000 North Korean workers and 800 South Korean staff. The total investment then exceeded $1 billion, approximately two-thirds of it coming from the tenant companies. This is a sizable figure when placed against North Korea's GDP of $40 billion in 2010.

For small and medium-sized South Korean companies, one goal was to compete with the Chinese export machine: Kaesong offered low-cost skilled laborers, who spoke the Korean language—unlike other contenders in China or Vietnam. For North Korea, the project eased its economic reliance on its main ally, Beijing.

North Korea was interested in Kaesong for other reasons: the 725,000 jobs that were planned to be created by 2012 (the number had reached only 50,000 by the beginning of 2012), an annual $0.5 billion as wage income for North Korea, and five years later an additional annual corporate tax income of $1.8 billion from the tenant companies.

In North Korea, these numbers are significant because they could help to correct the country's notorious negative balances of payment and trade deficits. Indeed, in 2010 North Korea imported goods and services totaling $3.5 billion versus exports amounting to only $2.5 billion, according to the CIA *World Factbook*. The planned tax income of $1.8 billion from Kaesong alone could more than offset this enormous gap. It could even allow the country to buy, for the first time, enough food from abroad, enabling it to shake off its decade-long dependence on foreign donors.

TIGHTENING THE SCREWS

Almost a year later, in March 2010, the business projects were put into further jeopardy when a South Korean navy corvette, the *Cheonan*, mysteriously sank. The incident left forty-six seamen dead. A South Korean government-led investigation, alongside experts from the U.S., United Kingdom, Canada, Australia, and Sweden, claimed that a North Korean midget submarine launched a torpedo at the warship.

Pyongyang immediately rejected the findings, which were also disputed by its quasi-allies China and Russia. Sweden, meanwhile, reportedly did not add any signatures to the report despite participating in the investigation.

Yet the *Los Angeles Times* wrote on July 23, 2010, that "challenges to the official version of events are coming from an unlikely place: within South Korea."[1] There were questions over the timing: the sinking happened just as one of the world's largest military exercises at the time, involving dozens of U.S. and South Korean ships, was under way. It also seemed strange that the *Cheonan*, and all the other American and South Korean vessels nearby, apparently did not notice the approaching torpedo and the North Korean submarine, despite having the latest technologies.

Because of the findings, the South Korean government ordered the halt of almost all trade between North and South Korea two months later, signifying the low point ten years after the "Sunshine Policy" brought hope to both sides. As doing business in the North became politically risky, customers cancelled their orders from the South Korean factories set up in the industrial zone, and several of them teetered on the brink of bankruptcy.

In addition, eight presidents of small- and medium-sized tenant enterprises complained in interviews that they lost hundreds of thousands of dollars as a consequence of the boycotts.[2] In September 2012, the right-leaning South Korean newspaper *Chosun-Ilbo* wrote that "Kaesong firms still suffer from N. Korea sanctions" imposed in 2010 by the conservative government in Seoul. It quoted a survey by the South Korean Chamber of Commerce and Industry, which reported that "some 61.8 percent of 200 firms said it has been hard to recover from losses."

For those companies, the worst was not over. In April 2013, a North Korean official who visited Kaesong announced that the government would withdraw all 53,000 of its workers from the zone. The KCNA complained that too many conservative South Korean newspapers and pundits, writing during a time of heightened tensions following the North's third nuclear test in early 2013, had doubted that Pyongyang would live up to its threats to close Kaesong if Seoul didn't back down.

Within weeks, the South Korean Ministry of Unification correspondingly ordered the hundreds of southern managers there to depart. North Korean authorities blocked some of them from leaving, claiming they had to pay "taxes," but ultimately all of them returned home. The decision effectively halted operations, although the northern and southern governments euphemistically called it a "temporary" suspension of operations. "Neither side wanted to be blamed for closing Kaesong first," said Lim Eul-chul, a South Korean researcher who traveled regularly to Kaesong after its founding in 2004.

In May 2013, North Korea offered to come back to the table on Kaesong, but with a caveat: the South Korean government wasn't welcome at negotiations. Rather, North Korean delegates said they wanted to meet directly with the businesses and managers whose operations had been shut down. The Ministry of Unification forbade the talks, arguing that Pyongyang was driving a wedge between the government and the people. On September 16, 2013, Kaesong was reopened after five months of haggling between the two sides. Though it was once a symbol of Kim Dae-jung's Sunshine Policy, its future remains uncertain.

In 2007, a year before Lee Myung-bak became president, I inquired about setting up a small packaging center in Kaesong for the PyongSu pharmaceutical factory. I didn't see much of a need to open a second factory there, but rather wanted to box and ship our low-cost Pyong-yang-made medicines to the lucrative South Korean market.

There was one upside: North Korean government officials thought it was a great idea, although we'd have to pay higher wages than those in Pyongyang. And unlike the more legally constrained South Korean managers, I was allowed to communicate directly with all the North Korean staff members. (South Korean factory directors had to com-municate through a government-assigned North Korean deputy who would deliver instructions down the pyramid.)

The problem, it turned out, was in South Korean tastes. A number of pharmacies in the South explained to me that our products would have to undergo a demanding inspection process. Even if they passed, buyers would be uneasy about ingesting North Korean-made phar-maceuticals that they assumed could be dangerous. Besides, Euro-pean investors like me could already invest in most parts of North Korea, and ironically, the more liberal industrial zone of Kaesong only put up more barriers. We scratched the idea.

Soon after Hyundai chairman Chung went to North Korea for business negotiations in 1989, other *chaebol* such as Samsung, Dae-woo, and LG started looking into projects and trade with the North. Daewoo invested almost $6 million in a garment factory in Nampo in the second half of the 1990s, and LG later set up a TV assembly plant in Pyongyang. These ventures were not particularly successful,

After the successful launch of Hwiparam I, a copy of the Fiat Siena, Brilliance China Auto's Junjie car (pictured) was assembled in Nampo by Pyeongwha under the name Hwiparam ("Whistle") II.

mainly because the quality of the products and communication between the two sides left much to be desired, as I learned from Koreans involved in those projects.

South Korean companies were eyeing business opportunities in North Korea, hedging on the Sunshine Policy of the 2000s. The chairman of one of largest South Korean construction companies, who was interested in securing a large chunk of sand from North Korea to make concrete in the South and other countries, invited me to look into opportunities for him. Though other companies had already been importing sand,[3] he thought that I, thanks to my connections in the North, could get most of the sand exclusively for his company. I also met a few representatives from larger business conglomerates in the South, all of whom employed small unofficial committees that discreetly studied the market.

With one *chaebol* I discussed opening a mineral water bottling plant at the foot of Mount Paekdu, known as the country's "holy mountain" because it was believed to be the birthplace of the Korean race. One highly competent South Korean industrialist and I thought up some more ideas over the years. The industrialist, working with a retired president of the largest dairy company in South Korea, Seoul Dairy, devised a plan to offer every North Korean child a glass of milk per day. The idea struck a chord with many farmers in the South who were of northern descent. We planned to first set up a milk powder plant and then gradually switch to processing fresh cow's milk; the practice of cow farming wasn't entirely developed yet in the North, and we needed to build it up while we worked on our plant. Charities and wealthy individuals committed to the project, but after Kim Jong Il's first nuclear test in 2006, the prospect quickly vanished. The North Koreans liked most of our intentions, but the obstacle was that both sides trusted the Swiss interlocutor instead of each other.

Other interlocutors have arrived from South Korea and overseas in the past decade, undertaking similar efforts to reconcile relations. One fantastic group started the privately funded Pyongyang University of Science and Technology (PUST), which opened its doors in 2010 despite the continued political strains between Seoul and Pyongyang.

A lot of North Korea watchers lost hope in the project, which was approved by the education ministry in 2001. Construction work and the inauguration were postponed several times. But on October 25, 2010, hopes were reignited when the university started its operations with twenty foreign professors, one hundred North Korean graduate students, and sixty undergraduates. Another hundred students joined classes the following year. Admittedly, the figures were not over-whelming—but they were a good start.

One personality behind the campus was Professor Park Chan-mo, an IT expert who took a post as one of the university's four co-chair-men. He came to the project with a good background. Until October 2010, Park headed the National Research Foundation of Korea—South Korea's top state body that doles out research funding, the country's equivalent to the Institute of International Education in New York. Before that, he presided over the Pohang University of Science and Technology (Postech), which he turned into South Korea's leading technical university and one of Asia's best universities. It ranked number one among the world's top universities under the age of fifty.[4]

Professor Park was particularly appropriate for this work because he was trusted by North Koreans, having lectured to the country's IT engineers before and trained engineers at the Pyongyang Informatics Center (PIC) in 3-D animation—helping making PIC the leader in 3-D animation software in North Korea.

Professor Park explained his vision in an e-mail to me: "Similar to other nations the future of the Democratic People's Republic of Korea will be largely depending on the young people, especially scientists and engineers and it is very important to educate those students to have a global mindset," he wrote. "It is well known that although there are political borders among the nations there are no borders in science and technology. Scientists and engineers should strive together for the betterment of human beings and world peace. That is why I am working for PUST."

FROM PRISONER TO UNIVERSITY PRESIDENT

James (Chin-kyung) Kim, a seventy-six-year-old Korean-American educator and former entrepreneur in the United States, was arrested at the Pyongyang airport in 1998 on suspicion of espionage. He was incarcerated for more than a month in a North Korean prison, even though the ardent Christian was delivering food from China during the famine.

Yet he and the North Korean government, which is quite pragmatic when things turn to its advantage, eventually forgave each other. At least that's how he tells the story. A few years later he started promoting the idea of setting up PUST, where he is one of four co-chairmen.

Professor Park, along with the other founders of the university, acted out of their own fervor for the Christian gospel. They were smart enough to know that open missionary work would have brought the project to an immediate end. But the reality of the situation—that most of them were ethnic Koreans, Christians, and businesspeople—must have been a headache for their counterparts in Pyongyang.

From my own work at the Pyongyang Business School, I was

aware of the North Korean worries. After long discussions on the agenda, we started with a trial seminar in front of party officials before receiving the green light to move forward. Even more telling of PUST's problems was that, although we submitted our school proposal years after the PUST chairs submitted theirs, the government allowed us to start classes six years earlier. Their reasoning was that we had no political, religious, or other agenda.

And unlike the Christian believers at PUST, I had to make a living and earn my dividends on earth and couldn't wait until going to heaven. The North Koreans needed to be sure that both of our ventures, established through foreign influence, conveyed scientific and technical knowledge but no ideology that could infect their apparatus. At some point in making their decision about PUST, they figured that the benefits of this privately run university, such as access to state-of-the-art equipment, outweighed the political risks, and they finally gave in, but with a few safeguards, of course. They were required to undertake a more rigorous selection of cadres than at the Pyongyang Business School.

One caveat, though, is that PUST doesn't hire truly secular lecturers, and those who do get jobs usually volunteer. "I tried to get a job with PUST but they ignored my application. I was willing to teach English and/or journalism," one university professor, an acquaintance, wrote to me in a rather humorous e-mail. "My wife was ready to teach English and creative writing. I may have failed their religious test. The application form asks: 'When did you accept Jesus Christ as your lord and savior?'"

Despite stereotypes that North Korea overwhelmingly represses the Christian religion, the government usually doesn't see the Lord as a serious threat to its earthly system. I once asked a senior security official if they did not feel threatened by Moon's Unification Church, active in North Korea in the hospitality and car manufacturing industries. He answered quite candidly: "Well, you know, it's a cat-and-mouse game." It's a never-ending contest that the North Koreans will make sure the other side can never win.

HARD-LINERS IN THE WEST WING

After two nuclear tests by North Korea, Chinese involvement significantly slowed down for a while. Later, the Chinese Chuangli Group and North Korea agreed to develop the number 1 dock at Rajin port while the Russians were renovating the rail line from Russia to Rason. The Rason port is ice-free and it gives landlocked Jilin province of China access to the East Sea. Chinese investment is on the rise, not only in and around Rason but throughout North Korea, particularly in areas rich with metals and minerals.

To the North Koreans, Chinese investment has a big advantage to North Korea: it is much less politically sensitive than investment from its capitalist rival South Korea. It may therefore not surprise that Chinese and other foreign investors are substantially privileged, compared to South Koreans. North Korean workers working for Chinese businesses or other foreigners in North Korea have to be paid a monthly minimum salary of 42,000 won, or 40 dollars (30 euros), but four times more when they work for South Koreans in Kaesong, according to the North Korean Joint Venture and Investment Committee.

But there may be another, more important reason for this. When I was working on some joint North-South projects, the northern side always demanded a substantial advance payment up front from the southern side. Informally, it looked more like a heavy entrance fee, something they would never have asked from other investors. When I asked for the reason, one North Korean responded, "Southerners helped destroy our country. That's why they have to pay for that!"

BUSINESS AND GEOPOLITICS

Ms. Kim Cha Yon, a Korean-American academic and strong supporter of the Rason Free Trade Zone, helped establish the Rajin Business Institute, a graduate school affiliated with the Rajin University, to train students in market skills required by foreign enterprises in the trade zone. The institute provided courses in business English, management, business finance, accounting, and quality assurance, among other topics, another sign that this regime is committed to some sort of business reform even if on its own terms.

Students told me that Ms. Kim, who gave lectures herself, was a popular character in Rason. She was deeply concerned about the growing influence of, as she put it to me, a "peacefully rising China" that might exert influence on them sooner or later—a fear widespread among Koreans. To counteract this trend, her goal was a politically and economically more balanced development in the region.

NORTH KOREAN CELEBRITIES

While the soldiers who carried out rocket and nuclear tests were national heroes, North Korea is home to many more stars who help define national identity. The country has its fair share of film stars and music celebrities, who are generally not known outside the DPRK. Some even showed up at the PyongSu booth during exhibitions, where they confessed they were happy customers—much to the delight of my staff and me.

Among the most admired sports heroes were the members of the legendary North Korean soccer team, which sparked a great shock in North Korea in the 1966 World Cup. On June 1, 2010, the AFP news agency reminded the world about a truly historic event: "North Korea 1, Italy 0. Four decades on, the sensational defeat of the two-time world champions by a team of unknowns from the insular nation ranks as perhaps the greatest shock in World Cup history."

Although they did beat the world's then-strongest soccer team, the North Koreans did not win the World Cup itself. Losing the World Cup did not lead to any punishment, as the Western media reported. On the contrary, the players were duly celebrated as heroes when they returned home.

The event occurred on July 19, 1966, when the North Korean national soccer team was victorious over the world champion, Italy, in Middlesbrough, England. For a few days in the summer of 1966, Pak Doo Ik, an army corporal, was the most famous footballer in the world; he was the scorer of the goal that knocked Italy out of the World Cup.

Games like these give North Koreans hope that their "pure and superior" race can defeat any foreign attacker. ABB sponsored a documentary film on the historic event, because I hoped the company could draw on its popularity.

In 2008 I was watching the Olympics on TV in my condominium in Pyongyang with some angst. One of the participants struck my eye. To me she looked weaker and more fragile than her rivals, but to my relief, she won the contest. Pak Hyon Suk, born August 4, 1985, became the weightlifting gold medalist at the Beijing Olympics in 2008, defeating athletes from Chinese Taipei, the Olympics label for Taiwan (bronze), and Kazakhstan (silver). She lifted 530 pounds (241 kilograms) in total in the 135-pound (63-kilogram) category.

Pak explained that she was trying to please her then-leader, Kim Jong Il, when she went into the last and decisive round. North Korean TV viewers were allowed to watch only North Korean athletes win Olympic medals in 2008. In 2012, though, North Korean authorities allowed their citizens for the first time ever to watch South Koreans win gold medals as well.

For her gold medal, Ms. Pak was rewarded by her government with a house in Pyongyang and a car. Compared to the advertising contracts awarded to Western athletes, her prize was modest. But it meant a lot to this patriotic North Korean. I expressed my heartfelt congratulations to Ms. Pak for her achievement when I met her at the airport upon her return. Her fighting spirit instilled confidence in millions of North Koreans. They were, as always, convinced that they are the best people in the world.

NOTES

1. Barbara Demick and John M. Glionna. Doubts surface on North Korea's role in ship sinking. *Los Angeles Times*. July 23, 2010. http://articles.latimes.com/2010/jul/23/world/la-fg-korea-torpedo-20100724.

2. Jung Eun-joo. Kaesong companies on the brink as sanctions continue. *The Hankyoreh*. January 19, 2011. http://english.hani.co.kr/arti/english_edition/e_northkorea/459520.html.

3. Sam Kim. S. Korea halts sand imports from N. Korea amid tension. Yonhap News Agency. May 18, 2010. http://english.yonhapnews.co.kr/northkorea/2010/05/18/88/0401000000AEN20100518007600315F.HTML.

4. Ami Sedghi. World's top 100 universities under 50: ranked by Times Higher Education. *The Guardian*. May 31, 2012. http://www.guardian.co.uk/news/datablog/2012/may/31/top-100-universities-under-50.

Epilogue
Winds of Change

Reform is China's second revolution.

— Deng Xiaoping

In February 2008, more than 400 Americans traveled to Pyongyang. It was the largest American delegation to step foot in the country since the Korean War. The New York Philharmonic Orchestra was performing, and it brought about 80 journalists from all over the world.

The group even included William Perry, the U.S. defense secretary under Bill Clinton, who always held a hawkish stance toward Pyongyang. In the 1990s, Perry was prepared to launch surgical strikes on nuclear facilities in Pyongyang and pushed for tough sanctions against North Korea after its withdrawal from the Treaty on the Non-Proliferation of Nuclear Weapons. The North Korean government perceived his plan as a belligerent act of war, but it was scuttled thanks to intervention from ex-President Jimmy Carter, who met with both President Kim Il Sung and then-President Bill Clinton in 1994.

On my way to the concert hall I passed Mr. Perry, who was smiling in front of the cameras, with other Americans in a country he once hated. How lucky, I thought, that this guy didn't get his way, so he could later visit a peninsula he almost turned into a crater.

Music helped open up China in the 1970s, when the Philadelphia Orchestra played there as the Nixon administration was following a policy of détente with Beijing. Indeed, music can also open the doors to change in Pyongyang. Perhaps the ball is already rolling.

After a symphonic performance of "Arirang," the foreign and North Korean audience applauds. "Arirang" is an old Korean folk song recounting the story of an unhappy woman left by her lover and yearning for him to return. It is a metaphor for today's divided Korea.

The Western media, in particular, were pleased with the North Korean program, which included composers like Dvorak, Gershwin, and Wagner. Even the American and North Korean anthems were a part of the show. Most of the pieces were not directly subversive, with the exception of the *"New World" Symphony*, a piece that Dvorak composed in 1893 during a visit to the U.S., praising the continent's blossoming democracy and free markets. The emotional highlight of the evening was the Korean folk song "Arirang."

ARE FOREIGN INFLUENCES BANNED?

At the end of 2006, Reuters published a German-language report claiming that Western music was banned in North Korea—the sort of allegation you would find in George Orwell's *1984*. The reporter claimed that the permitted tunes had titles like "Let Us Support

Our Supreme Commander with Weapons" and "Song of the Coast Artillery."

Reuters must have been puzzled, then, when the North Korean government held a concert on the occasion of the 250th anniversary of Mozart's birth in which, for example, "Figaro's Wedding" was performed. I attended the concert in the Moranbong Theater with a young French IT entrepreneur. Even though he didn't enjoy symphonies, he was excited to learn that North Korea wasn't just about revolutionary songs. "In the State Symphony of North Korea, they do Tchaikovsky from memory," Suzannah Clarke, a British opera singer who has performed frequently in North Korea, told the *Washington Post*. "The Philharmonic could probably learn a thing or two."

The appreciation of classical music has a historical precedent. Russian dance groups and orchestras performed regularly in Pyongyang for years, part of a palette that included European classical alongside communist Soviet songs. The affinity for classical music, then, was a result of Russians, the Korean composer Isang Yun, and others like Clarke.

Moving beyond the New York Philharmonic visit, artists from around the world were invited to perform every two years at Pyongyang's biannual Spring Festival. There was little censorship involved; these performances were even aired on TV for all North Koreans to see rather than being cordoned off as a playground for elites.

One year Swiss yodeling groups and alphorn musicians amused audiences at the festival and quickly garnered nationwide celebrity on television. That would simply have not been possible in their home country, where the market is flooded with talented musicians. Still, even some North Koreans have mastered the Western fine arts. My wife took piano lessons from a North Korean teacher who had mastered the classics on his instrument.

The Pochonbo Electronic Ensemble, one of North Korea's most popular orchestras, could be heard regularly on local radio stations and had an impressive repertoire of foreign songs ranging from "Lambada," a world hit by the French group Kaoma, to the German pop group Modern Talking's famous catchy "Brother Louie" to "L'amour est bleu" ("Blue, blue, my world is blue ..."), a song ranked second at a Eurovision Song Contest in 1967.

As a fan of classical music, I enjoyed concerts given by the National Symphony Orchestra on several occasions, whose repertoire included a wide variety of famous pieces ranging from Strauss's *Radetzky March* to the overture to Bizet's opera *Carmen*.

In the karaoke rooms around Pyongyang, amateur singers cheered over the ubiquitous theme from *Titanic*, Celine Dion's "My Heart Will Go On." The song, strangely, had been "Koreanized" with a Korean text and a more local background film that didn't have much to do with the original theme.

THE PATH TOWARD REFORM

So, how will reform come about, and what can observers expect based on past patterns? Political changes do not usually come as a "big bang"—and when they do, the results can be disastrous, as in the case of impoverished Cambodia after the U.N. hastily tried to set up a democracy in 1992. Rather, reform involves a gradual process of trial and error, a pattern that often consists of two steps forward and one step back.

Noteworthy changes occurred not only after 2002 but were already emerging in 1996 and 1997, the years of the huge natural calamities, when the Public Distribution System collapsed and was unable to feed the population any longer. Markets sprang up to fill the gap, and people started to wheel and deal in any way possible to make ends meet. Although it was then illegal, authorities reluctantly tolerated the development of this marketization and finally accepted and legalized the markets in 2002.

But what came as a surprise in 2005 is that the private sale of grain in the markets was banned again in an effort to roll back the markets and to revive the Public Distribution System. A host of other measures, described elsewhere in the book, against markets and traders were carried out until 2009, when a currency depreciation, the last and hitherto most radical action to restore the state-controlled economy of the past, completely failed. The currency reform in December 2009 was aimed at curbing inflation, tackling corruption, and reducing the power of the emerging merchant class. Money in the old currency had to be changed into money in the new currency at a rate of 100 to 1. But only a small amount could be changed, which meant that savings beyond the limited amount were lost.

Although salaries remained unchanged and after the currency reform were a hundred times higher, hoarding plus the sudden increase in purchasing power, versus the same quantity of products available, led to massive inflation expressed in soaring food prices. In March 2010, Pak Nam Gi, the secretary of the planning and finance department of the Workers' Party, who was held responsible for the disastrous result, was shot by a firing squad, according to the South Korean news agency Yonhap.

Responding to the imbroglio in May 2010, the state lifted all the restrictions on private trade it had introduced between 2005 and 2009, and a new period of liberalization followed. These developments have completely escaped the attention of conservative American outlets like the Heritage Foundation and *The Wall Street Journal*: in their 2011 Index of Economic Freedom, they rated North Korean economic freedoms low and unchanged from 1995 to 2005. From 2005 to 2011, the ranking dropped even further, from 10 points out of 40 to almost zero. Obviously, these talking heads made an ideological decision.

Although socialist China and Vietnam have very successfully carried out reforms while keeping their communist parties in power, they went through the same periods of progress alternating with reversals. Until 2003, economic reforms were widely discussed in China and there was a sort of a consensus that state monopolies or oligopolies should be reduced. That would allow the private sector to develop. The discussions have died down since then, and reforms have halted. A couple of private Chinese entrepreneurs told me that it has become more difficult for private enterprises to get bank loans. It may take a while until enough pressure has built up to get another round of reforms going.

But unlike in China and Vietnam, reforms in North Korea are very much either accelerated or slowed down according to the political environment. The July 2002 "reforms," quite bold by North Korean standards, were prepared when the Clinton administration in the U.S. started engaging more seriously with the country. The Bush administration, however, made a U-turn. It not only refused engagement but labeled the DPRK a member of the "axis of evil" and a target to be confronted.

The North Korean government did not use the politically incorrect word "reform" to describe the initiatives, instead calling them the "July 1 economic improvement and management measures," because they were introduced on July 1, 2002. They were meant to further monetize the economy by abolishing the coupon system for food rations. The new policy also allowed supply and demand to determine the prices of most products. It also depreciated the artificially high value of the domestic currency to a level close to black (real) market value to make North Korea more attractive for foreign investment.

To attract even more foreign investment, the government promoted special administrative and industrial zones, such as the Sinuiju Special Administrative Zone. Farmers' markets were legalized and allowed to transform into general markets. Other measures shifted managerial responsibility for enterprises and state farms from the central party to the local production units, which could no longer rely on state subsidies. They also had to cope with their own tough budget constraints from then on.

In addition, the conservative administration of Lee Myung-bak, which came to power in South Korea in 2008, abolished the pro-engagement Sunshine Policy of its predecessors and halted all aid to the North—a move that threw the North's leadership into disorder. The new catchphrases seemed intended to isolate, throttle, and corner a regime that was legitimately on the path to reform. Sunshine allowed family reunions, visits by South Koreans to North Korea, the setup of the Kaesong Industrial Zone, and the preparation of a host of other projects that brought hostile North and South closer together and made the Korean Peninsula safer.

Thanks to American and South Korean threats, the Korean Workers' Party had to place its emphasis on protecting its borders more than on economic reform. Of course, this country under siege was quite wary when it came to reforms, and it was not surprising to me when the *Rodong Sinmun*, the central organ of the Korean Workers' Party, called reforms "sugar-coated poison" by the imperialists aimed at undermining the socialist system.

When the U.S. started accusing North Korea of working on a nuclear weapons program three months after launching its July 1 reforms, it put more and more pressure on Pyongyang to reform itself. North Korea suspected the American advice of being part of a plot to overthrow its system.

And yet there had been many changes in North Korea that were not actually called "reforms." They were hardly noticeable for outsiders or even for expatriates living in Pyongyang, but they were still quite significant for this country.

For example, in the past, according to the DPRK's Daean management system, a factory management committee headed not by the CEO but by the party secretary had to run an enterprise. In 2002, however, the role of the CEO was upgraded and the CEO became the responsible chief executive of the enterprise. Factories were headed by the party secretary and a committee. The party secretary was a politician, not a technocrat, and would usually not have the background to run a business. The committee he headed also diluted responsibilities. From then on, a competent technocrat alone with no bureaucratic committee would be in charge.

Also, after the July 2002 measures, agricultural markets were allowed to transform into markets that peddled pretty much everything and those that already existed became legalized. Soon after, all kinds of industrial products were sold in these markets for the grow-ing number of private merchants.

It did not take long until additional street markets appeared, and more individual vendors began canvassing living areas with their goods as well. Of course, the state economy had started degrading in the eighties, and, together with the public rationing and distribu-tion system, had to a large extent collapsed by the nineties, when informal, illegal market activities emerged. The 2002 measures were intended in part to regain some control over these markets and to revive the state sector.

In 2002, the state let go of its fixed prices for rice and other food-stuffs, which rose to the market levels. The government correspond-ingly increased salaries to make up for the rising commodity prices. But the dramatic salary increases created an influx of cash injected into the economy, creating enormous demand for products and ser-vices that the state sector, with its low productivity, could not meet. As a consequence, inflation skyrocketed to 100 percent year-on-year.

Private citizens found ways to circumvent the state sector and make up for inflation. They typically found second jobs, often by set-ting up their own businesses. To keep their state employers happy, they shared the profits with those enterprises under which they oper-ated. For outsiders, this setup inevitably stoked confusion. I have done business with many companies, all formally belonging to state enti-ties, but I could not figure out for certain whether the managers were acting as government employees or actual business owners. Only a few would admit that they worked for their own interests; the major-ity deemed it wiser to be discreet with this legally delicate question.

The economic changes, of course, brought out fundamental changes in the desires of the North Korean people. Students had tra-ditionally seen the greatest prestige in working for the foreign or trade ministry, but now they suddenly spoke favorably to me about becoming businesspeople. The merchant class was, in this socialist country, despised in both the Confucian and revolutionary past.

Indeed, over the years, more students came to visit foreign business booths at exhibitions in Pyongyang. At first, they usually wanted to practice English. But eventually they expressed to me their wish to work for a foreign company or a prominent local one involved in the import-export industry.

Even the country's legal system no longer had the reach to rein in market activities. The Socialist Property Management Law of 1996, for instance, allowed only "enterprises, institutes, and groups" to use properties that were affiliated with the government. Still, in the 1990s and early 2000s, real estate swapping and trading discreetly emerged. Mr. Pak, an official at the Ministry of Light Industries, told me that he was happy to be able to get a better apartment by swapping with another person and then by paying for the difference in market value.

"Market value?" I inquired over a coffee in my office.

"Since there are more and more apartments and houses sold and bought, one can know how much people are prepared to pay for one," he answered.

Decades earlier this man had lived with his wife, children, and parents in an apartment allocated by his father's work organization. It was quite a hike, at one and a half hours away from his office. From his new residence he now could reach his ministry on foot in just a few minutes.

Tactics like this can be considered what the historian James C. Scott calls "weapons of the weak," or the endeavors of regular people to skirt around officialdom and determine the course of their own lives. Indeed, the North Korean people subtly forced the government to change its ways: the informal property market led the state to pass the new Real Estate Management Law, adopted in 2009 and including individuals in addition to organizations.

The rise of a business-minded technocratic class is also changing things for the better. In the early 1990s, when the former Soviet Union and allied Eastern Europe underwent a rapid metamorphosis, North Korea recalled all its overseas students to protect them from the "poisonous" influences of reform. A little more than a decade later, business-educated leaders are increasingly at the forefront:

officials repeatedly told me that they had received degrees in Hungary, sponsored by the Soros foundations; in England; in Germany; or elsewhere.

One example is Dr. Kim, a senior official at the Foreign Trade Ministry, who had received his MBA at a British university. This intellectual and career-driven fellow was always churning out business and investment proposals, presented in a professional way to me and other foreigners. Studying at a foreign university was no longer off-limits, but a trend among upper-class North Koreans.

But the students didn't always leave the country. In other cases, British and German professors were brought in to train students at the nascent and blossoming universities. Consider my own project, the Pyongyang Business School, which would have been unthinkable had I undertaken the endeavor ten years earlier. Yet the authorities conceded that it was more cost-effective and less risky to recruit students for training with foreign lecturers in Pyongyang than to send them abroad.

On behalf of Sandvik, a multinational firm focusing on mining equipment, I organized seminars for mines—of which North Korea had plenty. I did the same for other companies such as Dystar, the global leader in dyestuff. At seminars for this company, representatives of garment producers from all over the country came to Pyongyang. Though they wanted to learn about state-of-the-art science, the participants also became familiar with key products and how to use them optimally. Afterwards, some North Korean delegates became customers of these companies. The idea that foreign capitalist companies could talk directly to North Koreans, even from those outside of Pyongyang, would have been inconceivable a few years earlier.

The changes most visible to foreigners in Pyongyang could be recognized on Pyongyang's streets. Over the years people became better dressed, wearing more bright, colorful, and fashionable clothing, compared to when I arrived in 2002, when they wore dark clothes that were black, olive green, and blue. The "dark" fashion was economical at first: it was easier to keep these clothes clean. Most people had no washing machines and needed to wash clothes by hand instead with cheap soap.

In 2005, I noticed a wave of young women in Pyongyang wearing platform shoes, a style that made its way from the en vogue circles in China and Europe. The following year, the first wave of local women wearing foreign luxury brands emerged. They even patted their faces with good doses of makeup and donned jewelry.

That growth in cosmopolitan styles corresponded with an increasing number of cars driving around the once half-empty streets. Many of them belonged to state entities, but gradually more were actually owned by members of the newly emerging middle class who were using state agencies for their private business. It looked like a typical Asian route of economic development through the use of state enterprises. They were then called "umbrellas" for protection and for private gain, and were a centerpiece in China and Vietnam too.

Old meets new: three DHL courier vans drive in front of the Foreign Trade Ministry. The building's façade is adorned on the far left by a large painting of Marx and on the right with a portrait of Lenin. Yet their literature can no longer be found in libraries and book shops, and I never came across a single quote of theirs. It was a clear hint that North Korea wants to emphasize not an international form of socialism but rather its own national brand, mixed with the Juche and Songun ideologies, that no longer has anything to do with Marxism-Leninism. The highly visible yellow DHL vehicles, however, seemed at times to be just everywhere in Pyongyang.

While DHL is still in Pyongyang, Marx and Lenin have gone and therefore cannot be seen on the walls of this building as of spring 2012. Also of huge historical significance, in April 2009 the Supreme People's Assembly quietly removed the word "communism" from Articles 29 and 40 of the Constitution, covering the economy and culture, respectively. It added "Songun" (army-first policy) instead. This suggests that North Korea is planning to follow the political path of the former military regime of Myanmar rather than China's economic regime. General Ne Win installed a nominally socialist military government with the task of following the Burmese Way to Socialism after his coup d'état in 1962.

Surface changes, at least in Pyongyang, show that North Korea could now be entering the earliest phases of such developments. More shops are now selling a larger variety of products, including famous brands such as Disney, Nescafe, and Calvin Klein.

RISE AND FALL OF A TECHNOCRAT

North Korea pundits and Western media called Pak Pong Ju, North Korea's prime minister from 2003-07, a reformer, although it's hard to put a precise label on these leaders. He was a star figure who was replaced in 2007 in a move that many interpreted as meaning that North Korea was reverting away from its earlier reforms. Pak was born in 1939 and started his career as a manager of a food factory in the North Pyongan province (no relation to the similar-sounding city of Pyongyang). He later was appointed party secretary at a chemical complex and then moved on to become party manager of the DPRK's chemical industries.

During the 1990s, North Korea's most powerful party officials were Kim Jong Il, his sister Kim Kyong Hui, and her husband Jang Song Taek. Pak managed to get into Kim Kyong Hui's good graces and eventually rose to the rank of her first deputy at the party Central Committee. His ministerial post was ended in 2007.

But he returned in August 2010 to become her deputy again. *The New York Times* was quick to publish a headline reading "North Korea Reinstates Market-Oriented Official." The reporter speculated, "A former North Korean prime minister who was banished three years ago for pushing market-oriented reforms too far has returned to the center of economic policy, leading to speculation that the nation's leader, Kim Jong-il, might give such proposals a second chance."

The paper went on to quote a South Korean defense analyst as saying: "Pak's reinstatement indicates that North Korea is shifting back to market reforms, even if grudgingly, after its botched attempt to re-enforce state control on the economy," referring to the failed currency reform the previous year.

Still, even if Pak Pong Ju was a reformer, his 2007 replacement may have been unfairly maligned as a conservative. Prime Minister Kim Yong Il was Pak's Minister for Land and Marine Transport and chairman of the Korean-Polish Shipping Joint Venture Company, called Chopol, run together by a Korean and a Polish executive.

The Polish head, who was a committee member of the European Business Association in Pyongyang, told me that the new prime minister was a very competent and supportive chairman—and that he had a good understanding of business. He was not a staunch Marxist-Leninist, as the press made many believe. He was as much in favor of or against reforms as his predecessor.

The narrative that North Korea carried out reforms under Pak, then moved away from them, and then embraced them again was an illusion. Had the Western media outlets known Pak's successor, their still speculative headlines might have read: "North Korea Replaces

Market-Oriented Prime Minister with Another Market-Oriented Prime Minister." But this headline would not have signified anything newsworthy, so they would have probably glossed over this minutia.

There are other signs that North Korea is on the road to reform, at least in its infrastructure. In this country, which was cut off from the hyper-wired South, I managed to get an uncensored Internet connection in Pyongyang and to exchange e-mails with South Koreans. To learn more about IT opportunities, I wrote to my friend Park Chan-Mo, who was then the president of South Korea's leading science and technology university, Postech.

For the previous few years, Chan-Mo had been traveling repeatedly to Pyongyang to train IT engineers. He also introduced the 3-D animation studio at PIC (Pyongyang Informatics Center), which was at the time ahead of other IT companies in its expertise, business savvy, and skills. I appreciated his advice; we were negotiating the setup of the first IT joint venture, called Nosotek (Number One Software Technology Company). Chan-Mo was also a driving force behind the subsequently established Pyongyang University of Science and Technology (PUST), where he became the chancellor after retiring from Postech.

When I first arrived in Pyongyang, however, my company had not yet secured full Internet access at its offices. Rather, we found an e-mail function operated by the North Korean Telecom Company via a server based in China. The price was steep. Each e-mail cost at least $1.35 (1 euro) and the cost, according to the size of the attachment, could leap up to several euros, which was the currency we used.

To use the Internet, I went to a cybercafé operated by a state agency, which offered an uncensored connection. North Koreans also used the Internet there, and thus were not completely closed off from the information superhighway. Every session, though, cost me several euros. Later, in 2004, the World Food Programme installed several PCs with free satellite Internet access on its premises, geared toward the expatriate community.

That proved to be a strategic move for raising the WFP's profile in the country. The Internet office was suddenly transformed into a prime meeting point for expatriates, and the lines would get quite long. Later, a German entrepreneur set up Internet services together with a telecom company, which I used at my office and at home. Unfortunately, the telecom and its German partners lobbied very hard to maintain their Internet monopoly. Foreign-invested businesses could not install their own satellite dishes and operate a more cost-effective Internet.

The government did not give us the license to set up our own satellite dish. The cost of a satellite dish from China would have been less than $8,000, an investment that would be easily repaid after just a few months thanks to substantial cost savings. Embassies were allowed to set up their own satellite dishes, along with a few NGOs that subscribed to a Chinese Internet service provider. Foreign com-

Business strategy, business plan, marketing, human resources management? What the heck is that? Most North Korean business managers have never heard these terms. With the arrival of the Pyongyang Business School, that changed. All seminars were published and widely distributed. They reached numerous corporate executives, but also government officials throughout the country. Here, Dr. Heinz Suehlmann, a member of the executive committee and director of human resources at BASF Asia, the world's largest chemical company, chats during a seminar on human resources management at the Pyongyang Business School.

panies, though, were not allowed to have their own connection due to this lobbying.

I have been interviewed repeatedly by North Korean media, including the Korean Workers' Party central organ and the state council's newspaper. In one interview I was asked the standard question of what I thought about (North) Korea and the Koreans. I said good things, of course, such as that Korea was a beautiful country with similarities to my native country, Switzerland, and that its people were intelligent, well educated, disciplined, and hardworking. But then I possibly made a small gaffe. As Kim Jong Il had just returned from a trip to China where he visited industrial parks and top-notch Chinese enterprises, I added: "I am convinced that Korea under the wise leadership of Kim Jong Il will become a strong and prosperous nation like China, which he has just visited." While the journalists themselves adorned my remarks about their homeland, any allusion to China was dropped. After all, the Chinese Communist Party had carried out reforms, and newspapers in the DPRK still suspected that reforms could end up being a capitalist trap. Party cadres privately told me they did not consider China to be a socialist country any longer; some praised the country's development, while others truly believed the party line that was more suspicious.

In addition to industrial shifts, changes are also taking place for consumers. A bank in Pyongyang, for one, started issuing payment cards, almost like rudimentary ATM cards, which could be used at shops and restaurants. I was proud that the director of the innovative bank was a student of the Pyongyang Business School. Currently, two banks are competing for the attention of shops and restaurants to have their payment systems installed. Bank cash cards are widely accepted now. All pharmacies of PyongSu, for example, have installed the bank cash card facilities, which are increasingly popular among its customers. Even at the Pyongyang Metro, passengers "tape in" to a metro station using an electronic payment card—similar to the card systems used in subways around the world.

BACKTRACKING

After a meeting in early 2005 with one of North Korea's largest business groups, the vice chairman walked me to my car and lowered his voice. "Lengthy discussions on the course of the economy recently took place in the higher echelons of our party," he whispered, "and the old conservative guard asserted itself this time. Businesspeople just need to be more patient now." Obviously, he was aware that there would be a period to come that would make business life tougher for everybody. But he was optimistic that this was a passing phase: the course of the economy was, surely and predictably, going to change again later. And the change was set in motion after the "old guard" became too zealous in its ruinous currency reform.

It is an enigma as to why exactly the party's old guard has so fervently resisted reforms for a remarkable three decades, while Vietnam and China have opened at the behest of their communist-capitalist policymakers. In Vietnam, though, the political scientist Ben Kerkvliet has shown how pressure from villagers and farmers pushed the party onto the path of reform after food shortages in the early 1980s. If this is the case, perhaps change in North Korea will not be administered from the top down but will need to come from the bottom to be subsequently accepted by the party.

There are already signs that such changes, perhaps inspired by changes at the bottom of society, are taking place. The young leader Kim Jong Un implemented a number of personnel changes in April 2013 that revealed a shift from the conservative military to the more reform-minded, civilian technocrats. This is a significant reform in a country where the official policy has been "army first!" for more than a decade.

In the words of North Korea leadership expert Michael Madden: "These appointments appear to be important steps in moving key economic development projects and production away from the control of the military to the party and government."

In June 2012, Kim Jong Un gave farm managers more control over their decision making over their land. The Supreme Leader allowed farmers to keep surpluses for sale at a profit after they fulfilled state-mandated quotas. Some analysts believed he was experimenting with the early stages of a market-style relaxation, similar to the agricultural reforms that planted the seeds of change under Deng Xiaoping.

Other market-oriented shifts are under way. Before the agricultural reform, factories and other businesses had to pay salaries fixed by the state. From now on, enterprises can define their own salary policy and pay higher salaries for workers who are more productive.

It is true that, in 2012 and 2013, Kim Jong Un initiated a number of purges, firing top military commanders and even ordering the execution of his uncle and regent, Jang Song Taek. Many believed this signaled the end of any erstwhile hopes that Kim Jong Un, with his Western education, would initiate much-needed reforms.

But I disagree. There is no doubt that the government continues to attempt economic reform, even if through a system of trial and error. In *Korea Focus*, a well-informed author writes: "The objective of the New Economic Management System introduced by Kim Jong Un in North Korea is the building of an 'unplanned socialist economy,' or something similar to the 'socialist commodity economy' China implemented between 1984 and 1992."

But like previous reforms in China, the essay makes it clear that the implementation of reform is a messy business. There were few preparations before embarking on any changes, and the government simply didn't have the resources to get it done. Meanwhile, the beneficiaries of the old system opposed new ways of thinking. Perhaps that is less important than many North Korea watchers assume. Regardless of the resistance of an Old Guard, the country is indeed home to an informal private economy that is growing faster than the state economy, and with it a middle class.

In the mid to long term, the DPRK cannot survive without true economic reforms, and the party and its leader know this. If they refuse them, the state will collapse as badly as the socialist countries in Eastern Europe did two decades earlier.

General Colin Powell, the former U.S. secretary of state, gave credence to this mindset when he said that the North Korean leadership is not suicidal. For this reason, it will eventually embrace reforms as a way of self-preservation, even if it faces risks. After all, whoever leads the country in the future will be aware that the legitimacy of the one-party rule cannot be drawn primarily from a strong military defense against a declining enemy, the U.S.

But before a substantial transformation and a true divulgence take place, the international community will have to agree on some conditions. Leonid Petrov of the University of Sydney, a skeptical North Korea expert, pointed out in an online forum: "North Korea won't change nor will it follow Vietnam or China's examples without U.S. diplomatic recognition, solid security assurance, and fair economic treatment. But Washington does not need a reformed North Korea—instead the Americans and Lee Myung Bak [South Korea's hard-line president until 2013] expect Pyongyang to surrender unconditionally." He went on: "While cornered, North Korea remains consolidated ideologically with no room for domestic dissent or unrest. Confrontation will continue indefinitely until someone (either in DPRK elite or in U.S. administration) decides to interrupt this vicious circle and change the paradigm of relations."

It's a dream that hasn't been quite realized, but I remain optimistic. If the New York Philharmonic could be so well received in North Korea, then I place my hope in the coming winds of change.

Acknowledgments

Kamsahamnida!

I would like to acknowledge and extend my heartfelt gratitude to the following colleagues who have made the completion of this book possible:

Dr. René Zeyer, a best-selling author and friend whom I have known since we were teenagers. He offered vital encouragement and support, and gave me motivation and invaluable advice.

Geoffrey Cain, who just finished his M.A. in Southeast Asian studies at the School of Oriental and African Studies, University of London. Geoff is an outstanding journalist writing for some of the world's most prestigious publications, such as *Time, The Economist, Far Eastern Economic Review, Foreign Policy*, and *The New Republic*. Thanks to his background, knowledge, and insight, he offered me great inspiration and advice. I'm indebted to him for thoroughly editing my manuscript.

Most especially, I would like to thank my wife Huong and my daughter Linh for their patience, empathy, and support.

The Tuttle Story
"Books to Span the East and West"

Many people are surprised to learn that the world's largest publisher of books on Asia had its humble beginnings in the tiny American state of Vermont. The company's founder, Charles E. Tuttle, belonged to a New England family steeped in publishing.

Tuttle's father was a noted antiquarian dealer in Rutland, Vermont. Young Charles honed his knowledge of the trade working in the family bookstore, and later in the rare books section of Columbia University Library. His passion for beautiful books—old and new—never wavered throughout his long career as a bookseller and publisher.

After graduating from Harvard, Tuttle enlisted in the military and in 1945 was sent to Tokyo to work on General Douglas MacArthur's staff. He was tasked with helping to revive the Japanese publishing industry, which had been utterly devastated by the war. After his tour of duty was completed, he left the military, married a talented and beautiful singer, Reiko Chiba, and in 1948 began several successful business ventures.

To his astonishment, Tuttle discovered that postwar Tokyo was actually a book-lover's paradise. He befriended dealers in the Kanda district and began supplying rare Japanese editions to American libraries. He also imported American books to sell to the thousands of GIs stationed in Japan. By 1949, Tuttle's business was thriving, and he opened Tokyo's very first English-language bookstore in the Takashimaya Department Store in Ginza, to great success. Two years later, he began publishing books to fulfill the growing interest of foreigners in all things Asian.

Though a westerner, Tuttle was hugely instrumental in bringing a knowledge of Japan and Asia to a world hungry for information about the East. By the time of his death in 1993, he had published over 6,000 books on Asian culture, history and art—a legacy honored by Emperor Hirohito in 1983 with the "Order of the Sacred Treasure," the highest honor Japan can bestow upon a non-Japanese.

The Tuttle company today maintains an active backlist of some 1,500 titles, many of which have been continuously in print since the 1950s and 1960s—a great testament to Charles Tuttle's skill as a publisher. More than 60 years after its founding, Tuttle Publishing is more active today than at any time in its history, still inspired by Charles Tuttle's core mission—to publish fine books to span the East and West and provide a greater understanding of each.